For All the World to See

Best wishes,
Jean Aldridge
Phoebe Crouch
Eccl. 4:9-10
NIV

For All the World to See

by
Jean Peake Aldridge
and
Phoebe Fair Crouch

For Ginny, my beautiful friend who inspires me, and brings me joy. Happy 105th Birthday!
Love, Jean Aldridge
2/24/2024

Aldridge-Crouch Publishers
Rocky Mount, North Carolina 27803

For All the World to See

Copyright © 1993 by Jean Peake Aldridge and Phoebe Fair Crouch

1993

Printed in the United States of America
All Rights Reserved

No part of this book may be reproduced in any form or by any electronic or mechanical means including information storage and retrieval systems without written permission from the publishers. Reviewers may quote brief passages to be printed in a magazine or newspaper.

Published by Aldridge-Crouch Publishers
Rocky Mount, North Carolina 27803

Library of Congress Catalog Card Number: 93-72627
International Standard Book Number: 0-9637753-0-8

Printed on recycled paper.

Foreword

For All the World to See is a very personal look into the lives of two young North Carolina girls and the world they lived in for forty years—from the 1950's to 1990's.

Theirs is a real story that captures the flavor and history of the times as they re-live their moments in this most uniquely written dual autobiography.

It is an honest portrayal of the values they shared as they inherited from each other a friendship that has truly been their greatest gift to each other. This expression and description give new meaning to the world's search and appreciation for friendship.

There is much to be learned as well as much to be enjoyed as one senses the honesty and simplicity of their reflection on their own lives as they molded their values while encountering the events that influence society and the world around them.

How they face the good times, and the not so good times, are examples of how their faith searches the paths for tomorrow that continue to give direction to all our lives.

Yes, this is a very personal book and for many there will be no connection. But for those who discover its message, there quite possibly might be a remembrance of days gone by, or even better yet, the secret to how friendship can make us whole and how our own values give direction to our children and generations to come.

—Bryant T. Aldridge

We dedicate this book with love to Bryant who has been so patient and encouraged us daily; to Allison and Susan who believed in us; to Bryant, Jr. and Daniel because we know they will appreciate it; and to Dan's beloved memory.

Table of Contents

1. Jean 1
2. Phoebe 3
3. Peace College 5
4. College Orientation 6
5. Friends Meeting 9
6. Sylvia 12
7. Settling In 14
8. The Special Boys 16
9. Christmas Break — 1952 18
10. Happy Times—Sad Times 19
11. May Day and Summer Vacation 21
12. Our Dorm Room 24
13. The Engagement Ring 29
14. Tragedy at Peace 32
15. Graduation—May 1954 35
16. Marriage and Single Life 39
17. Life Goes On 44
18. Jean and Bryant Marry 48
19. Bryant, Jr. 50
20. Phoebe, Dan, Jean, and Bryant 53
21. At Home with Jean, Bryant, and Bryant, Jr. 56
22. New Homes 59
23. Setting Sail 63
24. A Trip to the Crouch's 65
25. Chicago Bound 67
26. Thinking of Going Home 70
27. A New Baby Arrives 72
28. Durham 74
29. Another Baby Arrives 77
30. Two Families Share Fun 80
31. Family Challenges 82
32. New Job 85
33. Separating Again 88
34. Rocky Mount 90
35. Vacation for All of Us 93

36. Life in Rocky Mount	96
37. At the Beach with Nannie	100
38. An Excursion	102
39. Together Again	105
40. Fear	108
41. New Beginnings	110
42. Friendship	115
43. The Crouches	118
44. The Aldridges	120
45. Growing Up and Stretching	124
46. Happiness, Grief, and Recovery	128
47. A Virginia Excursion	133
48. The Road to Disney World	136
49. Summer Days	142
50. Following Bryant's Instructions	146
51. Palm Sunday	148
52. Adjusting to Changes	150
53. More Changes	152
54. Graduation Day	155
55. Emptying the Nest	158
56. The End of the Tunnel	161
57. Strengthening a Friendship	164
58. Home at Last	165
59. Mema Failing	167
60. 1976—Celebrating the Bicentennial	168
61. A Lesson in Williamsburg	171
62. A Nightmare in November	174
63. Better Not Bitter	179
64. The Spirit of Christmas	184
65. Nannie	185
66. Dan, Jr. and Wingate	187
67. The Changing Roles of Parenting	189
68. Sandy	193
69. Another Milestone	200
70. A Strong Constitution	202
71. Our First Wedding	204
72. Allene	207
73. You Gotta Let It Go	210

74. That Last Year	213
75. The World's Fair	217
76. Paddling About	219
77. A Step Back in Time	221
78. Rewards	223
79. Out of the Fold	226
80. Taylor	228
81. Competing in Raleigh	232
82. Attractions of Home	237
83. A Corner Darkening	241
84. Brandon	244
85. Feelings Disturbed	246
86. Mema	250
87. Breathing Time	252
88. Surprise Ending	254
89. The Day Hospital	255
90. Millie and Jesse	257
91. Painful Departures	260
92. Love is Magical	263
93. Dreams Become a Reality	268
94. More Gifts from Heaven	274
95. Dan	284
96. Adding Chantilly Lace Memories	296
97. New Beginnings	300
98. Hawaii	304
99. Tadge and Daniel	308
100. Inspiration	311
101. Seeking Direction	314
102. New York, New York	318
103. Changing Positions	321
104. Easter Angel	326
105. 1991 Progressing	330
106. Capturing the Surprise	336

For all the world to see,
The simple joy of you and me,
We long for this for everyone,
Yet know it cannot be.

— Jean Peake Aldridge

*Memoirs
by two dear friends
remembering the times they shared
and how a treasured friendship grew...*

Chapter 1

Jean

Going away to school can be very traumatic. My brother was serving in the Korean War during this particular time in my life. Thanks to his love for me, his great appreciation for education, and his generous heart, he was able to send home $100 a month to my mother to help pay my tuition in college, and they made me go.

Sandy and I grew up together with a single parent, in a small southern town, living in our grandparents' home. We shared a room with our mother. He had the day bed in the corner, and mother and I shared the big double bed. It was a nice room. Mother and I were always trying to fix it up and make it pretty. I can see now the brightly flowered drapes we made from dress material gathered on a rod. It always worried me though, the big peeling area of plaster on the wall under the front windows. Our grandfather was in the cement block business, so our home was constructed out of cement block, and the moisture always came through, somehow causing the plaster to peel and flake. After thirty five years of keeping house myself now, I can better understand the time it takes to get repairs like this taken care of. And it was our home, the home my grandparents built for their children, and their children's children.

Mother worked at a local department store, providing for our needs; Sandy found his privacy in the piano; and I stayed busy and happy running from one school activity to another. We had the love and direction we needed to survive.

The bed I found at school was not double, but single — my bed! Mother and I covered it with fresh, sweet sheets with my name stitched on them, a new, bright red wool blanket (I wonder what ever happened to that blanket.), and a green J.C. Penney cord bedspread. My bed, my desk, my dresser, my closet—even a little throw rug beside the bed. At the windows were bleached muslin curtains Mother and I had made; they were all trimmed with fringe we made from tobacco twine, tied back and gathered on a rod, which allowed the sunlight to filter in through the huge windows. I could cry myself to sleep at night if I was upset now; I could turn over at night without disturbing mother; and she could do the same back at home.

Traumatic? No, my mother and brother had sent me to heaven. This was nice.

Now, Phoebe, on the other hand, was homesick for all the good things that I had discovered at school.

Chapter 2

Phoebe

Phoebe recalls, "I remember the first time I was homesick. I was ten years old, and my mama and daddy had taken me to Girl Scout camp in Gastonia right after my grandmother died. It was an awful feeling, and I knew I didn't like it! The next time I had that same sick-like feeling was the time they brought me off to Peace College, and I didn't like that either."

"We drove down from the mountains of North Carolina, and my Aunt Mary had to come with us. She was a school teacher and knew everything! She wanted to see where I was going to college, and she could tell us how to do! I won't ever forget the feeling I had as I watched them drive away on their way back home. I thought I would die!"

"I missed that home. I was sad. I missed everything about that house my daddy had built with his own hands. All of a sudden, I missed my mama's flowers. She always had flowers, flowers blooming all over, and she talked to the birds in the feeder at the kitchen window. I missed my mama. She was always there waiting for me in the kitchen whenever I came home, no matter when, be it from school, or a piano lesson, or voice lesson, or church. I missed my room! I had everything in my room that I could possibly want. My mama was a wonderful cook, and whenever I was studying in my room, she would always bring me one of her good sandwiches. She made the best! They were always filled with ham and cheese and lettuce, tomatoes, cucumbers, and onions."

"I was an only child. My parents were always there for me, doing whatever it took to make my life as comfortable as possible, and I was in love."

"It was not my idea to come to Peace, but more that of my future in-laws who thought it was the best place for me, and I can always remember my daddy saying, 'Gal, as long as you live under my roof and eat my meat and bread, you're going to do two things: mind me and get a good education.' So here I was, staring into a room I had never seen before, and they had told me I had to share this room with a person I had never seen before. They really expected me to live here away from all the things that I loved! And there she was, my blond roommate, in our room. Why couldn't she have been the pretty girl with the long, brown hair, all pinned back on the side with a silver barrette—the girl we saw when we got here today? She had on a white dress, a shirtwaist dress, with a bright red, ribbon, windowpane design. I never will forget that dress!"

Chapter 3

Peace College

 *P*eace College still stands today, just as it did forty years ago, surrounded by a well designed and pleasantly landscaped campus. Its Main Building, like a serene and stately antebellum mansion, is dramatically situated at the head of an avenue of gigantic oaks and magnolia trees. Although the signs of progress are evident today when one sees the new buildings surrounding the old, the charm of this woman's college has still not been lost.

 The impressive old Main Building is a handsome, red brick Greek Revival structure whose massiveness is lightened by Italianate and Victorian accents. Its huge, white Doric columns and swan work balustered porches remain the same, and it is the beautifully maintained dominant building on the campus.

 We arrived on campus on a brisk, fall day in 1952, and it became our home. Our arrival was relatively simple compared to freshmen of today going away to college. There were no stereos, televisions, microwaves, refrigerators, or other necessary appliances to be unloaded. We merely packed our belongings in the two pieces of Samsonite luggage each of us had received for our high school graduation gift, filled a foot locker with new sheets and towels, and with that, moved in and began this new adventure.

 As we reflect today on that experience, we never dreamed that it was the beginning of a friendship that would last a lifetime, but then what is a friendship? We had lots of friends, we walked to the corner drugstore with a friend, we went to the movies with a friend, we double dated with friends, we laughed and enjoyed many good times with friends, but what happened to all those friends, and where are they today? This is just another reminder to us of our unique gift.

 The story we are about to tell may not seem extraordinary to anyone else, but because we feel we have been blessed with a special gift, we have an overwhelming desire to record our feelings and emotions for our children and their children to hold dear.

Chapter 4

College Orientation

Phoebe and I were lucky enough to be assigned rooms in the Main Building of Peace College. The newer dormitory called East was connected to the main building by a corridor, safely enclosed with large glass windows and heavy French doors. We eventually found out that we had more in common with the girls in Main. They became our closer friends, and the ones we still keep in touch with at Christmas and on special occasions.

I was assigned to a room on fourth floor, on the hall with Miss Lucy Steele, our Bible teacher. At Peace, a teacher lived on every hall with the girls, acting as an advisor, even a mother figure if the need ever arose. Phoebe's room was on third floor, located just a few doors down from Miss Hall, our dean, and her suite of rooms.

Miss Hall was a short, little lady probably weighing all of 115 pounds. Her hair was greying slightly. She kept it cut short with a permanent to make it curly, and her expression was always serious. When she was persuaded to smile, her round face resembled that of a cornered chipmunk with fat, little cheeks. I'm sure she seemed much older to us than she really was at that time. She dressed very appropriately for all occasions, but we remember her most in her prissy, dark cotton dresses with big, white, lace trimmed collars, and her shoes! Her shoes — well, we really thought that she could do better with her shoes! Ugly, sturdy, laced up Oxfords, with thick heels! She was so prim and proper, so feminine, but those shoes were awful. Today, we know that she probably was looking for the most comfortable thing she could find to walk those long halls to take care of her girls. She had a distinct Virginia brogue, and we always snickered when she said, "Girls, go to your rooms!" It sounded like "rum" to us.

Miss Hall was an "old Peace girl," and she had taken on this brand new job, seemingly determined to prove her capabilities and authority. She tried hard to be tough, but we knew that she was as tender and soft as a kitten. She would be very proud of us today for recapturing these memories.

The President's Tea was a highlight that first Sunday afternoon at Peace. We walked the half block up Wilmington Street to Dr. and Mrs. Pressly's home. We must have been a picture all dressed in our crisp, white dresses and white gloves, parading to meet our new president. We were young girls, amazed at the first sight of this beautiful, old, white Victorian home. As we approached the ornately carved banisters surrounding the narrow porch across the front of the house, we could see the lace curtains moving gently inside the long, thin open windows on the first floor.

We remember the large terra cotta flower pots, brimming over with lemon yellow chrysanthemums on either side of the steps, as we very nervously waited our turn in line to greet Dr. and Mrs. Pressly.

Have you ever watched someone awkwardly trying to balance a tea cup and saucer, a dainty plate of party food, both hands full, and no place to set down either plate? Well, here was a long line of girls, standing in the heat, trying to look cool and refined, getting more and more anxious over that balancing act we had to face. Phoebe, in her usual comical way, passed the word to just pretend you're an octopus with white gloves on. My solution, on the other hand, was "If you don't know what to do with the goods, just stand there, hold it, and keep your mouth shut."

After standing there making all those brilliant, sarcastic remarks, we reached the door and were greeted by Dr. and Mrs. Pressly. We were immediately aware of his dignity and jovial personality. He had the wonderful ability of making you feel comfortable and at ease. Our worries were over! Lime punch and tea cakes never tasted so good.

Dr. Pressly was nearly bald, but his thick, black, bushy eyebrows made you wonder if he had had a dark, thick, full head of hair as a young man. His brown eyes, looking from behind those round glasses, reflected a kind and gentle man. He was tall and large in stature. He camouflaged his middle age spread well under dark, three piece business suits, and ever present was that gold pocket watch and chain, the chain hooked through the third buttonhole on his vest and the watch dropped into the right hand pocket.

In the days and weeks to come, we felt his strength and caring concern for each of us, even though we knew he was in full authority. Chapel programs weekly and Sunday night Vespers were always presided over by Dr. Pressly. His very presence, devotions and moving prayers added to our feelings of security. He made us feel very special by recognizing and addressing us immediately, and always as Miss Fair and Miss Peake. We knew his door was open to us whenever we needed him. He was truly our friend, our wise counselor, and we adored him.

Chapter 5

Friends Meeting

We quickly fell into the routine of schedules that had been assigned to us. We were awakened every morning at 7:20 by the sound of that familiar bell ringing. Ten minutes later, it would ring again to let us know that we had better get up! Breakfast was served, as all our meals were, in a large, warm dining room filled with round tables covered with white linen table cloths, and set for eight in the traditional Peace College white china trimmed with a green band. We stood behind our chairs and waited for Miss Hall to enter the dining room and have our blessing before we seated ourselves. We found our places marked with personalized napkin rings, our names stamped in the traditional emerald green school colors. We used these napkin rings every day for the duration of our stay at Peace. Seated at each table was always a teacher who acted as hostess, and without our ever realizing it, we practiced good table manners, intelligent conversation around a dinner table, and gradually gained more confidence and were comfortable in our new environment.

Every week we changed tables in the dining room and became acquainted with another faculty member and more students. It was always a thrill finally to get to "Miss Hall's Table." That was like an invitation to eat at the Captain's table on a cruise ship. By Thanksgiving, we were familiar with most of the students, our homesickness was forgotten, and we felt the security of a new-found family.

Rooming next door to me was JoAnn, a high school friend of Jean's. Because my blonde roommate and I had nothing in common, and were not compatible at all, most of my free time was spent in JoAnn's room. She was good natured and had a really sweet roommate. They had become great friends and greeted me with open arms and lots of understanding.

Back in those days, if a girl wanted to smoke, she had to go to a room designated "The Smoker." This room was over in the new East building.

Jean's roommate, Sylvia, loved to smoke, and Jean quickly found out that every time a bell rang, and there was any free time, Sylvia ran for "The Smoker." This is one of the reasons why Jean found herself in JoAnn's room, too. So this is where we finally met!

In getting to know each other during those first few weeks, we found that we were two individuals as different as East and West, yet we were comfortable together, having basically the same values and beliefs. As our friendship grew, we realized we trusted each other, could make each other laugh until we cried, and accepted each other simply for what we were.

I was happy in every aspect of college life but continued to have my share of roommate problems. My blonde roommate was a little weird! In fact, she was off the wall! She was born ten years too soon! She could have been a perfect flower child of the 60's. She would sit cross legged on the bed and say, "You know, we're really in heaven if you think about it, because anything above is heaven. Right?" I would look at her and think, girl, you are strange...all of your lights are on but you're not at home.

Needless to say, I had to get away from her, so I gathered up all of my courage after only two weeks and went to Miss Hall's office to ask if I could move into an empty room located next door to Jean and Sylvia. She agreed, and this worked out fine until they moved a new student in with me within a matter of a few days.

She was a real rebel and refused to abide by any of the long established rules that we had never questioned. One of the first rules impressed upon us when we arrived at Peace was signing in and out. This was asking no more than what was expected of us at home. It never occurred to us not to let our parents know where we were or when we would return. She refused to do any of this and was determined to have her own way. What a horrible conflict she created for herself. She scared me to death! I had never been around anyone like her. Eventually she was sent home .... wonder where she was sent from there?

By this time, Jean and I had decided that it would be a good idea for me to move in with her and Sylvia, and Sylvia agreed. She was so laid back, anything was all right with her. Their room was large and had plenty of space for another bed and dresser without crowding anybody. I gathered up my courage once again, but this time with Jean's support and with her right at my side, I asked Miss Hall to grant us this wish. She did. This was easier than we had expected. We were so pleased with ourselves. It had worked out just like we planned.

The days that followed were made even better now that we were

Friends Meeting

"Ruummates," and from that time on we have affectionately called each other "Ruum."

Chapter 6

Sylvia

Sylvia was quite a character! She kept us laughing just about all the time. She came from a beach family of, I think, eight children ... lots of sisters and a brother, and she had more tales to tell. I guess that comes from growing up in a big family. She was a beautiful brunette with a happy spirit, and her brown eyes would get bigger and bigger as Phoebe and I listened in awe to her wild stories. She would get our undivided attention and walk around the room talking, always with her hands motioning. Sometimes, she would start singing and suddenly break out into a crazy tap dance ... she loved to dance and was quite good at it.

We remember one story she told us about her daddy. She always fussed about how stingy he was, but with so many children he probably had to be! One night when they were the only ones at home, he ordered her to cook him some supper, and she kept telling him there was no food in the house. He said, "Sylvia, I know there's something in that kitchen to eat." Well, Miss Angry, Brazen Sylvia served her father a plate of lard, flour, and sugar, set it down in front of him, and ran like crazy! She didn't come home until late that night. She swore this was a fact, and all we could think of was, "what nerve." Imagine that nerve! Phoebe and I were afraid to raise our voices to anyone.

She was also kind of lazy or maybe was always in such a hurry to get to The Smoker. We really didn't know which. Consequently, she never had time to bathe or pick up her clothes or clutter. Phoebe and I tried to live around it and finally decided to do something about it. Halloween came, and this gave us a good reason for a prank. She had not changed her sheets since the first night at school, and we were afraid to say anything to her about it. We didn't want to hurt her feelings. Now, we had our chance! We began to scheme! We mixed up the worse concoction of goo, cocoa, peanut butter, sweet smelling powder; you name it, we used it! We spread it all over her sheet, short sheeted the bed, so when she came in from The Smoker, she would have to change her bed. She finally came in, went to bed, got up, and pulled those sheets off her bed, got back in bed, and never said a word. Phoebe and I just looked at each other. She slept from then until Christmas on the bare mattress. She really outsmarted us; it didn't matter to her, and besides, she only had one set of sheets.

Chapter 7

Settling In

We were settled now and understood each other. The order established for our lives at Peace was enjoyed and appreciated. We never felt as if any freedom had been taken away from us. We were always allowed to express our opinions and to grow and understand the feelings of others. We were content with our safe and secure environment and respected those who worked hard to provide this privilege for us. Like most college students, we stayed busy with the normal routine of attending classes, studying as much as possible, and participating in most of the extra-curricular activities on a college campus.

The fact that we had to dress properly, even wear hats and gloves when we went shopping, became a measure of pride for us when we were recognized as "Peace Girls." Dressing for dinner and being required to wear stockings sometimes presented a problem for us if we had a "run." We quickly learned a remedy for this, for the newest thing out in fashion was knee hose.

Our evening meals were really an experience in fine dining — relaxed, unhurried, and quietly served by women in black uniforms with stiffly, starched white collar and cuffs, and waiters who always treated us as ladies. Part of our Peace family were these kind, hard-working people. They were there to serve us three times a day. As we learned to call each of them by name, we developed a great appreciation for their service and a special affection for them. Unlike the random-access cafeterias in the colleges today, we realize we took all of this for granted. This peaceful atmosphere unknowingly prepared us for studying later, or it was supposed to.

We always had closed study in our rooms, with special permission to study in the library from 7 until 10 Monday through Thursday nights. Of course, closed study was not always spent studying although our grades never reflected this. We were caught many nights, laughing too loud over something very silly, with our door wide open, by Miss Hall when she was patrolling. Phoebe remembers one night when she caught us. We were

Settling In

trying desperately to study and had our feet propped on the wall over the headboard of our beds. Phoebe's feet were fat and her toes kind of stuck up, and my toes were long and boney. Her little toes stuck up so much that she never could make a print in the sand at the beach. Anyway, Phoebe got carried away with comparing our feet, and we got so tickled we never realized that Miss Hall was standing in our doorway or even how long she had been there. Suddenly, she appeared, glaring and peering over the top of her glasses wondering what we were doing. We gained control of ourselves. We quickly and mischievously declared that our mothers had told us to spend a certain amount of time each night with our feet propped above our heads while we studied. It was good for circulation and gave you a pretty complexion. With her stern expression, she pursed her lips, looked at us all knowingly, and said, "Girls, close your door!"

Do you think for one minute that she really believed the cocky little story we told her? She affectionately signed our annuals at the end of the year, "Close your door!"—M. S. Hall.

Phoebe recalls that we tolerated our physical education classes. We loved tennis; but when it came time for playing hockey, Jean had already figured out that the goalie did not have to run or get hit with a "stick"! Guess who always played the goalie? Jean said, "Field hockey was never very appealing to me. I always felt like it was a game for a bunch of men, all running back and forth kicking and knocking each other around with those sticks, nothing feminine about it. I didn't like putting on all of that garb of masks and gloves and leg pads. At least playing the goalie gave me an individual part without getting kicked as much." Phoebe was the one running up and down the field getting hit with a stick!

A special event that we always looked forward to was attending the Community Concert Series four times a year. We dressed in our finest party clothes, and at the appropriate time, we were loaded on city buses and hauled off to Memorial Auditorium in downtown Raleigh. There, we mingled with other concert goers. Meredith and St. Mary students were also bused in the same manner to the concerts, and it gave us an opportunity to visit with high school friends from these schools. We learned to appreciate the talents of world famous concert artists and to enjoy a cultural evening out.

Students never missed a concert; being in the infirmary was the only acceptable excuse. Some people would be amused at this requirement, and our hearts ache for a young girl of today ill at ease and unable to carry on a simple conversation at a social function, not even knowing the correct fork to use at a dinner party.

Chapter 8

The Special Boys

There were no planned activities for the weekends at school because so many girls went away, and this made it very lonely for me. Jean went home or to Durham every weekend. My home was three hundred miles away, so I was unable to go home except for Thanksgiving and Christmas holidays, and I missed my high school sweetheart! We planned to be married soon after graduation. Dan had joined the Navy and he was stationed in San Diego, California, so I certainly never had a date on the weekends. I made myself content by eating lunch at Walgreens Drug Store on Saturdays or attending a movie with one of my weekend buddies and writing love letters to Dan.

Sundays passed quickly with Sunday school and church and youth activities at First Baptist Church. I looked forward to Sunday nights because my "Ruum" would return, always just minutes before the ten o'clock bell rang. I could understand though, because I was not the only one in love. Jean was in love with her high school sweetheart, too, and Bryant managed somehow to time their return on Sunday nights just perfectly.

Unlike Phoebe who was so sure of marrying Dan, I was just happy and thrilled at this point in my life to be going steady with Bryant. He and I had been in the same class in high school and had never really paid any attention to each other until our junior year. We met the summer before that year on the beach, with a crowd of our mutual high school friends. The crazy, daring thing to do in those days was to steal watermelons and take them back to the beach for sharing around a bonfire. We piled into one of the fellow's pick-up truck and found a watermelon patch. The guys sneaked into the patch, grabbed a watermelon under each arm, ran helter-skelter trying to get back to the truck in the dark, hopped back into the truck, and off we went back to the beach. This was our first real meeting, not an official date, but a special memory for both of us today. I don't think he even called me on the telephone after that until after my sixteenth

The Special Boys

birthday that summer. He did surprise me with a box of chocolate covered cherries for my birthday that July, along with a simple but sweet card signed very shyly, "Love, Bryant." I thought he was absolutely the most thoughtful person I had ever met. (I think I really fell in love with him then!) Every time I see a box of chocolate covered cherries today, I am reminded of that precious 16th birthday present.

After that, Bryant and I became good friends and dated occasionally. It was not until after our senior year in high school that he asked me to go steady, and we realized how much we meant to each other. I wore that big class ring for nearly four years and faithfully changed that great wad of adhesive tape every month or so to make it fit my finger.

Bryant was our big high school hero. He was class president all four years, outstanding athlete, loved by everyone; and I was so proud to claim him. He accepted a football scholarship to Duke University, only thirty miles away from Peace, so it was easy for us to see each other often. Football practice began in August, and in his first week of practice, he hurt his knee badly. Some big linebacker ran over him and knocked his knee backwards causing hyperextension. After this injury, he spent the first four weeks in Duke Hospital trying to recuperate. I naturally took advantage of every possible ride I could get to Durham to be with him. Sometimes, his mother and father would pick me up and take me with them; at other times, his older brother Jesse gave me a lift, and still other times, friends going to visit him would give me a ride. We didn't realize just how serious his injury was until late in his recurperation when the doctors told us that there had been the possibility of amputation to that leg because of the extent of the injury. He was young and a good patient and eventually was released from the hospital only during the day to attend classes. He did this on crutches for the first two months of school, and not surprising to me, he was elected president of his freshman class at Duke. We lived for the weekends when we could see each other. I was either going home or going to a football game in Durham.

At Peace, we could only take phone calls at night after closed study. There were three telephone booths in the main lobby on first floor, and I stood in line nearly every night waiting for Bryant's call. He always called! I've always known I could depend on him. There were many nights when he would be waiting in the parlor for a thirty minute date, for we could only have callers after closed study on week nights from ten until ten thirty! He became a familiar face on campus.

Chapter 9

Christmas Break — 1952

Going home for Christmas that first year in college was eagerly awaited for and wonderful! I always felt important and grown up. Everybody was happy to see me, and the excitement of the holidays was so much fun. Two whole weeks of freedom away from books and classes, and for me I could see Bryant every day. It all passed so quickly, and Phoebe recalls," Mama had cooked me everything I liked in the whole world that Christmas," but we both found that we were anxious after this time to return to school. We were excited to see each other in January and to get back into the swing of things that we had already grown to love at Peace. Every new experience had been a grand and happy surprise for us. Going back home for a long visit that first year in college sometimes made us realize this. It just wasn't the same back home, it was different, and this was as it should be. We really belonged here now, growing and preparing ourselves for a new world.

We had made some great friends, three in particular whom we spent most of our free time with that second semester. We all lived on different halls but had found each other. Our roommate, Sylvia, was never around much. We had to catch her in between bridge games at The Smoker, or just catch her at The
Smoker, so we saw very little of her, although we loved her; and when we were together, it was truly enlightening! She brought us all the gossip from East!

Ann, Martha, and Sylvia Morrow were our buddies now. (Another Sylvia but very different.) Ann was the beauty queen and the teacher's pet! She was always perfectly groomed and smelled of Johnson's baby powder. We stood back in awe of Ann. Martha was reserved with a quick, dry wit that would catch us by surprise, and Sylvia was always laughing and happy. She was an excellent student, a wonderful, thoughtful girl, and we still can hear her cackling laughter.

Chapter 10

Happy Times—Sad Times

It seems so simple now, but what a pleasant memory we have of the afternoons we five girls spent walking to the Person Street Drug. We were so protected at school. We would sign out to the drug store and take off. We could only walk two blocks away in this particular direction, to the Person Street Drug, so this was one of our big afternoon outings. There probably has never been made a more perfect Cherry Coke than the ones we enjoyed on those carefree days. Strolling along those oak-lined streets, we were unhurried and free from fear. We giggled, gossiped, and light heartedly made fun of each other. We usually ended up doing the "Camel Walk" back to the green wooden benches lining the herringbone brick walkways around the fountain at the front entrance to Peace. Here, we would daydream and be as philosophical as an eighteen year old might be, listening to the water trickling over the fountain in the background.

We were dressed almost exactly alike sitting there on those old worn benches—those short-sleeved Angora sweaters with Peter Pan dickies, straight skirts, white bobby socks and penny loafers, or black and white saddle oxfords. There was no such thing then as jeans or slacks, tee shirts or flip-flops.

Surrounding the campus was a lovely, old, wrought iron and brick wall. We could be found on many of those lazy days swinging merrily on the huge ornate gate that separated Peace from the Raleigh streets at night. We still have pictures of five silly girls laughing, singing, and keeping time to the big old hinge squeaking on the main gate.

Many long and short afternoons were spent just simply waiting for the time when we had to fly inside to dress for dinner. Each of us could run up and down those four flights of stairs, sometimes taking them two at a time with boundless energy.

The side oak treads on the stairs leading up through the central halls of Main Building were already worn hollow from many years of traveling up and down by hundreds of other young women. We could stand on the fourth floor, look all the way down to the Main lobby, and see who was coming and going, as the stairs wound their way up from one floor to the next. They literally echoed with activity. Phoebe and I certainly contributed our share of wear and tear running up and down those stairs to and from classes, dates, parties, and meals. Looking back now, it's kind of nice to know we did.

Little things like this become such an every day way of life. You don't stop to think about where a stairway leads you. We realize now how that stairway led us to happy times as well as sad times. We remember not running with eagerness, as usual, but walking, frightened and sad, down the steps to meet Bryant in the Main lobby the day his father died. It was February, and Bryant was deep into spring football practice. He received a call that his father had died suddenly of a heart attack, his young father, only 47 years old. He never saw his son play the first college football game and would never know the successful man he would become. What do you say?

By the time Bryant arrived at Peace, Miss Hall had given Jean permission to leave with him for his parents' home. We had never experienced this kind of trauma in our lives before, and it was hard to understand. The tragedy we shared was just not supposed to happen.

After they left for home, Phoebe climbed her way back up the long flight of stairs to the fourth floor, feeling helpless, back to a lonely, quiet room, knowing that there was nothing she could do but wait out those long days until they returned.

Chapter 11

May Day and Summer Vacation

By the middle of the second semester, we realized it would be more to our advantage to change from the liberal arts courses we were taking to all business courses the next year. French, English, and math were a vital contribution to our education, and we learned to appreciate music even more from our Music History classes. What we had learned from Miss Lucy's Bible class was already affecting our lives, but Phoebe could not be convinced that dissecting a frog in biology would help her get a secretarial job after she was married. We had to be practical. Jean knew she would be financially unable to continue her education after graduating from Peace, so we made another major decision together. We would begin the Commercial Course the following year.

It was spring and time for us to sign up for our fall courses, and as Miss Lucy would say, "We made an about face and went in another direction!" That was the beginning of a new world, a challenge to learn secretarial skills that we hoped would better prepare us for work after graduation.

Spring also meant May Day. Now, how many of you have ever wrapped a May Pole? Well, Jean never has, but I have! Weeks before, we elected our May Queen and her court. Jean and Ann were our representatives on the May Court. The rest of us were assigned a part of the program for entertainment. I was one of the girls assigned to wrap the May Pole. Now, I have never thought of myself as a nymph, but there I was practicing to be one! Everyday for weeks, we would go through our routine. I went to sleep at night hearing Miss Fowler, our P.E. instructor, saying, "Make sure you have the right color ribbon, weave in and out, do it gracefully, slowly, in time with the music. Remember, you are a goddess of the meadow." I would die laughing and make some cute remark about me being a goddess! Finally, the big day arrived. Out on the front lawn under the magnolia trees and giant oaks, the scene was set. The May Pole was in place, and parents and families were seated, laughing, waving, and stretching to see their pride and joy. The music began, and all eyes were on the main entrance. There was my "Ruum" in her lavender, nylon net gown, worn over a full hoop skirt. She was carrying a matching taffeta, ruffled parasol with a bouquet of spring flowers attached to the handle. She was the prettiest thing I had ever seen. When the queen and her court were in place, the program began. The wrapping of the May Pole was the last thing in the program.

Enter the nymphs, dressed in rainbow colored, ankle length ballerina dresses with little ballet slippers. Now, if I wasn't a sight, weaving those ribbons in and out and around that pole! We whispered sarcastic remarks and tried to keep from giggling as the wrapping of that May Pole drew us closer and closer together. We felt very silly, and all Jean and Ann had to do was watch.

The May Pole and May Day festivities were a big success. When the guests and families were gone, the queen's maiden and the "Goddess of the Meadow" went to their room with another memory tucked away.

Spring fever affected us all. We were eager for final exams to be over and for summer vacation to begin. Phoebe headed for the cool of the mountains, and I went home to the hot, humid, flat lands of eastern North Carolina after graduation exercises were over. Ann and I had been elected as marshals for our class, so we stayed at school after all of our friends left for home that first summer. My cousin, Pat, lent me a long, white organdy dress to wear as a marshal, and we felt very important with our green and gold satin sashes over our white gowns, ushering for the graduation. Bryant came, and endured the heat in the chapel at Peace, just so that he could give me a ride home.

My summer was spent behind the counter of a local dry cleaners. A hot, dull, boring job, taking in and sorting dirty clothes, but it enabled me to earn $1.75 a day. (Even at that, Mrs. Tagmeyer, the owner, thought she was doing me a favor. My mother had always told me to tell employers to pay me what they thought I was worth. She was so afraid I wouldn't get the job. I don't know that I agree with that philosophy, but I did what I was told to do.) This would be my spending money for the coming year, and enough to buy Bryant and my family Christmas gifts. Oh, yes, I'll always remember Bryant's gift that year; it was a strawberry red Cashmere sweater, purchased for $21.95.

I looked forward that summer to attending Ann's wedding. She had been engaged the entire time that we had known her, and she was so excited that the big day had arrived! Clinton was only 65 miles away, so

May Day and Summer Vacation

Bryant and I had a wonderful, leisurely ride down there for all of the romantic festivities that day. Ann was even more beautiful as a bride, with those long, blonde curls, and every hair in perfect place. Her plans were to return to Peace in the fall and live in the dorm from Monday through Friday, just as usual. We couldn't imagine this ever happening, but it did, and it's still hard to believe she lived so normally for the next year with this arrangement.

Phoebe and I kept in touch throughout the summer. Her letters described shopping sprees, helping her mother with canning from their big garden, and regular trips to Lake Lure with Dan and his family whenever Dan could get leave. She would also elaborate in great length of the hours she spent helping Dan's mother prepare for dinner parties. She knows today that Mrs. Crouch and Cora, the maid, were grooming the new daughter-in-law to be.

The Korean War ended in July that summer of 1953. War was so unnecessary, such a waste, but we knew it was important to stop the spread of Communism during this conflict. I remember knitting Sandy an Army green wool scarf, and I found him a pair of battery heated socks that I sent to him the Christmas before that. Now, all I could think of was that he would be coming home, safe and well. There was a glorious air of relief everywhere. We rejoiced at the thought of a peaceful world.

Chapter 12

Our Dorm Room

*S*eptember arrived, and we found ourselves back in Raleigh at Peace, filled with happiness, excitement, and confidence. It was nothing like the previous year, and we could feel for all of the new freshmen, but we also knew what they had to look forward to. We were big seniors now! Second year out of high school! We were big deals! We were confident!

Our previous roommate had moved to East this year with one of her new friends, so they could be nearer The Smoker. (The last time we saw Sylvia, our roommate, was at our 30th class reunion, and she was still smoking.)

Phoebe and I made big plans for our new room. The room we had selected for this year was on the third floor, the same floor that all of our other friends were on. Ann, Martha, and Sylvia Morrow had gotten a triple just down the hall from us, and this was great. We had a very spacious room, the only one on the hall with an inside closet, situated just across from the bathroom. We thought we had the best location in the dorm until Phoebe's daddy saw it.

She recollects that first day, "My daddy was a fireman for the City of Asheville. When he set the last suitcase down in our room, he walked to the window and observed that our room was directly over the kitchen. According to him, we did not have a good escape route in the event of fire. When we went back downstairs, my daddy asked Miss Hall if he could inspect the kitchen. He told her 'his girls' did not have a safe location. I thought I would die! After the inspection, he told her, 'You should have the Raleigh Fire Department come out and go over the whole building, and have monthly fire drills!' Needless-to-say, when we had a fire drill at midnight, I never mentioned the fact that my daddy had anything to do with it."

Our little clique of five trotting off to the Person Street Drug was increased to seven as we included the two new girls living directly across

Our Dorm Room

the hall from us. Betty and Suzanne were only freshmen, cute and heaps of fun. We quickly related to them and became great buddies. Betty was from Richmond, Virginia, with the longest, most drawn out Virginia drawl we had ever heard. She first appeared in Bermuda shorts and matching knee socks! We thought she was straight out of Vogue! All the way from Richmond, Virginia! They were amusing and made great "Roomies across the hall."

The five o'clock train on Friday carried Betty back to Richmond almost every weekend, and Suzanne always had a ride to Greensboro as soon as she got out of class on Fridays.

Typing was a new experience for me, and with Jean always gone on the weekends, Saturday mornings were a good time to go to the typing room and practice. It helped fill the morning hours and increased my typing speed. One Saturday, I finished my typing practice and after lunch went by the post office to check the mail. There was almost always a letter from my mama, but this time I had not only a letter but a box of fresh apples from the mountains. When I got to our room, I opened the box, took one, and went out on the porch, sat in the swing, and enjoyed every bit of that Red Delicious. It tasted so good! When I had finished, I went back to our room and got another one. Well, to make a long story short, I didn't stop until I had eaten six apples. You would think I would have gotten sick, but I didn't. I just got happy, sitting there swinging and thinking about the mountains and my mama and daddy sending us those apples. Packed inside that box of apples was a quart size Mason jar full of Sourwood honey. I could hardy wait for Jean to return that weekend to show her our surprise and share the apples with her. She was delighted, but the thing that interested her most was not the apples but the Sourwood honey. She had never heard of a Sourwood tree and had never eaten Sourwood honey. I had grown up on this honey because my daddy had bee hives out in the country. The first thing we did with that Sourwood honey was take it to breakfast the next morning and put it on those piping hot biscuits they served us each day. Jean loved it, and I got more pleasure out of watching her eat it than eating it myself. When my daddy found out how much she enjoyed it, we were never without it. Daddy said that his "brown-eyed angel" would have as much as she wanted. That's what my daddy called Jean.

Jean's family today loves Sourwood honey. Every time she and Bryant are in Asheville now, they make a special trip out to Farmer's Market and stock up on this honey to share with their family and friends. She says this always reminds her of my daddy and hot biscuits at Peace College.

For All The World To See

No matter what our schedule was, I shot out of bed every morning like a rocket! I hit the floor running! Before the bell stopped ringing, my bed was made. (This always bugged Jean, and she would say, "It doesn't make any sense to make up a bed so fast and be in such a hurry all the time.") I headed for the showers. Jean began to stir when the second bell rang. She would be sitting on the side of her bed as I returned to the room. Me zipping around and Jean at a steady pace always ended with us going downstairs together for breakfast. For the life of me, I never could understand how she managed to be ready at the same time I was. All my zipping around never got me there any sooner.

After several weeks in the new Commercial Course, we could tell that our work was easier. We practiced on those business machines and typewriters in the afternoons, and we didn't have a whole lot of studying to do at night.

Three hours of closed study every night could be long! We were not allowed to turn on the radio, we couldn't leave our room, and we were usually through studying in an hour. Phoebe's mama sent us fudge that we would hide under the bed with the apples and honey, and that would keep us happy for awhile, but we were always looking for something else to do. One night Jean looked at me and said, "Ruum, let me cut your hair, let me cut all that frizz off." So we spread newspapers under a chair, and she cut my hair. It wasn't bad, but I haven't let her cut it since then!

Another night, Jean almost cut the end of her finger off. She was good at cutting things. We had stocked up on snack foods from the Halifax Street Grocery, just across the street from Peace, and we carefully squirreled that under the bed, too. We hid all of our "goods" under the bed, sure that no one would ever find our cache. The bedspreads hung all the way to the floor, and we knew that nobody would ever look under the bed. No telling how many roaches we fed! We had no intention of sharing our food.

Yeah, Jean nearly cut off the end of her finger. She was attempting to attack one of those devilish little Vienna Sausage cans with the key on top. You had to pull the key off and hook it in the little metal band that ran around the top of the can. You would turn, and turn, and turn that key until the top was free. When she tried to lift the top of that can, she cut her index finger really bad but taking her to the infirmary was out! No way were we going to explain those Vienna Sausage cans in our room to anybody! We played "nurse" quick for the remainder of that closed study and managed just fine. She's got a scar on that finger to this day from it. She doesn't eat Vienna Sausage any more, even though today access to

Our Dorm Room

those calorie filled sausages come in an easy pop-top can.

Warm autumn nights and restless young girls all closed up in a room are certainly not the combination that would create an atmosphere conducive to concentrating for very long. It was on one of these beautiful, balmy, Indian summer evenings that Phoebe and I had finished our work and felt brave enough to slip quietly out of our room, tip-toe down the hall and make our way out onto the front porch on third floor. We checked in every direction, as we eased ourselves through Central Hall to the porch, making sure we had not been seen. We knew it would be safer sitting in the big green rocking chairs stretching from one end of the porch to the other, rather than the swing that we all loved. The chains on the swing were notorious for squeaking when you were seeking a quiet refuge. We knew that would be a sure give-away!

We had our choice of rockers that night. We propped our feet on the banisters and reared back, much as I remember my uncle, Carlton, doing in a straight back chair in front of his little country store, ready to solve all the questions of the day. We complimented each other on this accomplishment and actually decided that we would spend the last minutes of closed study like this--weather permitting--whenever we wanted to. On this momentous night, I was expecting Bryant at ten o'clock for a thirty-minute date. Phoebe and I sat contentedly looking out over the front campus, enjoying the sound of the fountain, and the light from the lamp posts illuminating the walkways. The breeze was cool and gentle, and we discussed Bryant's miraculous recovery from the painful previous year. We were so thankful that he was able now to pursue his goal, and I could hardly wait to see him play in his first college football game.

Cars began turning in and filling the small parking lot. We saw Bryant's white '53 Ford Galaxy and ran to the end of the porch to greet him. He strolled up the wide brick walk toward the entrance, never expecting to see us on the third floor hanging over the banister before closed study ended. We whispered down to him, for we knew he saw us, but he wouldn't respond. We tried even harder to get his attention, waving our arms and calling softly. His eyes never left the second floor porch, and his steps nervously quickened.

The ten o'clock bell rang, and we left the porch. Phoebe sent greetings to Bryant, and I ran excitedly down to meet him. My heart literally stopped when I reached the second floor! There were Miss Hall and Miss Lucy coming in from the second floor porch. They smiled kindly at me in their refined manner, so familiar, fully aware of the adventure that had transpired on the porch above them. They said in unison, "Good evening, Miss Peake," and kept right on walking.

Hearing Bryant's version of their looking down at him in amusement, as we frolicked like two monkeys right over their heads, didn't make me feel any better. I was scared to death, and so was Phoebe when I explained later Bryant's perplexed expression on his arrival. Phoebe and I couldn't sleep that night nor could we dream up any excuse in preparation for a call-down. We had grown to love and respect Miss Hall and Miss Lucy, and the mere thought of their not approving of our behavior was devastating to us. The anxiety we suffered that night was apparently punishment enough. Miss Hall and Miss Lucy never mentioned it, but there was a certain twinkle in their eyes for us whenever we were in their presence. After that, we were content to be in the security of our room during closed study.

Could this have been so very long ago? Ah, to be nineteen again, filled with innocence and promise, to turn back the clock, and free the young people of today from the problems of this changing world. If only it could be that simple.

Chapter 13

The Engagement Ring

In the late afternoon of an October Friday, Jean had signed out to go to Durham for the weekend. We had to have written permission from our parents to spend a weekend anywhere other than our homes, and I knew that her mother had given her permission to visit a high school friend in the girl's dormitory at Duke. I always knew just exactly how to get in touch with her if I needed to, and she did me. She was going to the Duke vs Georgia Tech football game on Saturday, and her ride picked her up that day at four o'clock.

After the excitement of getting Jean off, I wondered what I would do with my time over the weekend. I didn't wonder long, because ten minutes after Jean left, Dan called. He had completed his basic training in San Diego a few months before and was now stationed in Memphis, Tennessee. He had gotten a long weekend pass and was calling me from Asheville. He was coming to Raleigh the next day. I was excited beyond all words! Why did Jean always have to be gone on the weekends? She would not get to meet my true love. (Miss Lucy referred to all of our boyfriends as "your true love" ... we know now that there was no way she could remember every name.)

One o'clock Saturday seemed like an eternity away. When he finally arrived, I proudly introduced him to Miss Hall and Miss Lucy. After a short visit with them, I signed out, and we were on our own for at least a few hours.

A friend of Dan's family lived a few miles outside of Raleigh and on their property was a beautiful little lake. The colors of the fall surrounded us as we drove out to this pretty setting. The oak trees deep red, the maples orange and yellow, and the evergreens of pine were breathtaking. Of course, the setting was prettier to me because I was there with Dan. We stopped by the lake ... to enjoy the view? No! Dan did not waste any time getting to the main purpose of his visit. It was evident that he was nervous. That wasn't like Dan. He took my hand, kissed me, and asked me

For All The World To See

to marry him ... again. After I said yes, he surprised me with what I thought was the most beautiful diamond ring in the world. I couldn't believe it! I hadn't expected a ring until Christmas, if then. (God love him, even then he always talked about never having any money.)

From that moment on, a million plans were spinning in my head. We drove up to his friend's home, but I don't really remember the visit at all. All I wanted to do was get to a phone to tell my mama and daddy, and I could hardly wait until Sunday night to tell Jean. Dan's visit that gorgeous day ended too soon. It's still hard for me to believe that it was the one and only date I had during the two years while I was at Peace College. Jean and I agree that these are the tender sweet moments that all young "true loves" should never forget.

The first thing I did after Dan left was walk straight to the telephone and call my parents. They were not at all surprised, but they were very happy because they loved Dan, too. They were eager for me to get home Thanksgiving, and we talked about the holidays and my trip home. I told Daddy, "I do not look forward to that long train ride, stopping at every pig path between Raleigh and Asheville. Wish I had the car. Daddy, couldn't you call Miss Hall and ask her if I could drive the car back after Thanksgiving, so I wouldn't have to get in all that Christmas rush in a few weeks?" Daddy said, "I'll see what I can do, gal." Whenever he said this to me, I knew he would work it out.

A few days later, Miss Hall called me to her office to tell me she had just talked with my father and that I had permission to park the car on campus after Thanksgiving until Christmas vacation began. Having a car parked on campus doesn't sound like a big deal, but when I say parked, it was just that ... parked! I had a mint green, four door '49 Chevy with white sidewalls that I drove back after Thanksgiving. I picked up my keys, and Jean and I would go out everyday, start the car, and let it run ten or fifteen minutes to keep the battery charged. We listened to the radio while Jean knitted furiously on navy and white Argyle socks she was trying to finish for Bryant's Christmas present. We talked about how nice it would be if we could drive somewhere instead of sitting there in the parking lot, but that's the way it was.

The six-and-a half-hour drive home was nothing. Jean and I figured that we had been in the car sitting still longer than that! I loved to drive and still do. My mama used to say, "You have to drive that car everywhere ... I think if you could get it through the back door you would drive it to the bathroom!" My mama never learned to drive a car. She walked everywhere, so she didn't fully understand my need for the car as a means of transportation.

My driving days ended after Christmas, and I was once again on the train going to school. Dan and I had set our wedding date over the holidays, so Dan's father gave me a book on "love and marriage" to keep me company during the long ride back. Dr. Crouch was not only my future father-in-law, but my pastor at First Baptist Church in Asheville. We were lucky to have a built-in marriage counselor, and any advice offered to me by him was gladly received, because I was eager to please and wanted to be accepted into the Crouch family.

Chapter 14

Tragedy at Peace

We decided that we really wanted to make the most of our final semester at Peace College together. Phoebe and I realized how very fortunate we had been to have each other for roommates, and we knew that this time would pass quickly. Neither of us had a sister, and we felt that this was probably as close as we could come to that kind of relationship. Our dependency on each other was strong, and we recognized this. I loved the way Phoebe made me laugh and could break my serious moods, and we never seemed to have any trouble getting along. We watched the girls all around us get upset with each other over actions and things that seemed trivial to us. Our time together was fun, and if we had any differences, we were always able to come to a quick understanding. Maybe it's because we've never felt any jealousy, and that made our thinking so simple. We were never in competition and took pride in each other's accomplishments. We tried to understand why others complicated their lives so much, and we humorously accepted our ways as "simple minded."

In this frame of mind, we began to plan Phoebe's wedding. After exams, we focused on the mountain of bridal magazines with which she had filled our room. She found the wedding dress of her dreams in one of these magazines and had her mother order it. If we weren't talking wedding invitations or wedding portraits, it was bridesmaid dresses or parties. Of course, all of this helped me push to the furthest part of my mind the fact that I didn't know what I would do after graduation, or where I would go. That was not something I could settle right then, so I kept pushing it back and concentrating with Phoebe on happier thoughts.

We had exhausted ourselves studying Modern Bride before "lights out" on an icy cold January night and were snug and warm in our beds still talking "wedding" as we listened to WPTF's "Our Best To You." This was a request program we often listened to on the radio until midnight, waiting for Bryant's familiar request. At least once a week, he called in this

Tragedy at Peace

request, "From a KA at Duke to his brown-eyed angel at Peace," and they played "How Do You Speak To an Angel". We just swooned! On this particular night, our sleepy spell was broken before any requests were heard by the sudden, deafening sound of the fire alarm.

We sat straight up in our beds and began fumbling hurriedly for our robes and shoes in the dark. All the time, Phoebe was saying, "I can't believe we would have a fire drill on a night like this! Why did my daddy have to be a fire inspector?" All of our sleepy friends stumbled along with us out of their rooms into the hall and down the stairs quickly in a reasonably orderly manner, only to be abruptly halted as we approached Central Hall on the first floor. Miss Hall was standing there with pain written all over her face. She waited until she knew every footstep was still before she said a word. You could have heard a snowflake fall. She finally spoke, "Miss Lucy was killed tonight around 10:00 p.m. in an automobile accident." We gasped in disbelief, and everyone began to cry, "No, not Miss Lucy! It can't be! What happened? Are they sure? No, no not our Miss Lucy. Oh, God, please don't let this be so!"

Moments passed, and we heard her speaking again: "Miss Lucy was returning from a speaking engagement in Wilson tonight when her car hit an icy spot in the road. She skidded, and in losing control of her car, she was thrown out of the car. It was a one-car accident, and she was the only one involved." This was just the eleventh day of January, 1954, the beginning of a new year. We stood motionless in our night clothes, weeping, trying to let this horrible tragedy sink in, grieving, one with the other. Dr. Pressly prayed, and we heard Miss Lucy's ever present comfort to us come from his lips, "Now we know that all things work together for good to those who love the Lord, to those who are the called according to His purpose." Romans 8:28, the very first scripture she made us memorize in her Bible class. "Always carry this with you," she would say, "because out of tragedy, you will better understand that good can come if only you will allow it." It helped, but we were weak as we were dismissed, and slowly climbed the stairs, endless stairs, back up to our rooms.

Wedding, requests, trivia, all forgotten! Phoebe and I fell into each others arms, grateful for our friendship, grateful for this friend so like a sister, and knowing all the time that Miss Hall had just lost hers forever.

We spent the next few days facing this task, thinking of this precious human being whom we had loved so much. The good that she had contributed to our lives could never be taken away. Her influence would always be there to help guide us.

Miss Lucy had been the Bible professor at Peace for twenty-two years, and we were blessed to have had her. She had a way of using illustrations in her teaching that would stick with you. In a minute, she could bring you to your knees by the application of one of her illustrations. The simplest illustration, for instance, was writing the word sin on the blackboard and circling the letter "i" reminding us that we are at the center of our sin. We never heard John 14, or parts of it, without thinking of the hours we spent memorizing this chapter from the Bible and standing, trembling as each of us recited it orally before her, but privately in her quarters.

    She challenged us to have healthy thought patterns and to develop positive attitudes. She touched us emotionally and spiritually and strengthened our beliefs in all that she had taught us. This was a gift that money could not buy. Remembering this helped us to move on.

Chapter 15

Graduation – May 1954

Before we knew it, Jean and I were picking out Valentines for Dan and Bryant. My mama sent us another little package of cheer. She was always doing this, especially on special occasions. I did not know until this writing that Jean still has the handkerchief covered with little red hearts that my mama sent to her in that package in 1954. It would make Mama happy to know that Jean has kept it all these years.

Knitting had become an element of creativity for us. If you didn't know how to knit, you had to learn. Everyone was knitting Argyle socks. The atmosphere at Peace was different now, quieter. Miss Hall's migraines were more frequent, and we tried not to disturb her. Every evening after dinner, we would hurry to our rooms and finish studying as soon as possible, just to get to our knitting. This was a calming outlet for Jean and me. We enjoyed figuring out the designs on graphs, choosing the colors, the challenge of keeping all the bobbins untangled, and it helped pass the time on those long winter nights. It was satisfying to spend this time creatively with only the sound of needles clicking for company.

The needles and bobbins weren't the only thing moving. I had a hard time sitting still for any length of time and would start shaking my leg. The more I knitted, the faster my leg would go. When Jean had had all she could stand of that flying leg, she would reach over, grab my knee and say, "Ruum, stop shaking your leg!" To this day when I catch myself shaking my leg, I stop because I am reminded of Jean's firm request.

Jean's mother really surprised us that March when she called Jean from Michigan to say she had gotten married. She had been dating this gentleman from Kinston for some time. His home was in Michigan, and she had gone with him to meet his parents. While they were there, they decided to get married and surprise the family back in North Carolina. Jean did not know whether to be happy or sad. She only knew that her mother would be that much farther away, living in Michigan; but if this was what her mother wanted, it was all right. I think it just left her numb and added to her feelings of anxiety about the direction she would take after graduation. My thoughts had been so consumed with wedding plans and things concerning my life with Dan that I could not imagine being in that situation or having that worry. My parents were at home working everything out for me.

Raleigh was as far east as Phoebe had ever been, and I had always wanted to take her home with me for a weekend visit. Now, I could. Mother was living happily in Michigan, and my brother was based in South Carolina, still in the Army, so my bedroom at my grandparents' home was available for Phoebe to visit. She was wide-eyed as we drove through the flat land of eastern North Carolina, down the long, straight and narrow, two lane roads. She couldn't believe you could see so far off in the distance without a hill in sight, but only freshly plowed farm land spotted with green woods connecting each little town to the next.

It was exciting to me sharing this part of my life with her, and I was amazed at her reaction, as much as she was at seeing this area for the first time. We stopped in LaGrange to speak to Bryant's Uncle Bob who ran a little hardware store with nail kegs for stools around a pot-bellied stove, sights she had never encountered. Bryant and I really got caught up in broadening Phoebe's horizons.

She had to see where my aunt and uncle lived out in the country. On Saturday, we went out to visit them in their little home, the kind some people refer to as a "shotgun house" because of the design. This is the place that I had spent many summers growing up helping my uncle "put in tobacco." They never had children, so my cousins and I were all adopted by them each summer as tobacco hands. All of this talk was so foreign to Phoebe. We walked down the sandy dirt road in front of their house, and I tried to explain to her about how we "took out" a barn of tobacco in the wee hours of the morning before we started "handing" and putting it in the barns for curing. As I walked and talked, I could remember so well the balmy feeling of powdery, hot and cool sand under my bare toes, the Pepsi Colas we poured salted peanuts into when we took a break in the shade of the tobacco barn, and I could practically taste the fresh corn, butter beans, fried chicken, and cornbread lunches we had each day around my aunt's kitchen table. Phoebe could not imagine gummy, dirty, green tobacco stain on my perfectly manicured fingers, nor could she imagine working this way during a summer vacation. Her father had never allowed her to work. My Aunt Selma still lives in the same house today and keeps us supplied with fresh vegetables from her garden whenever they are available.

Graduation-May 1954

On Sunday after Sunday school, church, and lunch, we took Phoebe to the early movie before having to return to Raleigh. We were surprised to learn afterwards that this was the first time she had ever gone to a movie theater on Sunday. In her family, Sunday was literally a day of rest, and she was not allowed to do anything on Sundays. Her mother always said to her, "What you sew on Sunday comes apart on Monday." She felt guilty but wouldn't dare tell us, because she wanted to go. She broke tradition, but it was all right this time. It had been an enlightening weekend for us, a fun time, and a nice diversion from the lonely weekends she had always spent at Peace.

Day by day, with spring blossoming and awakening around us, we could see our time at Peace coming to an end. Our attention centered on upcoming final exams and improving typing and shorthand speeds and grades. Many of our friends had gotten engaged as if there were a deadline to meet. Phoebe's wedding loomed before us with wonder and joy, but it was not to take the place of May Day or graduation. Ann, quite naturally, was our May Queen, gorgeous in her wedding dress worn the previous August, and I was her Maid of Honor. My mother had come from Michigan with a new movie camera to record all of the festivities, and I adored having her with me to share this special time in my life with my friends. Phoebe, Martha, and Sylvia Morrow danced and wrapped the May Pole again, and this chapter ended.

Exams were finally over, and we had done well. I didn't know until graduation that I had finished with the highest average in our class, and Phoebe was not far behind. My mother stayed in North Carolina until our graduation, which was like a cloud of white lined with red roses.

Graduations are never easy, for there are so many, many mixed emotions. We dreaded it, but we looked forward to it, too. We were very happy, but why did we cry? Our families were here; we were beautiful in our long, white dresses with gorgeous bouquets of long, stemmed red roses, holding hands around the fountain; yet we were sad. What were we made of?

We heard a commencement address that day in the chapel, but had we really heard it? Miss Lucy's spirit was there everywhere, echoing it seemed with all that she kept telling us: "We take a girl as she is and help her to be what she can be, and which, by the help of God, she will be." Oh God, let us fulfill this wish for her now.

We recessed out of the chapel singing together "God of Our Fathers" rather than the familiar hymn "Lead on O King Eternal," the exact same way we had done after every chapel program during the past two years.

Only this time, we knew it was different; we heard the final voice fade away, and it was all over. We were too young to realize the uplifting, spiritual impact these hymns would be for us anytime we heard them in the future or to know how engrained the words were on our minds.

Phoebe and I broke away from all the hugs and kisses and congratulations to take our roses to Miss Hall. We had been told that she was unable to attend our graduation because of another migraine headache, and we had to see her. Her suite of rooms was dark because the light hurt her eyes, and she was pale under the faint glow of a lamp light, but she saw us, and we were able to say good-bye to her privately and affectionately. We never saw her again, and it breaks our hearts when we think of that today.

We walked up the stairs and stopped, startled as we gazed into our empty room for the last time. Our luggage and belongings had already been loaded into cars for departure, and there was nothing left to do but change into our traveling clothes. We went back down to Central Hall and told Miss Thigpin, our ever-present little hostess, good-bye. We had done this earlier with all our friends. Now, Phoebe and I had to face each other and close another chapter in this relationship that had begun, what seemed like, just yesterday. We couldn't say a word, only hug each other; our hearts were full and our eyes were brimming over with tears. It was made easier though knowing that we would see each other again soon for her wedding day, and we dwelt on this.

I climbed into the back seat of my mother's car for a two day trip to visit her in Michigan, and I was miserable. Phoebe and her parents probably were back home in Asheville by the time we crossed the North Carolina line, and her feelings had to be similar to mine.

Chapter 16

Marriage and Single Life

My heart was in a tug of war as we drove away from Peace after the graduation ceremonies. I hated leaving my sweet "Ruum" behind on one side, and on the other side I was full of excitement and anticipation about the wedding. Jean and I waved and called our good-byes until we were out of sight.

The next day, the whirlwind of preparation began! In eighteen days, I would marry my "true love." Was it really happening? Yes, it was, because three gifts arrived that day, and I started writing thank you notes.

That next week, I was getting dressed for a luncheon, and as I took the new Carlye sundress out of the closet, I thought of Jean for the first time since getting home. Was that possible? Clothes are a real weakness with me, and on one particular weekend at Peace, I went on a shopping spree. This dress, along with two other outfits, was my treat for that day. When Jean got back Sunday night, I had all three dresses lying out on the bed for her to see and to get her approval. (Her approval always meant a lot to me, and it still does.) The first words out of her mouth were not, "Oh, 'Rumm,' they are beautiful and just what you needed," as I had imagined they would be; they were instead, "I can't believe you went out and bought more clothes when you already have more than you can wear now!" She also reminded me of how hard my parents were working to send me to Peace College. I put the dresses away, and a few days later returned two of them. I never will forget that night and the difference it made in my way of thinking. As I buttoned the last button and took one last look in the mirror, I smiled at the memory, wishing Jean were here, and I was glad I had kept this dress.

Dan arrived from Memphis four days before the wedding and was kept busy during the day by his dad. We saw each other when we could, in between the flurry of last minute activities. Jean had flown to Richmond from Michigan to meet Betty Womack. They drove in on Thursday in time for the rehearsal that night and the party afterwards. After two years of listening to me talk about him and looking at heaven-knows-how-many pictures, Jean finally met Dan. I sensed her approval with relief. It was as though they had known each other for a long time.

The Bridesmaids' luncheon was at noon on Friday. We picked up Betty afterwards and drove to my house, so they all could see the gifts. Dan's afternoon was spent with his father. They went to the club for a sauna and massage. Dan talked about how wonderful it was for many years after that.

Our wedding that night was lovely — like all weddings are. Dan's father married us, which gave it a special touch and extra meaning. After our honeymoon, we packed our gifts and moved to Memphis, Tennessee, where I knew I had facing me many more thank you notes to write. I had made up my mind that Jean's would be the first one I would write, so she would have my new address.

* * *

I was ready to get home after Phoebe and Dan's wedding. I had been away long enough and needed, for my peace of mind and simple economics, to make some plans for my future. I borrowed my grandfather's car and drove immediately, the following week, to Durham to apply for work.

My first interview was at Liggett and Meyers' Tobacco Company, not because I knew anything about tobacco but because I wanted the job, and it paid well. I was interviewed for the position of hostess, taking guided tours and explaining to guests the manufacture of cigarettes. The first question asked me was, "Do you smoke, Miss Peake?"

I never thought about the need for this qualification, and I felt the feeling of rejection quickly. My answer was "No sir."

"You know, Miss Peake, you can't sell a product if you don't know anything about it," the personnel manager told me.

I don't remember any more of the interview, only that I left and went on to the next one. I was set to beat the bushes until I had a job.

I was lucky again. I interviewed next for a secretarial position in the purchasing department at Duke University Library and got it. The pay wasn't much; it never is working for a university, but I was thrilled, and the benefits were great! I would be right on campus with Bryant. My next move was that of finding a place to live. After contacting a relative of one of my uncles, a wonderful tiny, one room, efficiency apartment opened up for me in her home, and I could afford it. It all worked out so perfectly, thank God, because I was terrified at all this responsibility on my own.

Marriage and Single Life

My grandfather was a dear, hard working soul, and was happy to help me out. He had married my grandmother when she was only fourteen, and after ten children and fourteen grandchildren, he probably was glad to see us all out and on our own. My grandmother always referred us to him for any advice, and I was lucky again to have him. He made me a loan of $150.00 until my first pay check which enabled me to get started. After utility and telephone deposits, rent and groceries, there wasn't much left, but it was a beginning, and I know how to "make do" and stretch a dollar. I could stretch a $.59 Chef Boy Ar Dee spaghetti dinner further than anyone could imagine. Bryant, as always, helped me out too by sharing his meal tickets with me in the Duke cafeteria.

I adjusted to this nine to five way of life and gradually gained confidence in being a working girl. I learned how to write orders for new and rare books at my job in that huge library. I had never stopped to think about how all the hundreds of books got there and, sometimes, the difficulty in purchasing one rare book. At Peace, we just walked in, found what we needed, put it back on the shelf, and walked out.

That first pay check gave me a new sense of relief, also, even though after taxes, I was surprised to find how little there was left again, but I was on my own and had to make it do. Bryant's brother, Jesse, was at this same time manager of an automobile financing company, and through him I was able to purchase my first car, a '49 black Fleetline Chevrolet. Jesse made sure it was clean and in excellent running order, so I had safe transportation, all for $300.00.

I remember writing letters to Phoebe that summer giving her a run down of my new life and getting perturbed because I never got any answers, but something made me think she was interested. I just knew she would be interested in hearing how Bryant and I stood in the beautiful building right beside Duke Chapel and watched Hurricane Hazel blow through with all her awful fury, as we watched gigantic oaks fall on the campus quadrangle. I knew that Phoebe and Dan were too far west ever to experience a hurricane of such force.

Three months after accepting my position behind the typewriter and desk at the Duke Library, I received a call from the personnel manager at Liggett and Meyers wanting to know if I was still interested in a job as hostess. I couldn't speak! He asked me to come in for another interview. I was so confused, not knowing how to work this out, but I was curious enough to go. He didn't ask me if I smoked this time; he simply offered me my first cigarette. I took it, shaking like a leaf with all my new found confidence; he lit it with his cigarette lighter, and I held that cigarette like

I had seen people do between that middle and index finger until I saw this long grey ash about to fall in my lap. His telephone rang, and while he took the call, something made my arm move toward the ash tray on his desk, and I dunked the ashes like a real pro, but I must have looked like a fool. I knew my life was on the line! By the time he finished his telephone conversation, the cigarette had burned completely down, and I found the strength in that right arm to put it out completely. I worked at Liggett and Meyers for the next year and a half.

* * *

How small your world becomes when marital bliss befalls you! All my thoughts were focused on Dan and being the "perfect" wife. We were so far away from home it was easy to think of nothing else but each other. I enjoyed fixing up our little apartment and learning to cook. Poor Dan, how he lived through some of the meals I prepared I'll never know. "Playing house" was fun and helped me push the nagging thought of having to go to work to the back of my mind. I had never worked a day in my twenty years of life, and although Peace College had done its very best to prepare me, I was scared to death.

Dan's father was a firm believer in the wife working, although his wife did not. "Until children are in the home, it is good to stay busy," he would say. So one Sunday afternoon after lunch, Dan circled some jobs advertised in the newspaper. The next morning, I rode the bus to downtown Memphis and started looking for a job. The good Lord was with me. The fifth office I visited was an insurance office and where I ended up working. The only thing I ever liked about that job was the location of my desk, by a window looking out over the Mississippi River. To this day, I can visualize the peacefulness of the paddle boats and barges pushing cargo up and down the river.

The first thing I usually did when I got home from work was sit down and read the mail. There was another letter from Jean. I tore it open, anxious to learn her latest news! I always enjoyed her letters.

This letter, however, was nothing like the others. I'm sure it had scorched the wind getting there. She was very upset with me, and rightly so. I cannot recall much of that letter today. I do remember that she reminded me of the unusual and wonderful bond we had had at Peace and how we vowed we would never let it die. How grateful I was then and am now that she loved me enough to write that letter. I did not lay my head down on the pillow that night until I had written her a long, long letter. I was shocked into the realization that although marriage was wonderful it should not be my whole world. This was the first time I had stopped to think about how important it was to keep in touch with family and friends. I did not want the relationship I had with Jean to slip away.

Chapter 17

Life Goes On

Only a girl in love with a college football star can understand the thrill of following his team and watching him play. I was free to do just that now, and it was exactly what I did. I adored my new job as a hostess, being an "authority" of the cigarette industry, as I met tourists and dignitaries from all over the world all week; but on Saturdays my attention focused on Duke football and one player, in particular.

I had moved into a one bedroom, but larger, apartment with three other hostesses by now. We achieved this successfully with four bunk beds, a general "kitty" fund, and taking turns one night a week with kitchen duty and basic housekeeping. We all shared basically the same interests and played on the weekends. It was nothing for us to leave work at 4:00 p.m. on Fridays and drive to Dayton, Ohio, to see Duke play Ohio State, or to Baltimore, Maryland, to watch the Duke vs Navy game. Bryant's big brother, Jesse, usually was our chauffeur, and the hours we spent on the road were always worth it. We didn't miss a game!

Duke had such a successful season that the team was invited to play Nebraska in the Orange Bowl on January 1, 1955. We immediately made plans to go. It was Bryant's sister and her husband who drove Bryant's mother and me to Miami, Florida, for a once in a lifetime adventure for us all. Duke beat Nebraska 35-7, and after being in Florida for 10 days practicing for the game, this lovesick 205 lb. football player gave up all the hoopla and victory celebrations just to ride all the way back to North Carolina in the car with me, sitting crouched down on the floor of the car. I don't think he would make that same choice today, but young love is wonderful — makes you do stupid things sometimes, but it's wonderful!

* * *

After hearing about all the excitement of Jean and Bryant's trip to the

Life Goes On

Orange Bowl, my return letter to Jean held news of a different kind. Dan's new orders were sending him to Port Lyautey, North Africa, the first of February. I couldn't think of anything that would shock her more. We had two weeks before he was to leave, and during that time, I settled in to live with my parents until the Navy sent me my orders to join him. All I knew about Africa was what I had seen in the movies — Tarzan swinging through the trees, natives in grass huts and crocodile infested waters. I did not want to go, but I was going because Dan was there, and it was the only way to be with him.

"Dad" Crouch felt that I should spend my time waiting constructively, so he arranged for me to go to Gastonia to brush up on my business skills at his sister's business school. Everyone felt this was unnecessary, but Dad's word was law, so off I went to live with my Aunt Zada and Uncle Bradshaw who also lived in Gastonia. It was a long boring month, and I told my mama and daddy as soon as it was over that I was going to Durham for a visit with Jean before I left for Africa.

My overnight visit with Jean was brief, but after living in Gastonia, it was heaven being with my "Ruum."

* * *

I had looked forward to Phoebe's visit, and we filled every minute into the wee hours of morning with "girl talk," each of us talking as hard as we could and at the same time. I wanted to know all about her new life with Dan, which seemed to agree with her, and she tried to comprehend the life of a working, single girl — all the time really concentrating on the orders awaiting her.

Bryant and I had become officially engaged a few weeks before she came. He had given me my ring on Valentine's Day, so I was naturally ready to hear all she could tell about married life as well as the process of planning a wedding. I knew she would probably miss sharing this special event of my life with me, which made us both sad and didn't help our having to leave each other the next morning. We were weary from too little sleep as we made plans to get together again before her departure to the other side of the world, but our plans never materialized as she left just two weeks later for Africa.

* * *

Mail call at the barracks was no different from any other day. Dan was

For All The World To See

happy he had received four letters from me. As he began reading the third letter, the words jumped off the page at him. He couldn't believe his eyes. He hurriedly re-read the page before him. Yes, he had read correctly. I was on my way to North Africa and according to his calculations would arrive that afternoon. He had three hours to get off work, find a place for us to live, and be there to meet me when my plane landed. He was able to get all of this accomplished and was standing there with his sweet smile and a bouquet of flowers when I stepped off the plane.

Port Lyautey was a beautiful little town with flower lined streets, tall palm trees, and white buildings. It was of strategic importance during the Second World War because of its location on the Sabo River. It was a pleasant surprise — not at all like the Africa in Tarzan movies.

The first week I was there, we lived at the hotel. While Dan was at work, I went exploring. All the sights, sounds, and smells that surrounded me were different from those I was used to at home. Peddlers were on the streets selling leather and brass, and there were Arabs leading donkeys with baskets on their backs overflowing with fruit and vegetables to be sold door to door. It was all very new and exciting. Everyday was a wonderful adventure.

We found a nice apartment that Friday and spent Saturday buying furniture. Our new landlady, Madame Sanchez, knew a man who sold secondhand furniture. She sent one of her twelve children to tell him he had a customer. We went with him in his truck to the Medina, the Arabs walled-in village, where he led us down a dark winding path that ended in front of a basement room full of furniture. We quickly picked out a bed, two bedside tables, and a dining table and four chairs. Dan and I often laughed about how naive we were to trust a strange Arab. The rest of our furniture we bought from an American couple who were shipping back to the States.

Our sixteen months in North Africa were like an extended honeymoon. We spent our weekends in places like Tangier, Fez, Marrakech, Rabat, and Casablanca. Jean would have loved haggling with the Arab merchants in the market places. In my letters, I tried to describe this new world in which I was living.

I remember one thrilling experience we had that I knew she could relate to. One of our ways of getting news from the States was the newsreel at the movie theater on base. Dan and I were settled in at the theater waiting for the main feature to begin when "The World News of Today" flashed on the screen, and we heard the announcer say, "And now from the world of football. In the game of Navy vs Duke, Bryant Aldridge, number 37, breaks away for an eighteen yard touchdown run." I choked on my popcorn. Dan and I both stood straight up and yelled, "That's Bryant, we know him, that's Bryant!" I fought back pangs of homesickness, because I knew Jean was sitting there somewhere in that crowd cheering for her "true love."

* * *

Phoebe was in Africa; I was working and counting my pennies; both of us were so wrapped up in our little worlds that we were almost unaware of the phenomenal "Elvis Presley Era" beginning all around us.

Chapter 18

Jean and Bryant Marry

Our lives were literally worlds apart now as Phoebe related her experiences to me of life on a military base in a foreign country. I thought about our conversation that night before she left of how our lives had changed with so much happening to each of us since leaving the daily, orderly routine of Peace College. I began to realize for the first time, I think, of how fast time passes and just how precious every moment is. Bryant and I set our wedding date for the day after Christmas, probably the worst day in a calendar year to have a wedding, but we had many factors to consider. Football season would be over, my mother would be home for Christmas, the 26th of December was his parents' and also his sister's wedding anniversary, and we didn't want to wait until after Bryant's graduation from Duke the next spring.

While Bryant tackled the academic world and serious football during his senior year, I worked and planned our wedding, drawing from every resource I knew. I saved every extra penny, knowing that the full expense of anything I planned fell on only me. I wrote to Phoebe to give her our news and asked to borrow her wedding dress. I remembered it being a beautiful white Chantilly lace with a cathedral train and matching veil. I could never afford anything like it so that helped me out financially, and it certainly made for a sweet memory.

I was just before ordering invitations to our wedding when Bryant got an invitation to play in the North-South All Star game on December 26th, so we changed our wedding to December 28. That would give him time to get back home after the game, if only he had gotten to go. He injured his leg in the final game of his football career and the final game of the season against the University of North Carolina and spent two more weeks in the hospital. I had learned to cope with many changes, and this disappointment was just another one.

Our wedding was small and simple but special to us in the Methodist Church in which we grew up. Unlike the elaborate ceremony and reception

Jean and Bryant Marry

Phoebe had, we said good-byes in the vestibule of the church. We honeymooned for three days in Williamsburg, Virginia, and have beautiful memories of freshly fallen snow covering this historic and picturesque little town, as we spent our first day as husband and wife. We also had to stay in a motel where Bryant could watch his college roommate on television play football, the East-West All Star game in California. This wasn't so bad because I enjoyed football, too, but it was aggravating to have to put 25 cents in the television every thirty minutes to keep it playing.

Like most experiences, and like the old saying goes, "You can only understand your brother's situation after you have walked a mile in his moccasins," I had to see what the responsibilities of a young married woman were before I could understand why Phoebe had not communicated with me the first few months of her marriage. I felt guilty now as I adjusted to being Bryant's wife and wondered if my letter to Phoebe at that time was right, but we had settled this knowing it was a turning point in our relationship.

The security of marriage and caring for each other was wonderful to me. I learned rapidly though that making a marriage work means working at it daily -- dirty socks dropped beside the bed left for me to pick up, wet towels thrown across the bed I had just made up, and buying tire chains with my savings when the big snow was gone before noon were not what I had envisioned. We worked hard at balancing all these little things with trying to concentrate on and appreciate the thoughtful and sweet actions. It wasn't always easy when your cooking, etc. may not be "like Mama's"!

Bryant and I were very happy making all of this work. He was kept busy with job interviews that spring until he finally made up his mind to take a job with the Prudential Insurance Company — selling. He was from the old school and was ready to graduate, go to work, and be the breadwinner. After his graduation from Duke, I gave up my job at L & M, and we moved to Fayetteville where he started his first big job. He disliked it immensely but was determined to give it the old college try.

Chapter 19

Bryant, Jr.

Our happiness only increased as we prepared for the birth of our first child. If only Bryant had liked his work, everything would have been perfect.

What did I know at that tender age; I was so young. My mother came for Christmas and to wait out the birth of her first grandchild. I tried desperately to get her to tell me what it was like, having a baby, and what to expect. She had never been able to talk freely with me and, as usual, avoided any direct answers. We had everything ready. We had made curtains for the nursery; she covered a wooden box with the same nursery print to use for a blanket chest; and we stocked the kitchen with baby supplies and more food. I was really beginning to feel like a huge walrus that would always walk around fat and ugly when at 6:00 a.m. on New Year's Day, I finally went to the hospital, too late for any prizes for having the first baby of the New Year and too late for a tax deduction! Our perfectly formed, big, beautiful son was born that morning, and my mother was right. She couldn't tell me what it was like, because no one knows until it happens to you just how it is. It had to be the most awesome day of my life. The feeling of relief and the surge of love that overcomes you at the first sight of your own flesh and blood are without doubts beyond all words. There, in my arms an extension of me and Bryant forever, his namesake, solely dependent on us for everything. What a tremendous and blessed responsibility. We would celebrate the coming of every New Year for the rest of our lives with thankfulness for this one glorious day.

When I could see my mother and Bryant through tears of pure joy and was able to think clearly, I said, "You have to call Phoebe."

* * *

Dan was discharged from the Navy in August, 1956, five months before Bryant, Jr. was born. Jean had written me before we left Port

Lyautey to tell us she was expecting their first child. I was going to be an "Aunt"! My "Ruum" a mother, it was hard to believe. We received a telegram the evening of January 1st. It read, "It's a fullback — Bryant Taylor Aldridge, Jr. — 9 lbs. 12 ozs. — Mother and son are fine." The message gave me a warm, strange feeling. The last time I had seen Jean she was leaving for work, dressed in her smart-looking Liggett & Meyers uniform, every hair in place. She was excited about being engaged and planning a wedding. Now, she and Bryant were parents. What a lucky little boy this new Bryant was.

Dan entered Mars Hill College near Asheville to continue his education after getting out of the Navy, and I worked as a secretary for two lawyers. In order to save money, we moved in with our parents, living one month with Mom and Dad Crouch, the next month with my folks. After living in "paradise" in Port Lyautey, North Africa, it was quite a change, and I hated it! Dan and I really did appreciate what our parents were doing, but we were looking forward to his entering N. C. State College in Raleigh that summer. We would once again have a place of our own, and it would put me closer to Jean. The thought of our being together more often was wonderful. It had been too long since we had seen each other, and I couldn't wait to see little Bryant.

* * *

I have always believed that everyone finds a niche for his life, and if well suited for it and satisfied with it, you have been given a rare and valuable gift. I know that I have been granted this gift. It didn't take me long after the birth of our son Bryant, Jr. to realize that motherhood and "feathering our nest" was truly my niche. It wasn't always easy, but I also know that nothing is.

The 2:00 a.m. feedings, and in "my day," the formula making, sterilizing of baby bottles, and mountains of cloth diapers to take care of, plus the general routine of homemaking could be a real strain on young nerves and patience. It helps to have a gentle, caring, and understanding husband, and a healthy baby, and I certainly had both. Bryant worked hard at a job he disliked to make sure that I could remain in the home as a full time mother and homemaker, and I adored him for it and loved every day of it. I knew what it was like to be in the working world, and I was very grateful that I could stay at home. We could have had many more material possessions if I had chosen to work outside the home, but the rewards we received from my being at home have far outweighed anything we might otherwise have acquired and are much more lasting.

Our little Bryant grew like a miracle unfolding before our eyes. He was a good and happy baby, which made my job easy, for I was so young and had to learn everything through him. We watched his development with amazement, as though none had ever seen a child like this. We were two new doting parents with hearts bursting with love.

Bryant's work in the insurance business led him to a new position with a newly formed insurance company in our home town of Kinston soon after our son was born. I was relieved to be leaving Fayetteville, as I had always lived with a slight fear of this military town and all that went on there. He, of course, hoped that this move would be what he needed to improve in his profession. Going home and being closer to our relatives filled us with sure and happy expectations.

Moving to Kinston at that time in our lives was heaven sent, and a move we needed and enjoyed. Bryant liked his work, and we shared those precious first months of Bryant, Jr.'s life with my grandparents and other loved ones. How grateful I am today that it worked out the way it did.

Chapter 20

Phoebe, Dan, Jean, and Bryant

Phoebe and Dan had been home from Africa for nearly a year when we were finally able to make plans to see them. It was like Christmas and New Year's all at once — a day we had longed for, time to celebrate, time to share our "bundle of heaven" with them, a time to make plans for being together again; and hopefully, this would not be as difficult now that we were living within a reasonable traveling distance.

* * *

Our apartment in Raleigh was small but wonderful. We were so happy to be settled at last. Dan was enjoying his classes at State, and I had a good job in the Sunday School Department at the Baptist State Convention.

The first real excitement after our arrival was a phone call from Jean asking us to baby sit! She and Bryant had an appointment in Durham and wanted to leave little Bryant with us for a few hours.

I didn't think Saturday would ever dawn! It had been two years and five months since I had seen Jean. They were coming shortly after lunch, but I started watching for them an hour before. I'm bad about doing that. "Watch pot never boils," my mama used to say.

The words still escape me when I try to express my feelings the first time I saw Bryant, Jr. I can close my eyes to this day and still see that sweet little face and those blue, blue eyes. The rest was a blur of hugs and kisses and greetings. Naturally, I remember the pale yellow shirtwaist dress Jean was wearing. Dan and Bryant shook hands and just stood there smiling, watching this long overdue reunion unfold before them. After we settled "Bryantie" for his nap, Jean and Bryant left for Durham. I stood by the bed most of that two and a half hours just watching him sleep. I thought he was going to sleep all afternoon. Having never been around babies much, I felt a little awkward at first. He was so good and easy to care for. We were fascinated by every smile, every sound, and every action no matter how slight. By the time his parents returned, we were his captives.

Over a spaghetti dinner, we tried to catch up, but time ran out all too soon. The good part was we were close enough now to see each other often. Knowing this made our good-byes easier that evening.

Isn't it interesting the things we remember? A little boy's face and blue eyes looking at you for the first time. A yellow dress, sunshine, two handsome young men. The joy of being together again, and there's another sweet memory. The first time we visited Jean and Bryant, we drove to Kinston Friday night after I finished work. This was the first opportunity Dan had had to be with them for any length of time. Dan and Bryant soon learned they did not have to say much when Jean and I were around. I believe it always amazed them that no matter how long we were together we never ran out of something to talk about.

This particular weekend, on Sunday afternoon, Bryant got one of his spur of the moment ideas. Dan and I mentioned that we couldn't get over how close we were to the coast. Bryant looked at Jean and said, "Let's take them to Tony's for supper." Well, we thought Tony's was a place there in Kinston. Not so! He was referring to the Sanitary Fish Market in Morehead City! He made a quick phone call, and off we went. We took Bryantie to Bryant's mother, and to our further surprise, switched cars. Bryant's brother Jesse had a new red Ford convertible and was kind enough to let Bryant use it to make our adventure even more exciting. What a sight we must have been to those we passed on the way. We were four young people laughing, our hair blowing in the wind, not a care in the world, or so it would seem.

That was just the beginning of many adventures to come. We became frequent visitors to Kinston, and on one of those visits we all drove to New Bern to water ski on the Trent River. We spread blankets for Bryant, Jr. to play on. We picnicked and enjoyed the cool shade the trees along the river bank provided. Now the only water skiing that Dan and I had ever done was at the Crouch's lake house at Lake Lure. The Trent River was a different story. It was narrow compared to the lake, and the water was black as tar. It was not like the blue green of a mountain lake. My skiing left much to be desired that day, and with each fall, I'm sure I drank half of the river. The Trent River never appealed to me after that. One thing of importance was decided that day by Dan and Bryant. They good naturedly came to the conclusion that they had to like each other because they had no choice in the matter.

Chapter 21

At Home with Jean, Bryant, and Bryant, Jr.

New husbands assume so much, and it is really commendable that they should have so much confidence in a new wife, but to think she can cook Christmas dinner for his family the first Christmas they are all together was asking too much. Bryant was determined to do this, and I knew that once his mind was made up, you hardly ever change it; so with much trepidation, I consented to try.

I remember planning menus and worrying about endless details, but with the help of a wonderful neighbor, whose husband also owned the grocery store where I shopped, I set out to entertain my in-laws. Of course, Bryant would not hear of my accepting any help and no one need bring anything—we could do it all, and do it all we did!

He played with Bryant, Jr. and tried to keep him happy while I set the card tables with our best china and silver or whatever I thought was the best we had. Our sweet neighbor had given me, literally, written instructions on how to roast a turkey — my first. The rest of the dinner, I could figure out from my new *Better Homes and Garden* cookbook.

My instructions were to thaw a frozen turkey, wrap it in clean cheesecloth (which my neighbor had given me), bake for so many hours, and baste frequently. I think the cheesecloth had something to do with keeping it moist. I was on my own. It was going to be lovely.

Bryant's family came for dinner, and it was lovely — buffet style, just like the magazines show in the pictures, Bryant carving the turkey, like the "fantasy" families do, but only half way through, for him to hold up in front of everyone a little paper bag he found inside the turkey revealing giblets. He not only found one bag but another inside that turkey, as if he was on some kind of hunt. He couldn't stop there and discreetly hide my

At Home with Jean, Bryant, and Bryant, Jr.

ignorance but, instead, he had to call me and say, "Jean, what is this?" My sweet neighbor never told me what surprises were tucked inside of frozen turkeys, only that you had to thaw them!

No new bride should ever have to experience such embarrassment, but I learned a lot. You turn turkeys and chickens inside out to wash and clean them, and your husband's ideas are not always the best. I thought about Phoebe and what she would have done, and how she would laugh at my stupidity. I knew she was in Asheville probably enjoying Cora's delicious cooking, turkey and all. I have learned to cook a pretty good turkey since then, though, and I don't mind accepting help for a family gathering when it's offered.

Our life in Kinston settled into a comfortable routine. Our one year old son kept me busy, and we were fortunate to be able to share his growing up during that time with his great grandparents. I missed having my mother close by to enjoy these magical moments, but it helped having Bryant's mother and my grandparents in the same town. I remember so well how my grandfather would walk the distance of a mile nearly everyday from their home to our apartment just to see Bryant, Jr. He was unable to drive now because of his failing eyesight. For as long as I live, I will never forget his baby-sitting for us. He came one night at 7:00 p.m., and Bryant, Jr. was already asleep, which upset him. He calmly told me that he was going to wake Bryantie, so he could play with him. Bryant and I believed in keeping our son on a schedule, so we left the house for our function never believing that Granddaddy would awaken him. When we returned later in the evening, my sweet granddaddy was sitting beside his crib in a straightback chair just watching him sleep. He had awakened him, and I tried not to be annoyed. They had played and enjoyed each other until Bryant, Jr. was sleepy, then Granddaddy watched over him until he fell asleep, always staying very close, so he could see more clearly. Breaking the schedule never hurts anything I realized from that one experience, and you get over it. One week later, my grandfather died of a heart attack. My little son lost his great granddaddy, and I will be eternally grateful that they shared a special love that one night, and I learned a valuable lesson: it is far more important to let grandparents enjoy these angels than it is to keep a rigid schedule, and "down the road" you'll be so glad you did. Our children today allow us this privilege, and we love them for it. Life is short, and time spent with loved ones is short, and you must fill it with happy memories.

Bryant continued to struggle with the direction of his life professionally. He couldn't seem to get satisfied in the insurance business, although he was doing well and enjoyed success in that field. More and more, his desire to return to school and try his hand at something else loomed before us. I couldn't even imagine what that would be like, especially since we had a child now. I could see the possibility of our comfortable life in Kinston maybe ending.

After days and weeks and months of analyzing, contemplating, and finally interviewing, Bryant decided to return to school. He wanted to fulfill his desire to become a hospital administrator, a relatively new field then, a profession he had considered very seriously while still an undergraduate at Duke.

Things really do work out. He found out that Watts Hospital in Durham offered a one year residency program and that would give him enough experience to know if he wanted to go further. That was all we needed to begin packing for a move to Durham. We knew that Phoebe and Dan would be only a few miles away; and Durham was like a second home to us, so the prospect of making this move was exciting.

Bryant began to set all the wheels into motion. He was accepted at Watts, and we found an apartment in Durham. Our plans were to move the first of August and try this new adventure. We had no money, only a lot of faith, and were convinced we could do whatever we set our minds to.

Shortly before we were to make this move, I received a call informing me of my father's illness and hospitalization. He had always lived in Virginia, and I only remember seeing him a few times during my life. My brother and I would ride the bus to Virginia to visit him occasionally, and I thought about the root beer sodas he always bought us and the pink Angora sweater he gave me when I was twelve. He wanted to see me now, and I felt compelled to go. I don't really know why; it just seemed the right thing to do. He had never been there for me, to send me off to school during my childhood, to see me graduate, to walk me down the aisle, or whatever daddy's are supposed to do, but there was an affection there that always made me know he was my daddy.

Bryant and I drove to Norfolk and visited with him in the hospital briefly, showing him pictures of his little grandson, sharing our life with him, and comforting an old dying man. We didn't have time to make up for lost time, but we left him peaceful. He died a few days later, and his going did not leave the void in my life that I'm sure it does for other daughters and sons when they lose their father, but my heart broke realizing even more the wasted time.

Chapter 22

New Homes

Durham was a big city after living in our little home town, and we were happy with the decision to make a change. Establishing a new home was easier now. Phoebe and Dan came over to help, and we were like children on a holiday making plans for more frequent visits and cookouts. We were more and more like family together rather than just friends. There was never any question that Bryant, Jr. was to call them Aunt Phoebe and Uncle Dan, and our lives were always better because we had each other.

Bryant had to spend only one day at Watts Hospital to know he had made the right choice. He could see a new purpose and satisfaction in contributing to the healthcare field, and his desire for management and creativity could be fulfilled. Having a husband happy in his chosen profession is wonderful, and we knew immediately that we were on the right course. He started making future plans for graduate school. We could hardly make ends meet on his $250.00 a month salary as a resident, but it didn't matter; we had a vision and intended to reach our goal.

* * *

It did not take Dan and me long to start feeling right at home in Raleigh. Dan was excited about becoming an electrical engineer, and I was happy that he had finally decided on a profession. Unlike his two brothers who had always known "their call" in life, Dan had not been that fortunate. We loved the college life, especially the sports. I had listened to Jean's description of football games and all the activities that went along with it but had never fully understood it until now. We really got into the spirit of it. The weekends and game time couldn't come fast enough for us. Jean and Bryant were amused at our enthusiasm. It was "old hat" to them, but it gave the four of us another point of interest to share.

Our weekend trips to Durham were a real treat. Bryant, Jr. was growing so fast, and before we knew it his second birthday had arrived! We went over for the celebration, and while Dan and Bryant watched ball games, Jean and I attempted to decorate Bryantie's cake. Jean wanted this lemon cake with white icing to be transformed into a carrousel. Now Jean and I are pretty creative gals, and when we put our heads together, we come up with some good ideas. My mama always said, "self brag - half scandal," but I'm going to brag on the cake anyway. We used candy canes to support the "roof" that we cut out of colored paper. Animal crackers were used for the carousel animals. We put peppermint candy around the sides with gumdrops in between. To top it off, we made a flag to "fly" atop the carrousel using a bright piece of material attached to a toothpick. The smile on Bryantie's face when he saw it was our reward. He was such a precious little boy and was so smart. He could recite one nursery rhyme after the other, so serious, almost standing at attention until he finished. Then, a smile would appear, and those blue eyes would dance while we clapped with delight. Being around him made me long to have a baby.

It seemed like everybody in the world was pregnant or already had a baby. My two sisters-in-law had three each, and Jan was expecting her fourth! Betty Ann later had twins which made five for them. When we were together, all they talked about was their children. Now, it wasn't that I had no interest in all the cute and clever things their children were doing; I loved each of them dearly, but I just couldn't relate. On the other side of the coin, they were far removed from their college days and that life, so I just listened to them swap stories and secretly longed for a child of my own.

Dan was now in his senior year at State, and we wanted to start our family. I had had some physical problems (which the Crouch's thought was all in my head) and was scheduled to see another doctor in Raleigh. He would be the seventh. None of the other doctors had found the cause of the pain I was having, and I was beginning to believe that maybe it really was all in my head because I wanted a baby so bad. At any rate, I was going to try this new, young doctor, and see what he thought. Thank goodness, Dan believed me and did not agree with his folks. Seven must have been the magic number because this doctor found my problem. The bad news was he agreed with the other six on one thing. He said our chances of having a baby were one in two million! He suggested I take the medicine he prescribed, relax, and enjoy Dan's last year in college; and when we were ready to adopt a child, he would be happy to help us in any way he possibly could. Dan and I were numb as we left his office that day. The drive home was long and silent. When we stopped in front of our

New Homes

apartment, Dan broke the silence with words I'll never forget. "Well, Honey," he said, "let's do what the doctor said, relax and enjoy this last year. He doesn't know everything; and if it's meant for us to have a baby, we will. God's timing is perfect." And perfect it was, because three months later, standing behind the rec center in Durham watching Bryant and Dan cook hamburgers, I mentioned to Jean that something was wrong with my nose and taste buds. "Coffee doesn't taste right, and the smell of smoke makes me sick." She said, "Ruum, you could be pregnant! Your sense of taste and smell changes you know." Sure enough, I was!

That May, Dan graduated from N.C. State and went to work June first for Bendix in Towson, Maryland. The baby was due June 16th, so Mom Crouch came to stay with me for a few days. Dan had worked two days on his new job when I called him to come home. I was in labor! Mom was usually a person in control, but she was in a tizzy that morning before leaving for the hospital. She changed clothes three times. I think my taking a shower, washing my hair, and shaving my legs with pains ten minutes apart unnerved her. We called Jean and Bryant before we left to let them know we were on the way to the hospital and to stand by for our call after the baby arrived. At 1:20 on that Wednesday afternoon, June 3, 1959, the same doctor, who had told us our chances were one in two million of ever having a baby, delivered a healthy, 6 lb. 10 oz. baby boy. Daniel Gay Crouch, Jr. had arrived to change our lives forever and to begin our love affair with him that continues to this day. What a precious miracle he was! When my mama and daddy arrived that afternoon, I proudly announced, "We have a boy!" My daddy said with tears in his eyes, "Are you all right, gal?" I answered, "Yes, Daddy." Satisfied that I was, he took Mama's hand and said, "Let's go see that boy." Jean and Bryant came over our first day home to see our new son.

Mama stayed with me two weeks after Danny was born; then Cora came for a week. I was waiting for Danny's four week check-up before moving to Maryland. The fourth and final week, Jean, Bryant, and Bryantie came and took me home with them. Dan attended to the movers and getting our apartment ready in Maryland.

* * *

When I look back now on that year we spent in Durham, I realize that it was probably one of the happiest and easiest years of our marriage. We no longer felt the anxiety of being unhappy in a job, our life was full and simple, and our needs very few. We enjoyed many good friends from our previous Duke days who resided in Durham. Everything seemed to fall into place for us, and the most important thing in our lives was a beautiful, healthy son.

I had never been around little children when I was growing up. I had many cousins, but they were all near my same age, so I was the first to admit that I never knew what joy a child could bring into your life. Bryant, Jr. was always a total joy to us. He was a calm, bright little boy and easy to manage. We could always depend on his behaving well, and he made us nearly burst with pride.

My mother gave Bryant, Jr. and me a trip to visit her in Michigan that fall, and on one of our shopping sprees with her, he fell in love with a "riding tiger." When she came to spend Christmas with us that year, she had not forgotten his excitement over that special toy and brought him the beautiful Stieff tiger on wheels that he rode with delight. He would pull the mechanism that made him growl, and his sparkling blue eyes would pop wide open as though startled by a ferocious jungle animal. He giggled and thrilled his "Mema" in a way that only a grandmother could understand. He was always our marvelous source of entertainment, and we adored him as we watched in total amazement the development of a two year old.

Chapter 23

Setting Sail

Good things kept happening to us, or so it seemed to us. In January of that year, we were told about an opening for custodians at a local recreation center. This meant a rent free, telephone free apartment with a small salary for custodial duties. Bryant applied immediately, and because of his previous experience of working for the recreation department in Kinston, he got the job. In two weeks, we were moving again, this time into a recreation building.

Our responsibilities began immediately. We were to move chairs and furniture back into place after meetings, lock the building after use at night, and clean the restrooms on Sundays. The latter was certainly the most difficult, but we managed that, too, with the aid of disinfectant and rubber gloves. We rapidly learned that nothing comes free, but we still appreciated this break.

It turned out to be even better, though, than we had imagined. We had a very nice one bedroom apartment with every convenience, the use of the community center, and private parking; and our little boy had his own private playground. It was a beautiful place to entertain him and his little friends. They rode tricycles on the safely enclosed sidewalks or played in sandboxes on sunny days; and on rainy days, we simply moved inside the huge open building. Rainy days were never a problem. Bryant and I thought we were rich now, no rent, so we were able to save everything for graduate school. We even treated ourselves to eating out occasionally, always hoping it wasn't being extravagant.

Phoebe's pregnancy came as a glorious surprise for us, and we had that much more in common and happiness to share. We knew this year was passing too fast, but we never doubted that we would always be close. I could hardly wait for her to experience the love of her own child as I had, but I dreaded her leaving us after their baby was born. We all knew again how soon we had to be separated after Dan's graduation, and that thought was depressing.

Bryant was accepted into the master's program for Hospital Administration at Northwestern that spring, so we began again to make plans for another move, only this time to the windy city of Chicago. Phoebe and Dan's little son finally came the third of June, beautiful and healthy, and we knew that God was good to us. We eagerly awaited our visit with them as soon as Danny could travel to Durham. From that point, we knew we faced the long dreaded separation, their little family going in one direction and ours in another. The fear of the unknown gripped us intensely. Our plans for the first of August materialized into a weekend visit with Phoebe and Dan in Towson, Maryland, on our way to Chicago where we would live for a year while Bryant attended Northwestern.

The weeks before moving to the windy city of Chicago were spent packing and deciding on the few necessities we would need and could get by on for a year away from North Carolina and home. The day finally came for our long awaited adventure to begin. With nearly all of our possessions carefully stored in Durham, we loaded our red and white Ford station wagon with clothing for the three of us, Bryant's books and golf clubs, Bryant, Jr.'s favorite books and toys, (his little red tricycle), and my portable sewing machine.

I had learned to sew as a little girl watching my mother and knew how to figure out how pieces of fabric fit together to create a garment. She worked in the piece goods department of J.C. Penney's for twenty years, and I watched her endlessly measure and cut fabrics, laces, and linings, and help ladies decide on patterns and designs, zippers and trims, never losing interest in her work regardless of how weary she was at the end of the work day. I am grateful to her today for creating this same interest and knowledge in me because it has always been a real source of enjoyment and creativity for me. Bryant teases me, referring to my sewing whenever I get upset saying that all he has to do is give me a piece of fabric, shut me up in a room with my sewing machine, and I can work off all my frustrations. I suppose some of my basic education comes from figuring out how to sew, measure, and make things work out. Naturally, we had to take my sewing machine to Chicago.

Chapter 24

A Trip to the Crouches

Bryant, Jr. was safely situated on the back seat of the car on his crib mattress, filling in the entire space behind the front seats creating a perfect crib. In those days, there were no seat belts or wonderful, safe car seats for children. They had free run of the car, climbing and playing as if in a play pen. I tremble at the thought of that freedom today. How much safer they are and more protected being confined in the car seats and taught from day one to be still and stay as secure as possible.

He was a good traveler and a happy little boy, so our trip was fun. We had planned to break the long trip by spending the first night in Towson, Maryland, with Phoebe and Dan and Danny, so after leaving very early on a Friday morning the first of August in 1959, we made our first stop. Bryant made sure we were well beyond the heavy traffic of Washington, D.C., before deciding on a rest stop. The three of us were really ready for a welcome stretch when he pulled into a newly opened Krispy Kreme Donut Shop just before our entrance to the Washington-Baltimore Parkway. Bryant, Jr. ran around and played for a while, we used the restrooms, and bought milk, soft drinks, and six hot, fresh donuts for our ride on to Maryland. We each enjoyed our treat and morning snack, and our littlest passenger fell asleep in his crib. Loving sweets as he always has, Bryant asked for a second donut, so I reached down into the bag for his donut, only to feel and find under a piece of waxed paper three "hard as rocks," at least a week old, donuts. He was furious, but there was no turning back at that point, as we were well on our way down the Parkway. We learned at lot! Our very first naive introduction to people not always being what they seemed, and how they will take advantage of you when you are innocently unaware. We never could understand what a mere clerk had to gain by cheating like that. Surely it didn't raise her salary or give her a promotion! Maybe we were the ones who actually gained from the experience, because we have never forgotten it and decided then to let it be a lesson to us: "Never trust a Yankee."

Dan had given us excellent directions to their apartment in Towson but hadn't warned us about the many confusing turns coming out of the Baltimore Tunnel. We missed our turn and ended up going through the tunnel three times before getting on the correct road. After that, we drove almost straight to their new home, and there was Phoebe, standing on the doorstep with two month old Danny resting peacefully on her shoulder, trim and neat, and already back to her Peace College figure. We all squealed with delight when we saw each other, so thrilled to be together and see familiar faces.

We had never seen such huge apartment complexes. The one they lived in was tremendous. It's no wonder Phoebe stayed in and didn't venture out much! It truly was a different environment from the quiet, slower pace of Raleigh. We took long rides around Baltimore and Towson becoming familiar to nearly all they would write to us about during the coming year.

The weekend with the Crouches was a happy retreat. Danny was growing up, cooing, smiling, and recognizing faces; and Phoebe and Dan were trying hard to be comfortable in the foreign land of the North. We all realized we were true Southerners. It was relaxing, and we were entertained by each other's company and funny stories but always hanging over was the cloud of months of not seeing each other or watching our little sons grow and change. We wanted so much to share this happiness but knew we would have to do this by mail for at least nine months. On Sunday morning, we said good-bye again and left for our long ride across the Pennsylvania and Ohio Turnpikes on to Illinois and into the big, strange city of Chicago.

Chapter 25

Chicago-Bound

Four lanes of heavy traffic headed south, four lanes of traffic going north, we thought we had seen traffic coming across the turnpikes in Pennsylvania and Ohio, but it was nothing like this. Bryant gripped the steering wheel tightly and settled confidently into the fartherest right-hand lane as we made our way north on Lake Shore Drive. Seeing a big city like this for the first time was awesome to us. On our left, the city of Chicago loomed before us with mammoth buildings, tall and grey, housing hotels, offices, department stores, and museums. We saw spacious, open parks, beautiful flowers in full bloom surrounding tremendous flowing and shooting fountains. On the right was Lake Michigan, her shores lined with sandy beaches filled with sunbathers trying to cool in the hazy, hot sun on this August Sunday afternoon. I don't know why, but I was surprised and never expected to see sandy beaches in the heart of the city, but there they were.

We loved pointing out all the new and interesting sights to our little son. I only wish now that I had written down all the precious things he said at his first impressions here. There is nothing any more honest or descriptive than the way a child describes something. If only I had been smart enough to record those sweet and adorable little expressions. We were in Evanston, Illinois, north of Chicago, before we figured out how to get off of Lake Shore Drive and make our way through eight lanes of traffic to our hotel.

We had budgeted ourselves for two nights in a hotel, so Monday morning we were up bright and early ready to find a place to live. We had studied the ads for apartment rentals in the classified section of the local paper the night before and had our day mapped out. Bryant, Jr. was a real trooper, always good at adjusting to whatever we had to do, so he climbed back into his "car crib" and was excited about helping his mama and daddy find a new home.

It was bad! Anything that we could afford, we couldn't possibly live in,

For All The World To See

and it would be in a horrible section of town. It turned out to be a very long day. Our excitement lead to depression and fear. With little sleep and anxious hearts, we started shopping again the next day. Still no luck! Every place we looked was awful, dreary, ugly, and scary. We decided around four in the afternoon to make one last try at the apartment building owned by the hospital where Bryant had found employment. We were sure it would be a long shot, but Bryant wanted to try, even though we had been told that only interns and residents got those apartments.

He left me trying to keep Bryant, Jr. entertained in the car while he made a call on the manager of the apartment hotel. Today, I would not wait in the car with a baby on the streets of Chicago. Bryant must have given the manager a real sob story: "Wife and baby waiting in the car with no place to stay, desperate, had to have help." No sob story at all, pure, and simple truth! It worked! Thank you again, God!

We looked out the car windshield and saw Bryant coming. All he said was, "We have a place, don't you say a word! No matter what it looks like, we're taking it." And we did. It wasn't so bad, small one bedroom, furnished with a "pullman" kitchen, day bed for Bryant, Jr. to sleep on, table and two chairs, and a desk for studying and typing. It was all we needed, and we were thankful for it. For two whole days, we had wondered what we were doing in this place and wanted to go home, but now we were able to look again to the future.

Bryant started his job in the Medical Records Department of Wesley Hospital, a large five hundred plus facility, and classes began for him at Northwestern University. We were lucky! He walked across the street to work and school, and I had a city park right in the front of our building for entertaining our three year old, even in the cold of winter when it was flooded for ice skating. I could skate and pull him in his little sled for rides in the park. Weekends were spent visiting the zoos and museums, evenings were spent studying and typing papers, and time passed. We made some friends, and the children played together, but we were all there for one reason: to get through with school and go home. Mema came for a visit, Jesse came for a visit, Bryant, Jr. celebrated his third birthday, Bryant worked, his golf clubs were stolen out of our car, I typed, and there were signs of spring finally. No more sounds of trucks scraping the ice and snow from the streets at night to wake us, no more being couped up in those two rooms on the eighth floor with only unfriendly elevator rides to the little market on the ground floor, but we still knew how fortunate we were to be so conveniently located in this big city, and time passed.

In May, Bryant decided to take the job offer from Watts Hospital after

Chicago Bound

the school year ended, and we began making plans to go home to North Carolina. We had been truly blessed again. Bryant had gotten the assistant administrator's position in Durham right where we wanted to live. We were expecting our second child, and our good fortune made us feel almost guilty, knowing from Phoebe's letters how miserable she and Dan were in Maryland and not knowing when they could get out of that way of life.

Chapter 26

Thinking of Going Home

In later years, Dan and I would refer to our fourteen months in Maryland as our wilderness experience. Thank goodness, the Lord did not choose to leave us there forty years! We soon realized that North Carolina was as far north as we ever wanted to be. Our little boy was the joy of our lives. He was a happy, active, and good natured baby, and such a miracle to us. Everything he did was wonderful!

The hills of home tugged at our heart strings when we went home for Christmas. The feeling had not lessened by spring. Danny had started walking in March, so the promise of warmer, longer days, and getting him outside was welcome. On one of our afternoon outings, I stopped to chat with a neighbor. After commenting on how much Danny had grown, she turned to me and asked in her Yankee brogue, "Is Diane a family name for boys in your family?" I said, rather amazed, "Did you say Diane?" Her reply was, "Yeah, isn't that your kid's name?" Even more amazed, I answered, "No! His name is Dan!" She said, "That's what I said, Diane!" In my next letter to Jean, I told her we had to get out of there. They don't even understand the way we talk!

* * *

Bryant and I drove to Pontiac, Michigan, on our way home from Chicago that summer and visited Mema. We adored sharing our precious son and her only grandson with her, and she found such a joy in being with us. She gave me her new raincoat to wear over my full stomach and insisted that we travel home by way of Canada and Niagara Falls. We did, and she was so right. It wasn't that much out of the way and was well worth the extra drive. From Niagara Falls, we dropped south until we reached Maryland and a long overdue weekend visit with our friends, arriving in time for Danny's first birthday.

After learning from them that "Dad Crouch" was speaking in Raleigh,

Thinking of Going Home

and Dan's vacation was coming up in two weeks, we talked Phoebe into riding as far as Raleigh with us and going to Asheville a little early. Dan didn't object because he wanted her to go home if she wanted to. Having her with us, and the two little boys together in the car, made our last leg home interesting. This was really an enlightening experience for all of us.

* * *

When Dan joined us for his two week vacation, he had decided to spend the whole time looking for another job. He secured one with another electronics company in Asheville. We even found an apartment! When the time came to return to Maryland, we were anxious to get started because we knew we would be back in North Carolina in a few weeks. The tears in my mama's eyes were from joy and thanksgiving as we waved good-bye this time.

The next few weeks, we were as busy as bees, but at last all the boxes were sealed, and the last piece of furniture was placed on the truck. We didn't even look back as we drove away from Lochraven Boulevard. We were on our way home!

Moving back to Asheville was good but different. We were young adults with a child now. Shortly before Danny's second birthday, we moved into our first house. It was small but suited our needs. We had a beautiful view of the mountains, and our little boy had children his own age to play with. We had a new appreciation for all the things we had taken for granted before we moved to Maryland. Our family listened to Dad Crouch's sermons each Sunday, and we were able to sing in a wonderful choir.

Chapter 27

A New Baby Arrives

Sunset Avenue! Even the name of the street was picturesque! Bryant found us a neat three bedroom house, one we could afford to buy, in a great neighborhood. A husband happy in his work, a wonderful, healthy, beautiful little son, a home of our own, and a baby on the way — what more could anyone want? Our life was so good!

It was a warm Saturday morning — September 17, 1960. We slept late, Bryant went to the hospital to give blood just in case there was a need for it when our baby was born. We had no idea that I would be calling him that morning because I had gone into labor, but as soon as I got up, I knew something was happening. Even though I thought I knew what to expect this time, it was six weeks early, and I was frightened. He rushed home from the hospital to carry me to the emergency room and hurried away to take Bryant, Jr. to stay with friends. By the time he got back to the hospital, I was in the delivery room! An hour later, God gave us an angel. Our life was surely perfect now. Our delicate and flawless daughter was born that September morning, bringing a dimension of love and warmth into our lives that we could never describe. We named her Myra Allison after our own mothers, and I think she has liked that. (And as I remember these glorious moments and try desperately to put my feelings into words, I could not write this paragraph without adding that this very day she celebrates her thirty- first birthday, and we celebrate with hearts filled with love and thankfulness for the day she was born.)

My mother came from Michigan to see her new granddaughter and to help care for her, and Phoebe came from Asheville to help me, also. Phoebe had a built-in babysitter now with her mother living in Asheville. We were living in the same state again, and we felt as though we were across town! We had the most marvelous time, all of us together, getting acquainted with our new little angel, and seeing our precious little boy gaze in amazement at his tiny sister.

A New Baby Arrives

* * *

Jean and Bryant now had the perfect family. Bryantie was so proud of his baby sister. He would stand by Allison's bassinet and gently pat her. I would never forget the expression of wonder on his face. Allison was so petite and beautiful. Jean and I laughed at ourselves, for we played with her as if she were a new doll — bathing her, dressing her, and brushing her hair. We were sure she would have curls soon. The memories we built that week filled my thoughts as I drove back home. We were only four and a half hours apart now. It was wonderful! The new expressway over the mountains between Ridgecrest and Old Fort, which had just been finished the year before, made any trip east easier. As I topped the mountain at Ridgecrest, the wheels could not turn fast enough. I had been away from home and my two Dans for a whole week. It was the first time since his birth that I had been separated from Danny. I found him and my mother playing in her back yard when I drove up. He was happy to see me, but my little fifteen month old son was already very wise. He was in no big rush to leave his grandmother and cried big tears when I put him in the car. I didn't blame him, but I have to admit it did hurt my feelings a little.

A few weeks later, the fall leaves were at their peak. I know they are always beautiful, but this year they were particularly beautiful because that was something else I had taken for granted while in Maryland. The fall of 1960 also brought the completion of the vacation home at Lake Lure that Mom and Dad Crouch had been building. It was to be a place of relaxation and recreation for the whole family. Dad Crouch impressed on all of us that we were to be in church on Sundays and not at the lake. When Mom had her first dinner party at Lake Haven, Ruth and Billy Graham, long-time friends of theirs, were among the guests. Before dinner, Dad asked Dr. Graham to say a prayer of blessing and dedication. It was a special moment when he stood in front of the fireplace and prayed.

Dan and I made plans with Jean and Bryant on our next visit to spend the summer vacation together at the lake. It was to be the first of many vacations spent together there.

Chapter 28

Durham

Durham was really home to us. All my life I had heard the expression, "Wherever you hang your hat is home," and it's true. Here, we had a great circle of good friends, a church we were already familiar with, and Duke University and all of its activities as well as an excellent day school and kindergarten for our son. We thought our little home was a mansion, all 1,200 square feet. I could actually drive up to the back door and unload our groceries, unlike the grocery shopping experiences we had while living in Chicago the previous year. Bryant, Jr. and I had to catch the elevator down from the eighth floor, walk three blocks to where we had to park our car, drive then to a grocery store, shop, drive back to our apartment building, unload groceries at the service entrance onto the elevator when we could catch it (Bryantie learned quickly what the "Open Door" button on an elevator meant, as that was his job to keep the door open while I unloaded), carry the groceries into our apartment, and then proceed to go back to the car, take the car back to the parking lot, walk the three blocks back to the building where we lived, catch the elevator again, and go home! We had had a big adventure but even that had been home. Unloading groceries at my back door since then has always been a luxury to me. I don't take it for granted.

    Bryant's new job continued daily to excite him and bring him much satisfaction. He had truly found his called profession, and he was good at it. Bryant, Jr. loved going to see Mrs. Rudin at play school twice a week, and it gave me time with Allison for our private time. Raising two children can get pretty hectic, and it was good for us to have some free time. In those days, we stayed at home all the time. Going out to play or for walks in the mornings and afternoons was our entertainment. Our lives were very routine and pretty much on a regular schedule. Our children napped every day after lunch. We always had our meals together. Our lives revolved around our family and home. I loved my life, too. I realized more every day that mothering and building a happy, stable home were very important and satisfying to me, and I was proud of our life.

1960 was an eventful year for us: Bryant's graduation, Allison's birth, and the Crouch's relocation. Bryant even decided that I didn't have to cook Sunday lunch any more, which meant no more roasts in the oven before Sunday School or congealed salad made late Saturday night. We could eat every Sunday after church at the hospital cafeteria. Now this was a big, big thing! People just didn't "eat out" that much in those days. It just wasn't in your budget, so this was a grand treat, and we looked forward to it. We soon established eating at the hospital for Sunday lunch as a family tradition for our family.

Bryant was always trying to figure out little outings for us as he kept our only car with him at work unless I had a doctor's appointment or needed to grocery shop. We learned of a new hamburger place that had just opened, one where he thought we could afford to eat, so this became another bi-weekly outing for us. It was named "McDonald's," and we could get hamburgers for 15¢ He could feed us all for under $1.00, and Bryant, Jr. loved it. It was a bright and colorful place catering to families, so we always looked forward to going to McDonald's.

Everyone's interest was captured in 1960 by the Presidential campaign and elections in November. Dwight D. Eisenhower had been our President for two terms, having been elected the year Phoebe and I graduated from high school, and we were probably more aware of him than any President before him. Eisenhower was a popular and respected war-hero before the American people elected him as their President. He chose not to run for another term at this time leaving the door open for his Vice President Richard M. Nixon to seek and win the Republican nomination. Nixon was opposed and challenged for the Presidency by John F. Kennedy. We were absorbed in their campaign as we watched Kennedy whistle-stopping across the country, mesmerizing the nation with his charisma. We were impressed and stirred by his youth and energy, and he was elected in November to be our new President, the youngest man to ever hold this office, changing the pattern of history for our country in a way yet to come.

Months passed, then a year, then another. Our young son was not only handsome with his crystal blue eyes, but he was proving to be a very bright, smart little boy. We adored him and loved watching him use his analytical little mind when playing. He and his sister were great buddies. The summer after his fourth birthday, we bought him his first dog, a Sheltie named Laddie. Phoebe and Dan had introduced us to this breed of dogs, and it was the perfect animal for us. We only had Laddie for a couple of months when he died at the veterinarian's. We were never convinced of the cause of his death, because we only took him in for routine shots, and he never came home. Our hearts broke! We immediately set out to find a new dog and soon found our tri-colored Sheltie. Bryant, Jr. named him Smokie. It's a very moving experience watching a child grow and love his pet the way Bryantie did Smokie. We were never without a dog as long as Bryant, Jr. and Allison lived at home.

During our third year in Durham, Bryant was offered a wonderful position in Greenville, S.C., presenting us with a very difficult decision. We weighed all the pros and cons and finally decided that it was definitely the right move. He would be assistant administrator in a much larger hospital, offering him an even bigger opportunity to develop in his career. We were moving again! We realized though that this was the way of life for most people at our age — moving, changing, adjusting, growing with every better opportunity.

We didn't like giving up our home, and especially up-rooting our son, but we were able to buy a little larger home in Greenville, and the move would put us only 65 miles from Phoebe and Dan. Phoebe and I began making plans immediately.

Bryant, Jr. had to start school in the very first grade in Durham because Bryant's job did not start until November 1, but he made the transition and adjusted beautifully. We celebrated Allison's third birthday with all of her precious, little friends and playmates. Then, I began to pack for our next bright horizon.

Chapter 29

Another Baby Arrives

With a few turns of the calendar, and shortly after Jean and Bryant moved to Greenville, S.C., Dan went into the construction business with a friend. At that same time, I found out I was expecting our second child. When I called Jean to tell her our good news, of course, she was excited. We both expressed hope for a little girl but agreed a healthy baby was the main thing.

Daydreaming about a new baby while watching children play happily can be abruptly interrupted by many things. This was never more true than on November 22, 1963. I was baby-sitting for my sister-in-law Betty Ann. The weather was cold and windy, so I had their twins and Danny inside. They were playing on the floor in front of me, unaware of the television playing in the background. My attention was drawn to the TV when a special news bulletin flashed on the screen. The announcer said in a somber and shaken voice, "The President has been shot." For the next week, we watched in horror as the details were unfolded before us. Kennedy had actually been shot down in cold blood while riding through the streets of Dallas, Texas, in a motorcade. Our young and energetic President, only 47 years old, and in the twinkling of an eye, his life was snatched from him; a family was thrown into utter torment and an entire country into turmoil. With unbelieving eyes, we watched Jackie Kennedy in a blood stained suit standing next to Lyndon Johnson while he was sworn in as President on Air Force One. The minute I walked through my back door, I called Jean. I pictured her in her pretty, bright new kitchen as she answered the phone. The tone in her voice matched my disbelief. All we could say to each other for the first minute was, "This can't be happening!" She was packing for a weekend trip to Durham. She and Bryant never missed the Duke/Carolina football game, but now their plans were uncertain. So much was happening so fast; most of it now is a blur.

At our before-Christmas get together with the Aldridges, we were still in shock over all the turbulence in our country since Kennedy's death. We tried to have a positive attitude toward the coming New Year and agreed that 1964 had to be better. Jean helped me put the finishing touches on the nursery, and we tried to turn our thoughts toward happier things.

The birth of a child brings such a rush of emotions. Happiness, love, excitement, and thankfulness are only a few. On May 1, 1964, Susan Elizabeth Crouch was born. God had once again blessed us with a beautiful, healthy child. She was perfect. I could not then, nor could I now, describe the joy I felt when Dan leaned over my bed and said, "Honey, we have a little girl." The next day, my parents came in my room carrying a huge arrangement of narcissuses. They had driven out to their mountain cabin and picked every single flower in the fields surrounding it and had the florist arrange them. I will never forget them coming through the door with those flowers. I had called Jean that morning to tell her about our precious little girl. Next time we talked, I shared this special moment and tried to describe the beautiful, lacy, white dress and slip my mama had brought for Susan to wear home from the hospital.

* * *

Buckingham Road! What could be more regal? And here Bryant and I had what was to us a palace on Buckingham Road. But we were in a foreign land! The adjusting came a little slower as we were unfamiliar with everything. It was a much larger city, and we knew no one and no place to go! I was very uncomfortable leaving Bryant, Jr. at his new school, but he grew to love it. It was Mother who couldn't adjust.

Before the first year was over, he had talked me into letting him walk home from school alone, about six city blocks, but it scared me to death. I remember waking Allison from her naps in time to drive to the school and follow Bryant, Jr. home. We had bought a second car (a '63 Comet station wagon) before we moved to Greenville.

Now, I had transportation at all times, so it was easy for me to plan my daily patrol to Bryant, Jr.'s school. I would follow about a block behind him until he was in sight of our home, and I knew he was safe, and then I would rush home in time to greet him. He was such a big boy! I have been criticized more than once for being an over protective mother, but peace of mind is worth a fortune, and I wonder how many other mothers have done the same thing.

Life in Greenville rapidly became similar to our routine back in Durham, different only because of two growing children and their increased activities. Allison was now old enough at four to start ballet

Another Baby Arrives

lessons. She was so cute to us, dancing in her "tutu"! Bryant, Jr. played the piano and swam on the swim team. And so it went.

Chapter 30

Two Families Share Fun

The assassination of Kennedy had changed our tranquil and transparent lives. We were more cautious, fearful, protective, and sensitive to anything slightly strange happening around us.

Our simple visits on the weekends with the Crouches were always a safe haven. Again, we enjoyed a pleasant social life in Greenville and kept in touch with many good friends we made while residing there, but our stronghold was always knowing we could take time out most any time with Phoebe and Dan.

Our weekend trips to Asheville and Lake Lure were fun and relaxing but were sometimes uncomfortable for Bryant, Jr. He and Allison would ride in the back of our station wagon and slide from side to side as we drove around the hairpin curves going up and over the mountain. By the time we would get to Asheville, he was nearly always green with nausea. He never did get used to that ride through the mountains

We were so fortunate that the Crouches would share their beautiful home at Lake Lure with us, and we looked forward to these summer trips. None of us could afford a vacation anywhere else, and this enabled us to have a real treat. Phoebe and I would always start planning our week's vacation together months in advance. We later realized that the planning was probably the fun. We would cook full meals, cakes and cookies, freeze, and work in order to get ready, then haul it all to the lake. We found ourselves sweating in a hot kitchen preparing meals for eight people three times a day, and it can be hot in the mountains in July!

We thought we were supposed to cook all those bacon, eggs, grits, and toast breakfasts every day! No one ever told us any different! Those other six people were out swimming, fishing, canoeing, kayaking, resting, sleeping, or whatever, and Phoebe and I were forever slaving in that hot kitchen. If we came out of the kitchen, they came in for something to drink and a snack; if we sat down, they wanted to know what we were having for dinner. We were always trying to figure out a way to get away!

Two Families Share Fun

One day, they let us out of the kitchen, and we went shopping - not for food - but for peace! We came back to an empty cabin, frightened, not knowing where they all were. We found them finally climbing Chimney Rock with our babies. Dan and Bryant never heard the end of that!

Phoebe and I would occasionally be allowed time enough to float out into the lake on big inner tubes, arms spread to the sun, looking dazed, bewildered, and tired. On one of these rare occasions, our calm was broken by the sound of a big splash! Three year old Susan had walked backwards, falling into the lake, and we saw Allison jumping in to "save her life." We jerked ourselves as quickly as possible back to the pier; our inner tubes were always tied there with ski rope, arriving in time to see Allison pull Susan out, exclaiming in excitement, "Susan, that was good. You did that so well!" Phoebe and I just looked at each other and said almost in unison, "This is a vacation?" Mothers protecting their young can be really nerve racking. I'm sure that the young mothers of today see us alone with no children around and think that we have no idea of what they are experiencing in rearing their families.

Chapter 31

Family Challenges

Three months after Susan's birth, the children and I were visiting Jean and Bryant in South Carolina. My mother called to say Daddy was in the hospital for tests. His health had been poor since an operation two weeks after Susan's birth. It was difficult for me to imagine him any other way but strong, healthy, and able to do anything. He had always been there to take care of any situation. I was grateful that Bob, Dan's brother, was his doctor. It was he who told us that next week Daddy had lung cancer. The many years of smoking and working as a fireman had taken its toll. When Jean and Bryant came to visit him, he was happy to see his "brown-eyed angel" and her family. Three weeks later, Daniel Raymond Fair was laid to rest. The little grandson whom he loved so much, standing by his grave, looked up at me and said, "Mama, can I leave these here?" In his outstretched hand were five smooth river rocks he and his granddaddy had collected on their last trip to the mountain.

A lot of changes took place in our lives that year ... Dad Crouch was elected General Secretary of the Baptist State Convention and resigned as pastor of First Baptist Church after twenty years of service. Mom Crouch was adjusting to her new life in Raleigh, but we knew she missed her grandchildren and the rest of the family. For the first time, I realized how much I depended on her wisdom, encouragement, and infectious laughter. She always made me feel good about myself and others. I missed her terribly but at the same time knew she was better off than my mother who was lonely and having to adapt to a whole new way of life. Mother had been very dependent on Daddy. She had never learned to drive. Thank goodness, we were there at this time to help her. Danny and Susan were a delightful diversion and filled many of her days with joy. Jean and I talked about Mom when we were together. Our roles had changed so suddenly where our parents were concerned. Somehow, we had never thought about having to take care of our mothers. They had always been there to care for us, and we were learning to cope with it.

* * *

We had lived in Greenville for nearly two years when our quiet sleeping was disturbed one night by the ringing of the telephone at one in the morning. Bryant and I both leaped out of bed; he grabbed the phone, and I could feel my heart pounding as I listened to him say, "Where are you?" I began to realize as he talked that it was my mother, and the pounding in my chest began to subside. When fear strikes me, I have always immediately felt this overwhelming beating of my heart causing me to become very still and quiet. Some people scream; I just get quiet.

Fear changed to excitement when Bryant told me that Mema was in Asheville, only 65 miles away, on her way to see us, but why one o'clock in the morning! We waited another hour for her to arrive. I could hardly wait; it had been so long, and I wanted so much to be with her and share our life with her.

In our all night visit after she arrived, we learned that she was homesick, tired of living so far away and alone, couldn't see her grandchildren or family, but most of all she just wanted to come home. She was only 49 years old at the time, ancient to us, still no grey hair, firm and beautiful. She had lived a hard, sad life in Michigan, another broken marriage, working again to take care of herself, alone! She had given up her good job, though, to come home; her confidence was back, and it was good to see her looking happy.

She was there now to get to know her grandchildren and for us to get to know her all over again. We talked her into staying, trying to make a home for her there with us.

I remember now her being there with us for Bryant, Jr.'s first piano recital. He had been a model student. My brother, being the musician that he was, had always told me that music should be as important in one's education as reading or writing. We were never given the choice of whether we learned to read or write, and music should be treated the same way. Because of his encouragement, we enrolled Bryant, Jr. in private piano lessons in his second year of school after he had learned to read.

The recital went well. Our precious little boy appeared before us, dressed appropriately in his first navy blue sport coat, tie, and grey slacks, took his seat at the long grand piano and began to play. I could feel my heart pounding! I truly thought it would burst with pride when I watched him turn slowly, look in the audience for his teacher, and finding her say, "I've forgot it!" I felt Bryant take my hand. You could hear a pin drop! We heard his teacher saying calmly, "It's all right, Bryant, just start over." He turned to the black and white of those keys, determined, and played his pieces flawlessly, overcoming stage fright, and continued piano lessons for another five years.

Mema stayed on with us, finding employment at the hospital gift shop, but she never was satisfied. After several months of trying to make this work, she decided to go on home to Kinston, North Carolina, where she would live with a widowed sister. That was a good thing, and the timing was perfect. We had had a good, long visit; and soon after she left us, Bryant found out about a job possibility in Rocky Mount, North Carolina, and decided to apply for it.

Chapter 32

New Job

Jesse and his family were living in Roanoke Rapids at the time, and he had heard that a bond issue had passed in Rocky Mount for a brand new hospital, and the city officials were looking for a hospital administrator. He called Bryant and told him in his big brother way, "You ought to apply for that job and come back to North Carolina."

We were comfortably settled in Greenville, contented, children happy, and close to the Crouches. Bryant loved his job at Greenville General. Could we possibly give up all this? He decided that he would apply anyway, probably a real long shot, but the opportunity of going into a place and planning and building a hospital from the ground up was a dream of a lifetime. He had to try.

Jesse had found out where to send his resumé and application. We waited, and after four weeks, he was asked to come for an interview. (Don't get your hopes up; it's only an interview! Pleasant, nice, businesslike!) We waited again! (He was much too young, only 32. Who would hire a man that young for such a tremendous responsibility?) We waited, no word; we finally decided to go on vacation and focus in on our real life.

We had hoped for a long weekend with the Crouches at Myrtle Beach, South Carolina, that summer and were able to convince them that this was a perfect time to go. In making the reservations at a quaint little motel we were familiar with, I was reminded of the special vacation we had taken with our children the summer before. I was glad we had been adventurous then, because now I knew Bryant would never consider such a trip with the new job possibility dominating our thoughts.

Our vacation the summer of 1965 was to Florida, and it was truly one of those memorable times. We had not been to Florida since the Orange Bowl trip in 1955, and Allison and Bryant, Jr. were excited about going somewhere other than Lake Lure. We were happy we could finally afford to give them this big adventure. It was great! The ride in our Comet station wagon, because it got better gas mileage, was comfortable and fun. We drove all over the state, pointing out lovely cloud formations on rainy days, watching rain falling in the distance, and feeling a thrill to see crayon colored rainbows as the brilliance of the sun cleared the sky.

It was the off-season. We found cheap motel rates and cooked breakfast in the room with my electric frying pan. We had to have those eggs and bacon. Allison and Bryant were wonderful, happy travelers, and we stopped to see anything they wanted to see: "Wickey Watchey," alligator farms, Cape Kennedy, and sandy beaches. We drove out of our way to the naval base in Jacksonville, Florida, to show them the "Gemini Space Capsule 4."

Bryant and I had heard on the local Florida news that the capsule had been retrieved from the Atlantic Ocean, off the coast of Florida, and was being held at the naval base. Being adventurous and always wanting to expose our children to educational opportunities, we decided to take a chance on seeing the capsule. We drove to the base and, without question, were given directions to the dock where we found the capsule on display with only a single marine to guard it. We were the only people there, amazed as we felt the parched and scorched heat shield that had protected Edward White, our first man ever to walk in space.

Bryant, Jr. had his own pictures taken of this Gemini capsule, on the dock, fresh out of water and space. Now, one year later, we were ending another family excursion. Myrtle Beach amusement parks, roller coaster rides, giggling in the salty surf, and finally being able to relax as we watched the Aldridge and Crouch children play "Marco Polo" in the motel swimming pool.

We arrived back at our home in Greenville, sent the Crouches on their merry way, and there in our accumulated mail was the letter. Rocky Mount wanted to talk to Bryant again, and he was to call for another interview if he was still interested. We thought we had put this question out of our minds. Allison started first grade in two weeks at a brand new school, Bryant, Jr. was signed up for midget football at the local Y, and we just couldn't move now!

The very thought of such a fabulous opportunity drew Bryant to Rocky Mount again.

Two weeks later, Allison started first grade, and I went to find us a home in Rocky Mount, North Carolina. Then, I had to call Phoebe to tell her we were moving 300 miles away from Asheville.

They wanted him to start work the first of October, one month after our children had started a new year in school. We were so young and

New Job

naive. Little did we know the challenge that awaited us.

Chapter 33

Separating Again

My father's death gave me a new perspective on life and the world around me. Being in the same town with my mom helped both of us adjust to life without Daddy. The realization of how quickly time passes crossed my mind a great deal. It seemed like only yesterday Mama, Danny, Susan, and I were driving toward Burnsville to have a picnic celebrating the beginning of summer vacation. Dan was on a business trip, so I had phoned Mama the night before to see if she would like to visit "the old home place," as she called it. She was thrilled and excited and insisted on fixing our favorite picnic foods. It was a perfect day in every way. We were the picture of happiness driving along without a care in the world enjoying each other and the breathtaking beauty surrounding us. Our first stop was the New Wray Inn in Burnsville and a visit with Mama's Cousin Rush who owned this now famous inn. The children loved sitting in the large white rocking chairs that lined the front porch and rocked merrily while their grandmother and I visited. The real treat was when Cousin Rush rang the dinner chimes to call his guests to the dining room for their meals. Our next stop was the Country Store. It is hard to describe the Country Store; you have to experience it. It fills up all of your senses. The smell of coffee, spices, dried flowers, candles, the sound of chimes, and the bell ringing over the door. There were handmade crafts for any age on every shelf and in each "nook and cranny" as well as homemade jams and jellies, and before me a whole shelf of Sourwood honey. What a picture that brought to mind ... Jean and me, hot biscuits with Sourwood honey in the dining hall at Peace. My picture faded quickly because Susan was tugging at me saying, "Mommie, I have to go pottie."

Leaving Burnsville behind, we drove toward the crossroads community of Pensacola where my mother was born. There stood the little three room cabin she drew her first breath in, surrounded by cattle, which now was being used to store hay in. The children were wide-eyed

Separating Again

with wonder to think their grandmother had actually been born in that place.

Now, it was time for our picnic lunch. Mama spread a quilt and began to unpack the handmade honeysuckle vine basket. We had chosen a spot by the Cane River. From the shade of the trees, we looked out over a pasture and grazing cows. Yellow flowers moved gently by the breeze. The sound of the river and the songs of birds and buzzing bees were the perfect trio to serenade us.

What a feast — fried chicken which Mama fried that morning, deviled eggs, pimento cheese, peanut butter and jelly sandwiches and my favorite, her macaroni salad, and for dessert, brownies.

Mother had promised the children a surprise after lunch, so when we had all the leftovers put back in the basket, we walked up the road a few hundred yards. As we rounded a bend in the road, there was a swinging bridge stretched across the river! The children had the time of their lives running back and forth on that bridge. Mother holding Susan's hand, the sound of their laughter — what a memory we built that day.

Jean's recent phone call telling us about their move to Rocky Mount kept haunting me. Our time together was so special; we didn't like the idea of so much time passing between our visits. Facing us again was the separation of our families, and we dreaded that.

We planned to visit them the weekend before they moved, which was only a few short days away.

All went well as long as we played the game of "pretend they're not leaving." We thought we were good at this. So — when the time came for us to head back to Asheville, Jean and I tried to be very grown up; however, as soon as our eyes met, the dam broke. The harder we tried not to cry, the worse it got. We stood there hugging each other, crying like two school girls and oblivious to the effect we were having on "those six other people." Suddenly, Susan was crying; then, Allison began to cry, trying to comfort Susan. We realized that Danny and Bryant, Jr. were standing there not knowing what to do, and Dan and Bryant were just shaking their heads. We began to laugh, silly and emotional, still crying at the same time. As tears gave way to laughter, we knew this was not the end of the world.

Chapter 34

Rocky Mount

Bryant and I had decided it would be best to rent a house in Rocky Mount with the hopes of building our own home in the near future, so our first weekend there was spent in a local motel after the long and tiring trip up from Greenville. Allison and I led the way in our '63 Comet station wagon, with Bryant and Bryant, Jr. and Smokey following at a safe distance behind us in the red and white '56 Ford station wagon.

We spent that first Saturday introducing our children to the new town they were to call home, showing them their school and neighborhood. None of us were real happy with what we saw, and with wide eyes and blank expressions, we toured all day.

We were greeted that afternoon by the chairman of the Board of Trustees of the yet unnamed, unbuilt hospital. That afternoon, he kindly gave us another tour of the area. When he learned of our plans to rent and that we were unable to get in the house until the following Monday, he immediately stopped the car at the nearest service station to use the telephone. When he returned to the car with cold Cokes for refreshments, he then drove us to the house we had rented and where we were met shortly by the realtor with a key, a service man from the city who quickly turned on water and electricity; and "voila" we didn't have to wait until Monday for anything. With the flick of a wrist and a few quick telephone calls, we soon realized the power of certain people, and that it's not always how much you know but who you know. Time and experience would reveal this to us more in the years ahead.

The weeks and months after that were spent literally trying to find our way. Allison and Bryant, Jr. settled and adjusted quickly in their new school situation. Bryant found an office and began the enormous task of planning and organizing a hospital for a community which made us very aware that only half of the population wanted us there. The bond issue for the new hospital had only passed by a little over 100 votes. Our children were seen as the new hospital administrator's children, and I was known as the new hospital administrator's wife. (We constantly were explaining to people just what a hospital administrator was.) We were on display everywhere we went, and everyone wanted to see this 32 year old "whipper snapper" who had come to town to spend their tax money. We had almost forgotten what it was like to live in a small town. As the politics of a small town and the politics of a county began to unravel and reveal itself, the reality of how naive and inexperienced we were set in, and it was scary. There was an "element" there who thought they owned the place and were determined to control.

Here we were, young and idealistic, excited, full of honesty and integrity, only wanting to do a good job, and at every turn, we were facing hostility among people we never knew existed. Bryant spent endless days and nights speaking, trying to educate the public of the facility he was planning, and trying to build a good reputation — something he had never been faced with before. He secured an architect and plans began to unfold after hours and hours of research; and consideration was given to every aspect of the perfect plan for this dream. Being back in eastern North Carolina gave us a wonderful
opportunity now to visit our families, and it was always a welcome break to be able to ride to Kinston or Snow Hill and back in a day to see Bryant's mother or mine. We couldn't get to the Crouches quite so easily now, so we went to see some of our family nearly every Sunday afternoon.

Mema was very occupied as a full time guardian to a five year old little girl at this time, so our visits with her were brief usually, but it was comforting knowing she was happy and well taken care of. Little Betsy had lost her mother at age four. She was an only child, so Mema had moved into her home to be her guardian, helping out her grief stricken and dazed young father. I felt sorry for Betsy but saw how very fortunate she was to have my mother as her mother. It was good for both of them, as Mother's world revolved around rearing another child, and she was needed once again.

Nannie had remarried the year we were in Chicago and lived only 45 minutes away from us in Snow Hill. She had married a long time family friend whom we all called, very affectionately, "Pappy." Pappy had a lovely family with grandchildren of his own, but he was also the only grandfather our children ever knew, and Allison and Bryant, Jr. loved him dearly. He had provided Nannie with a grand life, rescuing her from the dusty file cabinets and counters of the Register of Deeds Office at the local county court house, opening up to her a life of leisure and travel. He had a grand, old home on the coast of North Carolina, and as it became Nannie's home, it also became her children's. Pappy was an unselfish, wise gentleman we all admired and loved, and we were grateful to him for the life he had given to Nannie. Going to visit them on a Sunday afternoon always brought about excitement.

Chapter 35

Vacation for All of Us

After living in Rocky Mount for almost a year with new house plans underway, drawings and plans for the hospital developing, new friends (We really weren't sure of who was and who wasn't at that stage.), and sweet, patient children looking forward to the end of a school year, we could hardly wait to get back to the mountains of North Carolina and the cool waters of Lake Lure. It was hot in eastern North Carolina, so hot that I remember that first summer in Rocky Mount one of Allison's new found friends couldn't come to play at our house, but "Allison was more than welcome to play at her 'friend's' house" because they had air-conditioning, and we didn't!

Need I say more! The long ride back that year to Lake Lure was truly God's timing and rejuvenation for all of us. Allison and Bryant, Jr. had their daddy finally all to themselves, captive, riding in the car for eight hours, and their little minds never stopped; they were full of tales from school, laughing, fighting, playing, and eating from the picnic we had packed for our journey. It was good to get away.

* * *

Our house became a flurry of activity the moment Dan drove into the driveway. When he returned from work that Friday afternoon, Danny and Susan ran to greet him, both talking at once and anxious for him to know they had completed the tasks he delegated to them that morning. Everything in readiness was packed with amazing speed, and in less than an hour we were off! Our summer vacation for 1967 had officially started. We needed some fun, light-hearted adventure, and the company of good friends. The Aldridges would be joining us the next day. Mentally, I checked off the things to be done before they arrived. As we began the curving assent across the mountain, my thoughts turned to the week ahead and all the catching up on each other that Jean and I had to do. They had lived in Rocky Mount for eight and a half months now. A lot had happened to each of us during that time. Dan's mom had been diagnosed with cancer shortly after they left Greenville the year before. We were devastated. She came back to Asheville to be under Bob's care and for treatments. Once again, we were facing the loss of a parent. As we topped the mountain and started down the other side, my attention was brought back to the present by the conversation Susan was having with her imaginary family. Charney and John Harners had joined our family about a year ago. They and their three children Loon, June, and Croon went everywhere we did most of the time. Susan was explaining to "the children" where we were going and that Allison would be there tomorrow afternoon to play all week with them. I thought the Harners family was something I must remember to get Jean's opinion on.

Before breakfast the next morning, our energetic son had his daddy up early and down at the boathouse fishing. Dan Jr. loved being at the lake house. Everything about it kept him busy and excited — swimming, fishing, boating, playing in the woods. He certainly was in his element, and it pleased me to see him enjoy nature so much.

Finally late that afternoon, the moment we had been looking forward to all day was heralded by the "beep, beep" of a car horn. We hurried to greet the weary travelers. It was a happy and long overdue reunion. The week that followed was full of various excursions. We drove into Asheville one day to attend the Craftsmen's Fair. Booth after booth of beautiful handmade things lay before us. Everybody's favorite was the blacksmith. We were fascinated by the smith's skills. As his hammer hit the anvil, it played a rhythmic tune, and right before our eyes a mere piece of iron became a work of art.

The major part of our day at the lake house was spent in high gear, centered around the children and all their activities. We four adults enjoyed the cool peaceful evenings relaxing on the screened-in porch sipping iced tea and catching up on each other. During those times, Jean and Bryant shared with us the challenge facing them in Rocky Mount. We could not imagine some of the opposition they were coming up against. Short-sighted, self-centered people are always scared to death of a man with vision, honesty, and high integrity, which explained why Bryant was caught in the crossfire of that community. Dan and I could not fully grasp their situation. Our lives were so protected in comparison. Surrounded by family and friends, we very seldom met with any disapproval.

The week passed too quickly, and the time for good-byes had come once more. As we watched the little Comet wind its way out of sight, I feared it was the beginning of another long separation. We could not know that three months later, a week before Thanksgiving, we would be together once again, standing on a rain soaked hillside listening to Billy Graham read scripture and offer words of comfort to our family as we all paid our last respects to Mom Crouch. She had called all of the family together the week before to tell us she had fought the good fight, but she was tired and it was time to let go. As we joined hands around her hospital bed and listened to Dad's prayer for strength through the coming days, the words of John 14 walked through my mind once again: "Let not your hearts be troubled, my peace I give unto you." Miss Lucy had said this scripture would become one of the strong threads in the fabric of my life. Once again, she was right. It was hard to believe Mom was gone. She was only 59 years old and so full of life and love. Susan's three year old wisdom seemed to sum it all up when a few weeks later she asked me, "Why did Grandmother leave me?" I answered her with the usual, she was sick, she couldn't get better, she didn't want to leave us, etc. "It's all right, Mama, cause she left me her happiness."

Dan and I had much to be thankful for as 1968 began. His business was going well; our sweet children were healthy and happy and growing up so fast. They were a constant source of joy and pleasure to us.

Spring brought new beginnings not only to the earth but to our household as well. We bought a new house. Everything clean and brand new, a lot more room, and a whole mountainside for Dan, Jr. to explore.

Chapter 36

Life in Rocky Mount

Not only were Bryant and I trying to build a normal life for our family during 1967, in a community surrounded with uncertainty, we were greatly aware of the escalating and unbelievable war in Viet Nam as a background for all our plans. The American people never dreamed our country would be faced with the devastation of such a long and heinous war.

As we watched the war advance in the news, we also watched the citizens of this county, divided and bickering among themselves for months over where to build the new hospital in any attempt to stop its progress. In contrast, thousands of young men and women gave up their freedom and lost their lives daily in Viet Nam.

Our children were too young to understand the happenings of the real world, and that was wonderful. They brought happiness into our home with their growing love for school, piano lessons, and scouting. They became more and more active, their attention easily diverted from the discontent and animosity surrounding Bryant's work. Their activities were a peaceful distraction for us, as we were involved with them; I was serving as a leader for Allison's girl scout troop; and Bryant's Saturday mornings were consumed with coaching Bryant Jr.'s midget football team. I was very grateful that Bryant had made it possible for me to stay at home and be available to our children for activities so important to their growth and education.

Months passed, we kept plodding along, yet still uncertain of the hospital's rise, but we had completed plans for our new home and continued on our chosen course by breaking ground for our dream house, never really sure of just how long we would live here. We were excited about our plans and tried to explain our situation to Phoebe and Dan, but it was difficult for even them to comprehend what we were experiencing, for they were encompassed with their family and were in their protected environment in Asheville. It's like all things, one never knows what someone else's life is like until he "walks in his moccasins," as the saying goes. So much was happening all around us that our problems seemed insignificant. Lyndon Johnson, our President, had created a "Great Society" (supposedly) for everyone, bringing about unbelievable freedoms in our country — long haired, dirty "hippies" occupied our city parks, integration and forced busing of our school children was on everyone's conscience, and we shivered as we learned of the spread of drugs and alcohol in our country; and all this time Elvis Presley and the Beatles continued gyrating rhythm and blues throughout the world. We were glad our children were the ages they were, and we could "tuck them in" safely every night.

The humming of my sewing machine kept me company and satisfied my creativity, and I stayed busy designing and sewing clothes for Allison and myself, passing the lonely hours of many days, waiting for our children to come home from school. This sewing hobby of mine had convinced me of my ability to make draperies for our new home, now well underway since the 1968 winter season was behind us.

Phoebe and her family had come one weekend to see our house under construction. (I can see little Susan now parading around in her long-haired "wig" like a 16 year old. She always wanted long hair, like the big girls, so Phoebe got her a real wig!) After our weekend with them, saturated with spaghetti supper and house construction, I began early the next week on my sewing. Nannie came over to lend a hand, helping to hem the kitchen draperies. It was on one of these days that spring in April that we heard the news bulletin on TV of Martin Luther King's assassination. Another atrocious, senseless crime for our country to face which effected us all. It was hard to believe that a leader so dedicated to his cause, a great civil rights leader marching everywhere and proclaiming his "dream," now had been shot down in cold blood at the height of his career. What in the world could happen next? Immediately, every eye was drawn to the television as we tried to find an answer to this latest dilemma opening up the country to even more strife and filling our streets with protesting citizens. It was a frightening time with rioting and disorder erupting, and we became extremely cautious, wondering what this latest outbreak of violence would do to our country and the safety of our children. Our lifestyle in a small town cushioned us somewhat from the harsh realities of these events as we went about our daily lives.

Maybe it was a sign of the times, maybe the attitudes of people in a small, closed community, human nature, or our own sensitivity, nevertheless, we remember the friends we made when we moved to

Rocky Mount. Some were friendly and sincere, some merely acquaintances still, and we soon learned that it takes a lot of time and experience to know the difference. You can't wait for people to come to you; you have to be willing to reach out yourself and have time for them. Our church became a great source of strength during this time for us. Here, we were made to feel welcome and needed, a super source of comfort; and gradually our circle of friends and acquaintances grew larger as we searched for our niche in this unique community. We were more and more comfortable as we felt acceptance among some, and we could better understand the caution of others. Actually, you can't be friends with everyone, only friendly and pleasant. You have to relate to people in an open, honest way, and few people are willing or able to do this, and this is not all bad because what is right for one may not be right for another. Friendship is not always easy, as it takes time, understanding, compassion, and communication.

Somehow, I was never really bothered by the fact that we could only be so close to our new found friends. I was reminded of Phoebe and our friendship. We could be ourselves with each other even when we disagreed; there was caring and understanding between us, and we each had created space for the other in our lives, no matter how busy we became. This was friendship, special and sincere, and we were the lucky ones. The other didn't matter.

The site for the new hospital was finally decided on in the spring of 1968, and that, in itself, is another history lesson. There had been a certain "unhappy element" in the county doing everything in "their" power to obstruct this decision with the most bizarre incident being that a Catholic priest was going to build a rock quarry next to this particular site. This scenario ended when the priest supposedly ran out of town with some local woman. Nothing surprised us anymore!

We thought the worse was over. We could build our new home now joyfully and free of anxiety, and Bryant saw the combination of dreams, hard work, talent, and patience coming to fruition. It had taken a great deal of patience, and we wondered many times if we had enough to get us through. We had endured strain and stress, and all the time we were trying to rear our innocent children to be well adjusted with a sense of security, love, and family stability. Now, we relaxed some and moved forward.

The end of another school year and the beginning of summer were greeted by relieved, "promoted to the next grade," happy spirited children, filled with anticipation of what this freedom for a few months held in store for them. Our first order of business, before playing, was to move some

Life in Rocky Mount

furniture and stored articles into a cabin located on the recently purchased hospital site in preparation for moving into our new home. This also gave us much needed extra storage space, and we could "spread out" in our rental home.

Chapter 37

At the Beach with Nannie

Nannie had invited us to the beach for a week as soon as school was out, and this was really all we wanted to do. It was aggravating to have to take time out to move furniture, but it had to be done. Going to Nannie and Pappy's house on Bogue Sound had been a highlight for us for several summers, and we were always ready to go when the time came.

It would be different this summer though. Pappy had died suddenly the year before, and we had never been to his house when he was not there. Nannie would be there alone waiting for us to help fill her loneliness, still keeping up a brave and cheery front, still grieving.

We drove down early on a Saturday morning arriving in time for lunch, and it was just as Pappy had left it. Bryant, Jr. and Allison raced out to the long wooden pier stretching out over the shallow waters and sea grasses leading to the deeper waters of the sound. We followed close behind watching, arm in arm with Nannie, drinking in the beauty of this place again, and relaxing without realizing it. Bryant promised Nannie he would help her replace a few boards that had blown off of the pier during a winter storm.

It was a big, old beach house with a covered front porch, surrounded by a lush carpet of St. Augustine grass reaching all the way down to the edge of the water. Looking back at that comfortable old home made us appreciate even more what Pappy had provided for us all. We sat on the benches at the end of the pier starring at the rippling waters of Bogue Sound, glistening from the reflection of the summer sun like a sea of tiny brilliant diamonds. Pappy had been with us before, talking, describing, watching the constant parade of fishing boats and luxurious yachts, sail boats and barges, some loaded, some empty, cruising up and down the intercoastal waterway directly in front of their house. We could see Shell Island just beyond the deep channel, and we remembered our many little boat rides with Pappy and Nannie over to pick up shells, always being

At the Beach with Nannie

careful that everyone wore old tennis shoes to protect their feet.

Bryant and Allison and Bryant, Jr. were calling for lunch now, and the spell was broken. I thought about the aroma of Nannie's crab concoction boiling on the kitchen stove. Pappy would set those big, wire crab pots early in the mornings, and late in the day, he would drag them in and fling them up on this same pier, loaded with freshly caught blue crabs. In the house, the seasoned concoction would be boiling, just waiting for Nannie and Pappy to drop the live crabs into the hot water for steaming. (I am still amazed today at the idea of their dropping those creepy, crawling live crabs into that hot water without even flinching.) There would be no crabs for lunch today, only banana and peanut butter sandwiches and a myriad of memories choking us.

We had the full week ahead of us, a week of laughter and fun, of restful nights, and of steaming hot coffee as we watched the sun burn the early morning fog off the water, waiting for a lazy day to begin. And the Crouches were coming all the way from Asheville for a long weekend.

Chapter 38

An Excursion

The trip to Bogue Sound was an eight hour drive, but in true Crouch fashion, we left at five a.m. and arrived at the beach house by early afternoon. It was good to be together again. The warm breeze gently blowing the marsh grass at the edge of the yard was a sharp contrast to the mountains. As we sipped a glass of iced tea, I commented on that fact. Bryant immediately began to plan one of his famous excursions. The next day, Thursday, we spent taking the children over to the beach, resting and enjoying a wonderful seafood dinner at the Sanitary Fish Market in Morehead City. Come five a.m. Friday morning, we all piled in that little ol' beige Comet of Jean and Bryant's and off we went on another adventure through the still deserted streets of Morehead City, over the bridge and past Beaufort, through each little sleeping village, all the way to the very end of Highway 70. We had no idea where Bryant was taking us, but we finally ended up at the Cedar Island Ferry for a two and a half hour ferry ride across the Pamlico Sound to the Island of Ocracoke. It was the first time any of us had been to Ocracoke. After the long ferry ride, we were looking forward to breakfast. The cafe we chose did not disappoint us. We enjoyed generous helpings of grits, eggs, bacon, buttery homemade biscuits, and heavy mugs of hot coffee. We let the children wrap the leftover bread in a paper napkin to feed to the sea gulls. Ocracoke was a beautiful, picturesque little fishing village. It was like being at the end of the world to me. I commented to Jean that Mom Crouch would call this a "couldya place." Could ya live here and be happy?

The free twenty minute ferry ride from Okracoke to Hatteras Island passed quickly as the children fed their leftover biscuits to the sea gulls hovering over the bow of the boat begging for food. Each of them squealed with delight every time a gull caught a piece of bread in mid air or actually took a crumb from their hand. When we got off the ferry, we didn't have to ride too far to the Cape Hatteras Lighthouse. All of my life I had seen pictures of this black and white spiraling landmark, a 208 foot tower

An Excursion

keeping its silent watch over the sea. The children wanted to climb all the way to the top so Jean and I told Dan and Bryant to "be our guest." We found a comfortable bench near the entrance to the lighthouse and settled down to wait. It was a bright, sunny day, not too hot, but hot enough to be thankful for the strong breeze coming in off the ocean. I noticed the waves were much rougher here than at Atlantic Beach. Jean began to talk about her Grandmother Wise. I remembered her being called Miss Ersie, but like Jean, I called her Mama.

Jean said, "My grandmother was a young girl of only fourteen when my grandfather discovered her living with her family in the little town of Buxton, only a few miles from here. He grew up in Pamlico County on the mainland. At that time, he was serving in the Coast Guard, and on one of his trips across the same waters we just traveled, he met my grandmother. He was older and loved her at first sight. They were married soon after that, and when she was at the tender age of fourteen in 1908, he carried her away from Buxton and Cape Hatteras, the first time she had ever left this desolate island, to live in Pamlico County where she raised a family of ten children."

I said to Jean, "How did she know how to be a wife or what to do? Did she start having children right away? Thank goodness he didn't have more than ten tours!"

Jean continued, "Thinking about it, I know Nancy Ann, the "help" my granddaddy had hired for Mama, actually raised Mama because she was only a child herself. She raised her right along with the rest of the children."

We drove from the lighthouse down to Buxton to see Mama's birthplace. As we turned around in this out of the way little fishing village and headed back up the coast, I thought that in all these years of knowing each other that Jean and I had not shared our ancestry. As far as the mountains are from the sea shore, they were that far apart.

We could see the Pamlico Sound to our left and the Atlantic Ocean breaking on our right as we drove north toward the end of the island. We were looking forward to crossing the newly completed Bonner Bridge that connected the island to the mainland. The view as we rounded the crest of the bridge was breathtaking. Bryant slowed the car and there before us was a panoramic view of the Atlantic Ocean, the Pamlico Sound, and the Albemarle Sound, all breaking beneath the bridge into the Oregon Inlet. From here, we could see the outline of this part of the North Carolina coast. It gave me a new appreciation for the Outer Banks. Our next stop was lunch, greasy hamburgers and french fries from a local drive-in at

Nags Head, then on to Kitty Hawk. Bryant wanted us to see where the Wright Brothers took their first flight. As we looked at the monument marking this historical moment in history and while the children ran off the marked distance on this grassy knoll, I said, "Wouldn't the Wright Brothers be amazed to see aviation as it is today?"

We knew we had to meet ferry schedules late that afternoon but had saved enough time to let the children run off some of their pent-up energy on the big sand dunes at Nags Head. We parked the car on the side of the road and watched the children as they ran way ahead of us climbing and falling, using all fours, hands and feet, racing to reach the top of this mountain of sand like I had never seen before. As we made our more leisure climb following the children, Jean pointed out a piece of property at the foot of the hill on the south side owned by her family. I was dumbfounded as I listened to her spin another story about her granddaddy.

She said, "My granddaddy always loved Nags Head and one day got a good buy on this piece of property. It was before the day of motels, and he knew that fishermen coming to the coast needed a place to stay. On this land, he built six little tourist cabins that he rented out to tourist and fishermen. It's only 150' wide and 200' deep, and this presented a real problem at his death. In his will, he had forgotten to leave this land to any one person. His ten children never could agree on who was to get it or how it would be used, so it was eventually divided up into ten strips of land 15'x 200' with the lines actually going through the middle of some of the cabins. What can anybody do with a strip of land that size? We know now that the children sold their portion off to each other as time passed. Some of the family still reside there."

These same sand dunes that we watched our children romp on are known today as Jocky's Ridge. It makes us feel good to know that it has been preserved as a state park.

It had been a long day. We met our ferry schedules; and with four tired sleeping children, we back tracked our way to Nannie and the house on Bogue Sound.

Chapter 39

Together Again

Vacations are bright spots, but no matter how many you have or when, whether it is summer, winter, spring, or fall, you still have to come home to reality, only rested, hopefully. There are always what seems like mountains of wash, empty refrigerators, new schedules, tons of mail, unread newspapers, and not enough time in the day to change gears.

Bryant and I quickly fell back into our usual routines and kept busy, savoring the memories of our Bogue Sound vacation and exploration of the Outer Banks of North Carolina. Celebrating my thirty-fourth birthday in July that summer brought pleasant thoughts to my mind, as I recalled a conversation Phoebe and I had had on our long ferry ride gazing out on the beauty of God's sea. We thought we were getting so old, and time was passing so fast, perhaps because the year had been extremely eventful for us. Both of our birthdays were in July, and we realized as we had discussed the events of the summer that we would celebrate our 34th birthday only a few short weeks after hearing the grim news of Robert F. Kennedy's death. He was shot down in a hotel in Los Angeles after claiming victory in California as the Democratic candidate for President. It was difficult for us to comprehend. It was another senseless assassination, and no one had any answers to why! The world seemed to be changing so fast all around us, and we agreed again that it was good that we didn't know what tomorrow would bring.

* * *

Dan knew I was dying to get to Rocky Mount to see Jean and Bryant's new house which was still under construction. I was good at dropping "one liners" like, "Jean said the house was really taking shape now. Wish I could see it. I told Jean I hoped that house wouldn't be finished before I got down there to check it out."

For All The World To See

I did not know any of this had registered on Dan one little bit until he came home from work on Friday evening and said, "I did some checking today and found out you and the children could fly to Raleigh for under a hundred dollars. If it's convenient with the Aldridges, and Jean can meet you in Raleigh, you all could fly down Monday, and I'll come pick you up next weekend."

He had been asking me for weeks what I wanted for my birthday and figured this would be a gift he didn't have to worry about my returning because it didn't fit or wasn't the right color. I totally agreed and was thrilled to death, as were Danny and Susan. It would be Susan's first plane ride and the first one Danny would remember. The timing was right for Jean and Bryant, so the preparations to go began. I had a lot of work to do. Not only did I have to get mine and the children's clothes ready, I had to make sure a week's worth of clean underwear, socks, and dress shirts were there for Dan. I also did extra cooking, so he would have an easy-to-prepare supper each evening.

By the time Monday morning rolled around, I was ready for a relaxing airplane ride. However, the weather did not cooperate! It was a stormy, pouring down, rainy day. Susan and Danny enjoyed the bumpy ride, but it was a fixed smile, white knuckle flight for me. Happily, we beat the storm front to Raleigh and landed in bright sunshine. Jean, Allison, and Bryant, Jr. were there to meet us and our unexpected treat of being together again so soon had begun. The hour's drive to Rocky Mount took us through small communities and past tobacco farms that stretched as far as the eye could see. This land was as flat as a pancake but pretty. Once again, I said a silent "thank you" to the good Lord for letting us be back in North Carolina. Before we knew it, we were pulling in the driveway on Clifton Road. After a cool glass of lemonade, we changed into cooler, more comfortable clothes, and drove over to the house site. It was really coming along nicely and was going to be beautiful. Each day of that week was full of activity. We took the children to the club for late afternoon swims; to the Children's Museum to see real live alligators, snakes (ugh), and other unusual species of animal life; to little league baseball games; and to, at least, two trips a day by the house. One afternoon Bryant, Jr. made a delicious pound cake for our dessert that night while Jean and I cut and taped newspapers together the exact size of their breakfast room table. Then we measured and marked the center. That afternoon we took the "table top" over to the house, placed it where the table would stand, and x'ed the spot where the light fixture would hang to be perfectly centered. That was my small contribution to the building of the house!

Together Again

On our way back home that weekend, I thanked Dan more than once for my birthday treat. The trip and the hours spent together were a lovely and lasting thing for him to do. To this day, I can still see Jean and myself placing that pattern and measuring. The light hangs perfectly centered over that table now where we share meals, laughter, endless conversation, and countless cups of coffee.

Chapter 40

Fear

It happened on a Sunday afternoon late in August, 1968. We knew that school would be starting soon, and we faced the hectic schedule of September, so we spent this particular Sunday afternoon with Nannie in Snow Hill, rocking on her big front porch, watching Allison and Bryant, Jr. playing under the huge pecan trees in the side yard. Occasionally, they would find a long lost pecan, left on the ground like hidden Easter eggs, and keep a running account of who found more than the other. The days were still long, and after a simple and relaxing stay, we unhurriedly headed back home to Rocky Mount.

It was always hard for Bryant to enter town after being away, now that the hospital site had been selected, and not ride by and check the "property."

We had to do this before he would take us home and while it was still light! No amount of moaning and groaning from his three captive passengers changed his mind! He was so eager to get this project started.

The property couldn't even be labeled a corn field, only a barren piece of land stretching out over 100 or so acres taking in a small wooded area and two very small lakes on the back side. Our only access was over a path, rutted and bumpy, put there by the many trucks hauling people in and out surveying the land. Bryant could maneuver it very well in our '63 Comet and proudly drove through explaining all the time and visualizing where every building would go.

It was on the back side, near the wooded area and almost at the end of the path, when he stopped the car abruptly. We all gasped and couldn't believe our eyes as we sat motionless wondering what to do. There, looming up before us was a barricade that could have only been built by a group of very strong people. The huge wooden gate, wide enough to drive a car through and probably fifteen feet high, had been ripped from its hinges on the fence that safely enclosed an acre of this land for the previous owner's weekend retreat. We could go no farther. Bryant locked

Fear

us in the car and very carefully slipped behind the barricade in between the trees. The gate had been tied to the trees with electrical wires and chains, preventing any possible movement.

I was petrified! We were all scared to death, waiting, watching, and wondering what Bryant would find, praying all the time that he would be safe. (Looking back, it was probably a stupid move for him to go alone, but he was compelled to check.) He found no one and came for us shortly. We climbed, as he had done, between the trees, and he led us quietly toward the lovely cabin located inside the enclosed area of land. There, we found utter chaos. All of the furniture had been stolen, all of our stored belongings gone, and whoever did it wasn't satisfied with just stealing; they had ripped out the light fixtures all over the house, pulled all of the wiring out of the walls, broken all the windows, and ripped the doors from their hinges. No one person could have accomplished this evil act on his own, and we had never in our lifetime been confronted with such evidence of meanness and violence.

We were frightened! Was this evil directed toward us personally? Could people actually be this mad to get at the building of their new hospital? And if they would do this, what else?

How do you explain to little children the reasoning behind acts of hatred and sickness like this without creating even more fear in their little hearts? Bryant and I did the best we could, and we knew we would no longer be able to protect our children from the human evil and violence of the world. They had to be warned and protected as best we could.

Bryant reported this crime to the local police, and we never heard any more about it. As far as we know today, only a few people ever knew about it, and it was never discussed.

We wanted to move away from Rocky Mount to a safer place, but we were too locked in with our commitment that we knew it was not the right time. We were thirty four years old, and very young, naive, and had a lot to learn about people and life. Phoebe and I were right about one thing — it is good that you don't know what tomorrow might bring! You cannot live in fear. You take one day at a time, live it to its fullest, and be grateful.

Chapter 41

New Beginnings

The beginning of a new year is always a mixed bag of emotions for me. There's that "blah," letdown feeling after the holidays. Yet, at the same time, there's a bit of excitement about the new months ahead and what they might bring. 1969 was no different. The American people had gone to the polls in November of the previous year to elect the 37th President. They chose Richard Milhous Nixon. After five years of L.B.J. and Ladybird, we were looking forward to the change. On January 20th, I got my household chores done quickly, so I could stay glued to the television and not miss a minute of the inauguration and all the festivities scheduled that day. Dad Crouch had spent the night with us but left when Dan did that morning. Dad's mind was not on the inauguration. Since the Baptist State Convention last November, his thoughts were on a lovely lady from Virginia. She and her husband had been friends of Mom and Dad's through the years at various church meetings. For the last six years, she had been a widow. While she was attending the N.C. Convention, she and Dad renewed their friendship. He asked her out to dinner, and from that moment on, he "set his cap" to win her, and win her he did! They were to be married on February 8th. Dad had started dating a few months after Mom's death, which was a shock to me and something I had a hard time accepting. I didn't get upset with Dad as much as I was angry with Dan! Don't ask me to explain it. I didn't understand it myself! I got fighting mad at him one day over something that I don't even remember what now, but I ended my "mad spell" saying, "I know one thing: if I died tomorrow, you would marry again before I was cold in the grave!"

He started laughing and said, "That's what this is all about, isn't it? You're mad at me for something my daddy's doing! Honey, I can't help what my daddy does. That's none of my business, but if it makes him happy and helps him through this time, who am I to judge!"

New Beginnings

The word "judge" hit a nerve. Dad didn't fit the picture in my mind of what a grieving loved one should be. I was feeling hurt for Mom and her memory and, at the same time, was thinking how quickly one could be replaced! By the time Kitty came on the scene, I knew Dad was not trying to "replace" Mom. He was just trying to deal with life without her. It was impossible for me to understand the loss and loneliness he was feeling at that time.

Kitty, a petite, very attractive and charming woman, was also very brave to take on a family the size of the Crouch clan. She was easy to love and accept. It was wonderful to see Dad so happy. The wedding was in Charlotte, presided over by Henry, Dan's oldest brother. After the ceremony and picture taking, Kitty's three children and their families and all of the Crouch families met for the first time at the reception. It was a happy, emotional day, full of new memories, new beginnings. On the way home, Susan asked Dan, "What do we call her, Daddy?" Dan, Jr. said, "We call her Grandmother, don't we, Daddy?" Dan answered, "Let's call her Grandmother Kitty. Ok?"

* * *

January of 1969 found the Aldridges moving into our new home. It had taken almost a year for its completion, and we moved in with a comfortable and secure feeling as if we had finally come home. There was a different feeling for us as we settled into this house that we had dreamed of and planned so carefully. It was ours and only ours.

We watched it rise day by day, nail by nail, from only a sandy clearing in a wooded area. Unlike other homes we had had, this one truly was a profound part of each of us — the hidden "cubbies" under the eaves in Bryant, Jr.'s room for his baseballs and bats, footballs and gloves, or scouting and camping materials, and wonderful built-in shelves in Allison's room for displaying her dolls and little girl mementos. Yes, it was us and home, sparsely furnished, but warm and comfortable and safe, and filled with love and appreciation for the many blessings surrounding us.

Bryant had left much of the building decisions of our house to me, as he was totally consumed with the new hospital now (and I add miraculously) underway. We had many anxious moments, fretting and worrying over finances or colors, or trucks backing into trees. It was difficult for me not to burden him with little things when his mind was on the construction going on at the hospital and the colossal, mind-boggling

For All The World To See

responsibility he faced. All of these seemingly "so important" issues faded as our new home became a distraction and a haven for us.

Bryant, Jr. was twelve years old now and entering adolescence. He was bright and handsome, anxious to excel, with a broad spectrum of interests — sports, scouting, school activities, and piano — with raking leaves on a fall day and making up his bed gradually being pushed to the bottom of his list. (Much like most normal twelve year old boys, I would say.) He had followed the development and growth of the space program from its beginning and with an even more fervent interest since seeing first hand the Gemini capsule on our Florida vacation when he was only eight years old. Now, he looked forward to seeing, as we all did, with unbelievable anticipation, what was to be the first man ever to walk on the moon. People throughout the world waited for the day. Everyone knew the names of the astronauts on that mission: Neil Armstrong, Edwin Aldin, and Michael Collins.

We had watched the lift off of the Apollo II on that Wednesday morning in July, holding our breath, as the mammoth, brilliant burst of flames and power forced the rocket into the air that would send the space craft and these courageous men into space. Four days later on July 20, after watching and following the mission with thankfulness for the safety of these men, yet in almost disbelief, we settled ourselves comfortably in our den to wait for the incredible view of man first setting foot on the moon. It was a long day, and at times it was hard to keep everyone awake as the television reception was not always clear. The announcers gave us a constant account of the progress, even describing the footage disappearing as the lunar module made its approach to the surface of the moon; and finally, we heard with great joy Neil Armstrong say, "The Eagle has landed." We all listened and waited and realized what an incredible time it was to be alive. No one can ever forget Neil Armstrong's words as he put his left foot on the surface of the moon and uttered, "That's one small step for a man, one giant leap for mankind."

Bryant, Jr. and Allison managed to stay awake until the wee hours of the morning, absorbed and fascinated with the wondrous sights that lay before us on the television screen. Grown men in bulky space suits were bouncing around on the moon and planting an American flag there. What a brave and trusting sight, and we were all together sharing this historical event and etching this moment of history on our minds forever.

It became increasingly more difficult to find a time to get together with the Crouches now. Our children's activities played a more important

New Beginnings

role in our scheduling, and it always seemed impossible for Bryant to leave town because of his commitment to the new hospital. He felt the need and desire to be on the site everyday, overseeing all aspects of its rise from a pile of brick and steel pipes to the most excellent medical facility he could help produce, down to the most minute detail. (He even had us sleeping on different pillows, testing their softness in an effort to decide on the one most comfortable for the patients.)

Our children were content in a new home and with their new friends. They were "busy little bees" keeping me dizzy driving them from one grand activity to another. Bryant, Jr. attended summer camp for the first time with a friend and loved it. Leaving him there was one of the hardest things Bryant and I ever had to do. We arrived on a rain soaked Sunday afternoon, and deposited him, his gear, and clean camping clothes in a wet musty cement block cabin. Even the mattress appeared wet! All we wanted to do was bring him back home, but he was oblivious to all this. He found John, his special friend, and they saw the river and the boats and an opportunity to play and learn and grow and have fun away from home for the first time.

Allison was not so fortunate with her first camping experience. She had gone to a different camp at the same time with a special friend, also. We had been convinced by friends that it was "the place" to go, and Bryant and I wanted our children to have a good camping experience contributing to their growth. We did not realize until after we had gathered her and her belongings on the last day of camp and were riding home what an unhappy and confused little girl she was. Questions like "Mama, what makes people black with sin?" made us know immediately what was wrong. It apparently was a more charismatic church camp than we had been led to believe, preaching "hellfire and damnation" and had our daughter never wanting to go to camp or leave home again.

If we have learned anything in our lifetime, we have learned that nothing happens by chance. When we arrived home that same day, Bryant, Jr. called from camp begging to stay for another week. He and John had already worked everything out, and we were happy for him to do this. It occurred to us that we might possibly be able to get Allison in at the last minute, and we had the good fortune of everything working out again.

I washed her clothes and packed her off, after a weekend at home, for another week at our own Methodist Church camp on the Neuse River. She was only nine years old, and it was not easy leaving our baby, so hesitant, but she knew Bryant, her big brother, would be there with her. We had the delicate task of helping her to understand the differences in environments and religious beliefs and convincing her that our convictions were what was right for us. We felt that this was the correct way to handle this situation. It worked! In only a few days, she was an ecstatic child with "best friends" enjoying her precious childhood again.

Chapter 42

Friendship

Almost a year had gone by before we were able to make any plans for a holiday with our dear friends from Asheville. Their lives and ours were just too busy. An eight hour drive still separated us. It was apparent that we had to make a more concerted effort if we wanted to see each other.

Phoebe and I communicated by phone as often as Dan and Bryant would allow us to make a long distance telephone call, and we resolved that July 4, 1970, was to be our next vacation together.

When they came to Rocky Mount that summer, I realized just how much I had missed seeing Phoebe. My new friends here were cordial and nice but still held us at a distance. This feeling of guaranteed loyalty that comes from a genuine warm-hearted friend is very relaxing. The freedom of honesty and openness in sharing our thoughts, approving or disapproving — we recognized without question that we could always rely on this trust.

Bryant, Jr. and Allison had learned to sail at camp the previous summer, and both adored water sports, and we had discovered Gaston Lake, a beautiful man-made reservoir only 45 minutes from our home. A July 4th picnic and a trip to the lake was the big entertainment we planned for Phoebe and her family.

I know Bryant well enough to know that when he sets his mind to something that he doesn't usually stop until he accomplishes what he has in mind. In the early spring of that year, he decided that we had to have a boat. (He's pretty easy to read, too, especially when he starts asking questions like, "If we could buy a boat, what kind would you like?" or "If we have a boat, would you water ski and fish?") It wasn't long after that that he and Bryant, Jr. had found a boat we could afford. It was a used wooden, power boat with a 35 horsepower motor that was strong enough to pull us on water skis. (We tried pulling Bryant one time, but that didn't work.)

Most every Saturday or Sunday afternoon after that found us heading for Gaston Lake. We scouted around until we found a wildlife area where we could launch our boat and an unoccupied grassy lot where we could picnic. We spent long hours riding around enjoying the beauty of our brief retreats. Bryant, Jr. and Allison quickly learned to water ski, so they took turns skiing, and I was always relieved when they were too tired to ski and just wanted to boat ride.

We were excited to have a lake of this size and so close to home for entertaining our friends. The Crouches were familiar with Lake Lure, which was surrounded by the North Carolina mountains, and this was a different sight for them. They were surprised to find that it was larger and the water much warmer, yet cool and refreshing on that hot day.

Susan and Danny had really grown so much in a year that we hardly recognized them. Each of them, it seemed, had had a real growth spurt. Susan had learned to swim at the "Y," so for the first time, we could all relax more around the water. After giving Phoebe a quick spin around the lake, she and I were content to ready the picnic and stay put.

Bryant and Dan took the children boating and skiing while we took advantage of the solitude. The water was slick as glass in the cove where we settled that day. It was perfect for skiing; only the hum of motor boats and summery water, lapping lazily on the shoreline, broke the quietness of the moment. Phoebe and I talked non-stop, uninterrupted, with eyes always following our amateur skiers, holding our breath each time one fell and giving a sigh of relief when we saw the little head pop up out of the water.

Eventually, all of this activity wore us out, and everyone was ready to eat. We picnicked and floated out onto the lake on big inflated inner tubes from tractor tires. No matter how fancy a store-bought float was, these were always the best kind we thought, for there was room for two people to sit on and rock back and forth until we tipped it over. There were always silly, ingenious games being thought of by the children to play with the aid of these inner tubes.

It was a day when the Crouches met many of our friends and their children for the first time. They were spending July 4 the same way we were, and we all had an idea of where each family "lighted" for the day (always ready to move on, in case an owner of the property might show up). We visited back and forth, getting a boat ride from one spot to the next. The mamas waited on shore stretched out, relaxed in webbed, aluminum folding chairs, satisfied to let the daddies drive the boats and pull the skiers.

These were wonderful memories, another time, another place,

Friendship

another experience, and the silken thread of our lives being woven together a little bit stronger.

Chapter 43

The Crouches

*M*ama had called early, wanting to know my plans for the day. She had some last minute Christmas shopping to do and wondered if Dan, Jr., Susan, and I would like to tag along. My answer was, "We would love to; we'll pick you up around ten." Now that I had our annual open house behind me, I was really free to enjoy the remainder of the holidays. This time last week, I was not so relaxed, but I decided it was worth all the work and poured myself a second cup of coffee. This was the sixth year we had given this party for friends and their children. The menu Jean helped me plan when we were together Thanksgiving was a big success, especially her recipe for Brown Sugar Pound Cake. (I still bake this cake to give friends at Christmas.)

 I glanced at the calendar to make sure I didn't have anything else scheduled and noted it was the first day of winter. Where had this year gone? It had been a good year. Dan's business was doing well, and we were all in good health. Our life was wonderfully ordinary and busy. We had much to be thankful for. January started off like any other. Our days were filled with church, work, school, trips to the dentist, hair cuts, grocery shopping, the usual. Dan, Jr. was growing much too fast, I thought. At 5'2", he was almost as tall as I. Susan was loving school and doing well. I will never forget her first day of school. Remembering it always brings a smile. The long awaited day finally arrived. "Miss Independence" didn't want me to take her. She wanted to ride the school bus with her brother. Dan, Jr. promised to look after her and get her to the right room. After kissing me good-bye, she got on the bus and never looked back! What she never knew was I drove to the school thirty minutes later and peeked in her room to be sure she was all right. That afternoon as the bus stopped in front of our house, I ran out to greet my children, anxious to hear all about their day. Dan, Jr. got off the bus first and said, "I don't know what's wrong with her, Mama. She won't tell me." There she was, tears streaming down her face. I could not imagine what had happened. She fell into my arms and cried,

The Crouches

"Oh, Mama, I didn't learn to read or write or anything!" I didn't let her see me laugh. It wasn't funny to her.

Dan was working hard to meet the demands of his customers. Business was better than ever, and it promised to be a banner year. He was unaware of the deception going on behind his back. When the board met in late February, my trusting husband found out what greedy men can do. They claim to be your friend while at the same time they have cast their lot against you. By the time Dan knew what was going on, it was too late. He chose to resign as president of the company.

There are no words to describe the feelings you have when something like this happens. You feel hurt, angry, frightened, totally devastated. One minute, you feel secure and successful; the next minute, you realize how fragile your life and your surroundings are. After a few days of numbness, you start trying to get your life back in order. Blessings are counted, and you get your priorities lined up. We learned a lot about ourselves and others during this time. The Lord supplied all our needs, and this ol' world kept right on turning, and we had a new appreciation for things that were always there, but we took them for granted.

Through contacts in the industry, Dan learned of an opening with a lumber company in Burlington. He went for an interview and came home very impressed and hopeful. It was another family owned business, which made us have some concern. However, when the owner called three days later, the offer was so good that Dan decided to accept it. I couldn't wait to call Jean! We would be only two hours away from each other now. That was one of the best parts of the move, along with the relief and gratefulness I felt for his having a job again.

Dan started work in April, the week after Easter. His new boss helped him locate a trailer to live in until the children and I could join him. Dan Jr. and Susan loved staying in the trailer the few weekends we went down to house hunt. They said it was like camping out. Since we had never camped out, nor would we ever, I let them think that! We were not having any luck finding a house. We tried to keep a positive attitude, knowing something would be there for us.

Chapter 44

The Aldridges

These days held many unexpected surprises for us. It seemed that Bryant was never at home. We didn't know from one day to the next if he would be home for dinner or at the last minute have to have dinner with an architect or a doctor who happened into town "just shopping around." It was nothing for him to leave town unexpectedly for an overnight trip to examine more hospital equipment or a change in architectural plans.

This was a big adjustment for all of us, one we never liked but had to accept. Bryant had to juggle his time now, all of the time, to suit everyone else's needs; and his family got what was left over. Family time was a special time for us. We enjoyed the privacy and looked forward to the solitude of dinner together at the end of a busy day. Holding hands, saying grace, sharing and listening patiently as each one had his or her chance to spill out the events of the day was part of our bonding. It was frustrating when Bryant couldn't be with us, but when he was, it was a complete and joyous time.

He did manage to save time for coaching midget league football and Bryant, Jr.'s team. The love of football in the beginning, and an even greater love for our son, set this time aside without question.

Bryant, Jr. had informed us in the fall that he no longer wanted to take piano lessons; and in his caring way of always wanting to please us, he told us he would continue if we wanted him to but that he wouldn't enjoy it. Our teenager had made a choice all on his own, very carefully thought out, testing the reins, and tugging at our heart strings as he reached out for more independence and control so vital to his growth. We knew his interests were more now in sports. We were satisfied as our mission had been accomplished and that was to contribute the knowledge of music to his basic education and to have him enjoy it and not dislike it.

From then on, it was football or basketball or track, whatever the season, and Allison and I were the most enthusiastic spectators. She had the piano all to herself now, except on still and quiet occasions when we would hear Bryant, Jr. playing confidently by himself. We would listen from another room and smile at each other, knowing that he was unaware of his own relaxing, as his growing, young fingers methodically touched the keys of the old piano.

These were the days of forced busing in our schools, which brought about more balanced integration leading to no more neighborhood schools, which brought about major decisions and upheaval for the entire community. Private schools were popping up near and far trying to beat the establishment. This major ruling by the U. S. Supreme Court for desegregation in our public schools had put everyone in a state of panic, especially in the south and particularly in eastern North Carolina.

I remember the divisions and sadness we felt among our friends as the deliberating went on, trying to reach a better solution other than busing innocent young children miles away from home for the sake of integration and satisfying political needs. There was no stopping it, and the big, yellow school buses began to roll. The idea was to pick up children at their neighborhood school, bus them sometimes ten to fifteen miles away to another school, and bus them back in the afternoon to their neighborhood schools. It didn't seem to make any sense, but somehow each family figured out its own way of adapting to the problem.

Bryant, Jr. assured us that he would be fine. He was in junior high and quite capable of taking care of himself, being surrounded by a close circle of friends who trusted and depended on each other. We felt comfortable with Bryant, Jr.'s situation but worried about Allison's; she was only ten years old. We finally decided that I could take Allison to school and pick her up each day and at least avoid the busing.

This was our solution, and life went on. Nothing was more important to me than Bryant and our children, so my days were planned around school hours. I had from about nine in the morning until two in the afternoon to "do my own thing," and my favorite pastime was still sewing. I tried needlepoint, creweling, and knitting, but my creative love was sewing; maybe because I saw the results faster. I usually set aside every Tuesday and Wednesday for sewing, filling in the other days with church work, volunteering in the Junior Guild, or playing an occasional game of bridge or golf. Bryant had encouraged me to learn to play golf before we moved away from Greenville, South Carolina, a "sport we could play together in our old age."

We enjoyed a relative calm now with the school problem quieted somewhat. We waited for the opening of the new hospital that spring with an almost childlike enthusiasm, just knowing how much easier our life would be after this project was completed. We had looked forward to Phoebe and Dan sharing in the excitement with us, but they were unable to come, and we accepted again something out of our control. The past few months had been very difficult for them, and a great, dark cloud was lifted when they informed us that Dan had found work. We were enjoying the fruits of success as they watched so much of theirs fade away. Dan had to start all over, but we were confident that "it would all work out." (These were Bryant's words of wisdom during tough times.) Sometimes we laughed at him, but most often we ended up only ill when he was nearly always right.

The Crouches were moving to Burlington, only two short hours away. In the midst of all their hardship and uncertainty, Phoebe and I knew we were being selfish but couldn't help being happy and excited. Was it actually possible that we might end up living this close to each other?

May 16, 1971, will always be another memorable day in our lives. Our family had waited so long. Only we knew the great efforts that went into making that unforgettable day possible. Nash General Hospital, its buff-tinted brick, each one placed so carefully, now in position, creating the gently curved six-story cross of corridors and rooms, proudly outstretched and gracing the very heart of the 100 acres selected for its home, so long only a dream, now a reality, opened its doors and admitted patients to the first "all-private room" hospital in North Carolina. It had come to life, not without strong pangs of nervousness or "opening jitters," but it was alive, magnificent, and on its way to becoming one of the leading medical complexes in North Carolina. What a beautiful contribution to the welfare of this community, and Bryant had helped with his vision to make it possible.

* * *

In the seventeen years I had been married to Dan, divorce had never entered my mind, but there were times I could have killed him — like the night he called from Burlington to tell me he had just bought a house I had never laid eyes on! I don't know what he thought my reaction would be. Let's just say he wasn't expecting the one he got. I could not believe he would buy a house without my seeing it! From his description, it sounded lovely, but I was still in shock when I hung up the phone. It was hard to absorb all that was happening. Dan was very happy with his new job. For that I was thankful. Nevertheless, there was that dread of moving, of facing new beginnings, of once again leaving this place I loved so much. Two thoughts always lifted my spirits. Soon, the four of us would be together again, and the Aldridges would be two hundred miles closer.

We were scheduled to move June 4th, the day after Dan, Jr.'s 11th birthday. The moving van was loaded and on its way. After one more walk through the house to make sure we had everything, we were ready to leave. Dan, Jr., Susan, and Dandy, our dog, were in Dan's car. The house plants and I were in mine. It was a relief to be on our way. I hate goodbyes, and there had been too many. I would enjoy the four hour drive to Burlington. The peace and quiet would be wonderful.

Chapter 45

Growing Up and Stretching

You only have to spend one summer with a thirteen year old to know that he or she soon needs help in filling the long idle hours of summer with structure. In our county, one needed only to be fourteen years of age to obtain a worker's permit, so the first summer for the new hospital was also the summer of Bryant, Jr.'s first job and branching out into the real world.

As his parents, we felt a responsibility to help our son learn good work ethics and self-reliance, and he needed to learn the value of money and the great challenge of working with the public. With this in mind, he was given employment in the maintenance department of the hospital, much to his chagrin. He started out with a "dummy stick" picking up discarded paper or cigarette butts on the grounds, graduating to cutting grass or general yard work, and soon driving a tractor or whatever the job called for. Needless-to-say, he began to appreciate more and more, free time, idle hours, "spending money," and his parents. He didn't complain now of being "bored" or "not having anything to do" and was certainly motivated to do more than have to carry a "dummy stick."

These are tough times in a young person's life, tough on them, tough on parents. All of a sudden it seems, overnight, you are each faced with a wonderful individual, too young to be an adult, too old to be a child, frustrated one minute, loving the next, and no textbook guidelines to go by, each one doing the best he or she can, enduring the pain, holding dear the tenderness, digging deep for patience, and loving throughout, if you're lucky, and we were.

With Bryant, Jr.'s days so filled now, and working basically the same schedule that his father was, it presented me with much more flexibility of my own leisure time. When Phoebe called wondering if we could work out time together to spend "lots of birthday money" from her mother, we were amazed that Bryant would suggest that Allison and I go to Burlington and

Growing Up and Stretching

visit for a week without him and Bryant, Jr. We had never done this before, leaving our men alone, but it was very appealing. Allison and Susan were still happy playing dress-up and Barbie dolls together while Phoebe and I chattered and "played house," so we only needed the one suggestion to go before hauling off for an all-girl trip to Burlington.

* * *

It did not take our family long to adjust to life in Burlington and our new surroundings. We had nice neighbors and a good church, and Dan Jr. and Susan liked their schools and were making new friends. Things were going well, and we were grateful. I was trying to adapt to life in the country. Our house was pretty, the setting picturesque, but it was thirty minutes away from everything! Now that may not sound like a lot of time to most people, but to me it was. I felt like I lived in the car. It reminded me of what Cora, the Crouch's faithful housekeeper, said one afternoon. Mom had been in and out all day between meetings. As she left, for what must have seemed like the twentieth time, she overheard Cora say, "Huh! It's one thing fo sho. When de Good Lawd come for dat woman, he gonna haf ta meet her on de highway, cause she sho nuff ain't gonna be home."

There were a few things we would like to have done in the house as we moved in, but our top priority had to be the installation of air conditioning. The realtor had given Dan some song and dance story about the house not needing it because it was so shaded. Well, that was a joke, and no one was laughing. The humidity was awful! We would have to wait a little longer on living room furniture and other decorating projects I had hoped to do.

On the morning of my thirty-seventh birthday, I was enjoying the view out our kitchen window as I made a pitcher of tea. It was a beautiful July morning, birds singing and squirrels busy doing whatever it is that squirrels do. The flowers I had planted on either side of the white pebble walk leading to Susan's red barn playhouse were blooming. Susan and her little neighborhood friend were happily playing as only little girls can play while Dandy, our Shetland sheepdog, lay close by watching their every move. Dan Jr. was in the mountains experiencing camp for the first time, and there was a big void in all our lives with him gone. The mail truck, winding its way up our long driveway, interrupted my thoughts. When the mailman handed me a package, wrapped in brown paper, bound with yards of tape, the familiar handwriting told me it was from my mom. Like a child,

I began tearing the layers of wrapping off. The old shoe box was full of white tissue paper. There was a small piece of paper rolled up like a scroll and tied with a pink ribbon nestled in the middle of the box. I untied the perfect little bow and unrolled the "scroll." It was a check for one thousand dollars! The attached note read, "Happy Birthday, Honey; Mama loves you." I ran in the house to make a thank you call. Mama told me she had sold some timber on her mountain property and knew Daddy would want me to have some of it to "fix up my place."

When I called Dan to tell him, he said, with a smile in his voice, "That's great! You can take us to dinner tonight, and I can pay some bills."

"You wish!" was my reply. "I'm going to call Jean and see how soon she can come and help me do some things around this house."

"OK," he said. "Sounds like a good idea to me. See ya tonight."

Jean and Allison came the second week in August. It was a special time, and we savored every moment. Dan always left early for work. That gave Jean and me time for a second cup of coffee and uninterrupted conversation before the girls came bouncing in to breakfast. It was wonderful to get caught up on each other. We had all been so busy. Susan and Allison were good little troopers. Both girls have a happy, easy-going nature, never lacking for things to do. They were perfectly happy with whatever the day brought. It was the first time we four "girls" had ever been together like this, to "do as we pleased." I don't know if the phrase "shop till you drop" had been thought of, but we sure did do just that! It makes my head spin to think about all we packed into that week, and how far we stretched that thousand dollars! First, we shopped for fabric to cover the old couch and chair Dad Crouch had given us. We also chose fabric to make dining room chair cushions and a cloth for the table we would get Dan to make from a bar stool and plywood. After those purchases came a wing chair, coffee table, and a chandelier for the dining room. I was so excited I could hardly stand it. After seventeen years of marriage, we would finally have a living room we could use! Jean should have been an interior decorator. She has a wonderful eye for color and can do things to a room I would never see to do. We have always worked well together; therefore, we get a lot done in a short amount of time. If you have ever heard the expression, "We killed the bear, but Papa shot it," that was us making the cloth cover for the table Dan made. I have to have a pattern for everything I see. Jean just measures a little and starts cutting! The result is always something beautiful and just right. So I pinned and pressed while she cut and sewed. Our living room was transformed from a cold uninviting room with only a mismatched couch and chair into a colorful, warm, and inviting place to enjoy. That was one birthday present I will never forget.

Chapter 46

Happiness, Grief, and Recovery

Seasons followed seasons, each one creeping up, it seemed, before you were ready. Crispy golden autumn again (Where did time go?) and our children growing up so fast. We had made the tremendous decision before school started to send Allison to the new private school. She missed her best friends, and we just couldn't get satisfied with the school situation. Fearing the unknown, we agonized over what to do. We felt this was the right move to make for her education, and she moved into a new environment, adjusting quickly, and we gladly made the financial sacrifice.

Sunday afternoon trips to visit Mema or Nannie, always hurrying back in time for M.Y.F. for Bryant, Jr., Duke football games, scouting field trips, football practices and games, slumber parties — everyone had a schedule, and it consumed our life. Phoebe and I realized once again that we never would see each other if we didn't set aside our time, too. We arranged for a regular luncheon date each week and would meet in Raleigh to shop or just visit, always careful to get back home before school was out. It was wonderful being able to meet half way, and having a good friend to share one's thoughts with is cheap therapy and a valuable gift.

We didn't know when we planned those weekly meetings that it would be the only times that year we would see each other. Our families met in Durham in November for the Duke versus N.C. State football game. I have no idea today of who won the game, but we were good "sports fans," and what really mattered was the tailgate lunch of fried chicken and pimento cheese sandwiches and brownies, and we all came out of the picnic without a bee bite. It's not who wins or loses, but all the fun and "hoopla" and sportsmanship surrounding it, and we were masters at fun and especially the "hoopla"!

* * *

Happiness, Grief, and Recovery

It was a cold, rainy Friday evening. Dan was laying a fire with Danny and Susan's help for us to enjoy after supper. The children were hoping the weather would clear by the next evening, so they could go trick or treating. I had just asked everybody to wash their hands and had come to the table when the phone rang. Dan answered it, and I heard him say, "Hi, Dad. How are you?" Dad never called just to chat, so I figured he and Kitty were probably coming through Burlington the next day and wanted to stop by for a visit. However, judging from Dan's part of the conversation and the change in his expression led me to believe that something had happened, but I couldn't determine what. As Dan hung up the phone and turned to face us I said, "Honey, what in the world has happened?" "Johnny's been killed in an airplane crash. The plane went down in a snow storm over Colorado," was his answer. Johnny was Dan's nephew, and they had been very close. We just stood there looking at each other in disbelief.

The next hour and a half was a blur. Dad and Kitty came by to pick us up. The drive to Asheville gave all of us time for remembering this wonderful, energetic, young man. Pictures of John flashed through my mind like a fast forward motion picture. The eleven year old who cried after our wedding because he thought "his Dan" was gone. That same boy, a few weeks later, visiting us in Memphis. The teenager driving off to college in his first car. The handsome young groom standing at the altar watching his bride coming down the isle, and the last picture I had of him: the father, tenderly carrying his oldest daughter to bed. Someone so precious, so loved — gone. I will never forget what his mother, Ruby, said as I hugged her when we arrived at the little house on Fairway Drive. "We must remember to let this make us better, not bitter."

When Jean and I met in Raleigh the week after John's funeral in Mississippi, she and I had a lot to talk about. We tried to do a bit of shopping because Christmas was five weeks away. We finally decided to stop shopping (if you can believe that) because we couldn't think about gifts and visit at the same time. At lunch, we talked about, among other things, how a phone call can change your life so quickly. We agreed it was wonderful that the good Lord protected us by not letting us know what our tomorrows would bring.

The holidays passed amid the usual rush, festivities, and excitement. My mom spent Christmas with us much to our delight. She was so much fun, and like all grandmothers she was perfectly willing to sleep with her granddaughter. Each night, I fell asleep listening to her delight Susan with the story of "The Little Red Hen" just as she had done with Danny when he was seven years old. Mama also enjoyed helping Dan, Jr. and Susan with the training of the newest addition to our family, a puppy. Our sweet little Dandy had gotten killed while we were in Mississippi. Rebel, our new dog, was a beautiful little Sheltie with a personality that matched his name.

The day after Christmas, my mama was ready to go home, so we all piled into the car early that Sunday morning and headed for Asheville. We must have looked like "Out Our Way," Ma and Pa, the kids, the dog, and Grandma! As soon as we got Mama settled and said our tearful good-byes (Mama, Susan, and I always teared up when we left each other. Don't ask me why? We just did.), we went by to see Betty Ann, Bob, their children, and their Christmas bounty. The whole family was going skiing that next week, so all of them had gotten ski outfits and equipment. Our visit was short. We wanted to get back home before dark. If only we had known that that was to be the last carefree, untroubled visit we would ever have with them again. As we drove away from their house, I commented to Dan that Bob's color was bad. He looked like ashes. Dan said, "He's just tired. If I know Bob, he is doing too much. It will do him good to get away next week."

Bob fell while ice skating at the ski resort and broke his wrist. Not a good thing for a busy surgeon to do. After his fall, he began having headaches and other symptoms that were alarming. Dad even called Dan expressing concern after being with him at a committee meeting in Raleigh. The twins had made the trip with him and told their granddaddy, "Daddy kept running off the road."

Once again, a phone call came that changed the course of our lives on a quiet Sunday afternoon. Betty Ann called us from the hospital to tell us she had taken Bob to the emergency room that morning. The tests his colleagues ran had some frightening possibilities.

The family met in Asheville the next day to hear the final results of testing. When the doctor entered the waiting room, his expression told us what we feared before he ever spoke a word. Bob had a malignant brain tumor. We were frozen, like statues, unable to move, not wanting to believe what we were hearing. This beautiful man, the perfect example of physical fitness and good health. It just wasn't possible, not Bob, but cancer is no "respecter" of persons. It's a thief that strikes without warning and shows no mercy!

Every Friday for the next six months, Dan and I would pick up Dan, Jr. and Susan after school and drive to Asheville. Dan would spend the night with Bob, rest a few hours Saturday morning, then go back to spend more time with his brother. We did whatever was needed to relieve those who were with him all week. Hopefully, a little break on the weekends helped.

Happiness, Grief, and Recovery

We felt so powerless, unable to stop time, unable to change anything.

Bob was only forty-two years old when he died that July, a dedicated Christian father and husband, an outstanding doctor, a leader in the community. His wife and five children were blessed with supportive friends and family, but nothing could fill the void left by their tremendous loss.

* * *

Only a few short weeks after our families' happy gathering for the football game in Durham, we learned of Dan's brother's horrible illness, and we had no idea of when we would have an opportunity to enjoy fun of that nature together again. As the cold, dreary days of winter came and went, we busied ourselves with what Phoebe and I always say, "the same old one and two," but we maintained our contact and support each week in Raleigh over lunch.

Knowing how much we were enjoying Gaston Lake and our day trips there that spring, I was not surprised when Bryant came in one late afternoon, filled with excitement over a used mobile home he thought we might be able to purchase and put up at the lake. We already had rented land, thanks to Bryant's older brother, Jesse, who had befriended an elderly farmer whose farm land had been flooded, leaving him with 23 miles of waterfront property. Bryant and Jesse and five friends had each rented a lot and had worked hard clearing the beautiful wooded property and had even built piers for each of us. The idea of a place actually to spend the night was thrilling, so again the wheels went into motion; and by July the fourth we had the mobile home in place on our rented lot at Gaston Lake, and we had a vacation home. It was only two bedrooms and a bath, a great little kitchen, and living area with a view of the lake from every window, and we loved it. Not many things have we done that we enjoyed as much as our peaceful retreats at Lake Gaston, close enough to Nash General, yet far enough away for a day or two of fun and rejuvenation. This, too, came at a good time in our lives. Bryant, Jr. (Was he really old enough for driver's education?) was strong and agile, and a great help to his father caring for the boat and driving all over the lake; and Allison was approaching twelve, swimming, skiing, and content with fishing for hours off the end of the pier for what we called our "yearly bass." There were no boyfriends or girlfriends; days were simple and uncomplicated, just friends and family to feed and laugh with, and look up at the stars with on a clear night.

I had kept Phoebe abreast of all our lake work and sometimes felt a little guilty knowing the awful year they had had with Bob; but I knew she was happy for us, and after his death, we made plans for the Crouches to come for a visit.

It was the first convenient weekend they had that August, and cramped as we were, on a hide-a-bed and sleeping bags, we were together. Tranquil and relaxing, hectic and noisy, but enough time to pause, enough time to reflect and appreciate this gift of friendship and healthy families.

Chapter 47

A Virginia Excursion

I felt "as free as a bird" driving out of our driveway heading for Rocky Mount. It was a gorgeous day; the fall colors were beginning to show which heightened my excitement. Jean was ready and waiting when I arrived at her back door two hours later. We loaded her bag and placed her contribution to lunch in the cooler which was conveniently resting on the back seat. We would have lunch on the ferry. We talked non-stop, our words and stories overlapping each other, interrupted only by our laughter. We were so proud of ourselves for "stepping out on our own" like this and still a little shocked that Dan and Bryant would allow us to make this trip alone.

I was in strange territory never having traveled this area before. When we turned off I-95 at Stony Creek, the Virginia countryside stretched out before us. Harvested fields lay empty of the crops they had yielded. Tall old trees intermittently lined the two lane highway covering us with a colorful canopy. The sun's rays shown down through the changing leaves like hundreds of spotlights pushing against the shade. The next treat was the ferry ride. We arrived a few minutes early and took our place in the line with cars waiting for the ferry. We had just enough time to get our lunch of melon, fruit, cheese and crackers, and a cold bottle of Tab out of the cooler before we boarded the ferry.

"Good God, Phoebe," Jean whispered, as she punched me in the side, her voice full of fear. "Look at that drunk! He's headed straight for our car."

"Where? Huh! He is heading straight for us. Damn! What is he doing?" I realized we were staring at this scrawny, dirty, bearded, completely intoxicated middle aged man, who staggered and fell against the front of our car.

"What are we going to do, Phoebe?"

"I don't know!" I said.

"I've got a fingernail file in my pocketbook," Jean retorted.

"I've got a ballpoint pen," I said quickly.

"Damn! Jean, the two of us could pick him up and throw him in the water if we have to. Right now I'm so scared that I think I could do it by myself," I said loudly!

At that moment, something caught my attention in the rearview mirror. "Thank the Lord! Here comes a patrol car, Jean." By the time we both turned and looked out the rear window, a sheriff's car, with lights flashing, pulled up and stopped right beside us. They arrested the drunken fool and relieved the front of our car, not to mention us!

"Jean, Dan and Bryant would die if they knew what just happened!"

Jean chuckled, with a sigh of relief, "I swear, that's what we get for coming off by ourselves like this!"

As luck would have it, our place on the ferry was the first car in line on the outside lane. This gave us a view of the James River with the Jamestown settlement in the distance. As we ate our lunch, feeling safe with the windows down again, the short ferry ride gave us time to relax and focus on the view, the feelings of the moment and the rest of the day still ahead of us.

We had just packed the last remnants of our lunch back in the cooler as the ferry docked. I was expecting a longer drive into Williamsburg, but before I knew it the College of William and Mary was on our left, and Jean instructed me to turn right and follow the signs leading to the historic area. I followed her directions as this was my very first trip to Williamsburg. Instantly, I was captivated by our surroundings. Old world charm jumped out at us everywhere we turned. Our reservations were at the Williamsburg Lodge. We checked in, unpacked, and drove to the Pottery Outlet! The old world charm was put on hold. We were there to shop for bargains! Each of us had made a list of the things we wanted, and each of us had a limited amount of money to spend. This first afternoon was spent walking through the pottery shops taking mental notes and writing down prices of anything that looked interesting. When we finished "casing" the place, we returned to the lodge to clean up and go out to dinner. We had taken time, before we left, to make dinner reservations at Christiana Campbell's, an eighteenth-century tavern, which was said to be one of George Washington's favorite places to eat. The spoon bread and rum cream pie remain in my memory to this day.

After dinner, we walked back to the lodge through the quiet streets, seeing families strolling together, laughing and talking in soft voices seemingly not wanting to disturb this peaceful setting. There were couples leisurely walking, holding hands, oblivious to everyone but each other. This

A Virginia Excursion

truly was a step back in time, one that allowed us to glimpse what seemed to be a slower, easier pace of life. I could see why Jean and Bryant chose this place for their honeymoon, and why she was anxious to bring me here.

The next morning, we ate breakfast at Mama Steve's House of Pancakes and rechecked our notes. The night before, we had used the process of elimination and had come up with a serious list. Now, we were ready to join the throng of shoppers! No one would believe all we packed into one and a half days and all that we bought with our small allowance. China, glasses, and some brass for Jean; candlesticks and a pair of brass sconces for me. I first saw the sconces at the Craft House, but the price of $47.50 each was not in my budget. However, $8.00 each was. There they were on a dusty shelf at the Pottery, just waiting for me to take them home! We found everything on our list and were pleased with our purchases.

After breakfast Sunday morning, we retraced our way back home. At that time, the Pottery shops wrapped each item in newspaper. The trunk of the car was packed with newspaper wrapped "treasures." If I live to be a hundred years old, I will never forget the expression on Dan's face when I opened the trunk of the car. For a moment, he had that look of disbelief; then he broke into laughter and said, "Well it looks like your trip was a profitable one! I'm glad you're home safe."

Chapter 48

The Road to Disney World

A memorable and emotional event took place on January 27, 1973. The Viet Nam War ended. This bitterly disputed war that had started in 1960 and had torn our country apart was at long last over. It was a good way to start the new year.

Our weekly get togethers at the Capitol Room in Raleigh were more like planning sessions, as it became more and more difficult to mesh the schedules of four children of different ages and diverse activities together. Phoebe and I liked the Capitol Room, a relatively quiet cafeteria with a pleasant atmosphere and excellent food. It was an easy meeting place, and here we could get our fill of collard greens and cornbread, something we never cooked at home. Plus that, we could splurge devilishly on a piece of coconut cream pie. Who had ever heard of fat grams or cholesterol then?

Life was really good to all of us about now, and our minds seemed to just race with ideas. We also knew that in order for us to get our families to vacation together that it had to be something really great! Bryant, Jr. was driving now, at sixteen, and had a schedule of activities that would wear anyone down, not to mention his interest in a cute, little brown-eyed girlfriend who kept him on the telephone for hours every night. Allison was thirteen and enjoyed being with her friends more now than with her parents, and Dan, Jr. was feeling much the same growing pains. Their interest was "being at home with their friends where the action is," so we had our work cut out for us, because as our children grew older they seemed to have less and less in common.

It was after one of those rich, moist servings of coconut cream pie that I suddenly remembered to tell Phoebe of a "deal" on a trip for a family of four to "Disney World" in Orlando, Florida, that I thought we should take. Bryant and Dan had been such good sports about letting us take off for Williamsburg. Surely, we could talk them into this. The price was certainly right! That always got them! Only $180.00 for two adults and two children, three nights and four days at the Contemporary Hotel, with

The Road to Disney World

tickets to the Magic Kingdom. Disney World had only been open for a few months, and the promotion sounded like a great notion to us. Phoebe and I were giggly and excited as we threw out our ideas. We knew our children would love it, and we vowed that we could save that much out of our grocery money to help pay for the trip. This was by far the most excited and the happiest departure we had ever had from each other. We could hardy wait to get home and test our plans on our families. Bryant and Dan thought it was wonderful, another "piece of cake." They were such pansies; anything that made us happy made them happy. The children were jubilant when we discussed the surprise trip with them, so elaborate plans for our Easter vacation went into high gear.

Not long after we set our sights for spring and the anticipated trip to Florida, Bryant and I found ourselves making arrangements with three Rocky Mount "couple friends" for our annual get-away at the North Carolina coast. There is something very romantic and cozy about slipping away from the rigors of one's daily routine for a couple of days in the warm sun at the beach in the dead of winter. You always hope for a perfectly sunny, unexpected spring-like weekend, but if you're not blessed with this, it doesn't really matter as long as you get the much awaited solitude.

At the last minute, one of the couples decided they couldn't go, and it opened up the perfect opportunity to include the Crouches. At this stage in our lives, it was much easier to leave on the spur of the moment. With all of our children older, we could "farm" them out with friends and know they could pretty much take care of themselves, or Nannie was usually available to come and spend the night with ours. This worked nicely for all, making her feel needed and giving our children another opportunity to spend valuable time with their grandmother. Phoebe and Dan joined us that March at Wrightsville Beach at the Blockade Runner Hotel for another "package deal."

I'm sure our friends would remember those warm, relaxing weekends. Without question, it was wonderful — fried seafood platters on Friday nights, brimming over with french fries and onion flavored hushpuppies, laughing and joking over a bottle of wine in one of our rooms after dinner, walking the beach bundled up to keep warm the next day, and Saturday night, dinner and dancing all dressed up in our party clothes. We packed long, plaid wool skirts with wool blazers for evening, and the men complained good-naturedly of having to wear a coat and tie. When you have a delicious four course dinner in a room overlooking the ocean, with a live band playing "fifties" music in the background, you forget about an

For All The World To See

uncomfortable tie.

It was at this time that we learned something new about the Crouches. In all the time we had spent together, we never dreamed they didn't dance. I knew that Phoebe could "mountain clog" and assumed that she danced the same way that I did. Dan, although he could sing like a bird, didn't know his right foot from his left, and being staunch Baptists, neither of them had ever learned to ballroom dance, so we set out on that particular night to get them on the dance floor. There was no way we were going to allow them to sit at the table and watch. I doubt if Dan ever "danced" again after that night, but we surely had a laugh or two together then.

April 16 finally arrived, and our meeting place was Howard Johnson's in Fayetteville for breakfast. We were all on time eager to begin the long drive down Interstate 95 to Florida and Disney World. Income tax returns were filed once again — that was behind us, and with that always comes blessed relief. Bryant and Dan could have driven to Alaska! In those days, traffic was not as heavy as it is today, so we made good time following along together, stopping for lunch, then switching passengers, so all the girls could ride together for a while. With so much excitement, we never realized how fast we could get all the way down to St. Augustine, which was where we planned to spend our first night before going on to Orlando. We were a little upset to think we could have driven all the way in a day, but arriving in St. Augustine before dark gave us a brief opportunity to see the waterfront and some of the historical landmarks in this beautiful, old, moss covered city.

Disney World was even more than we expected, truly a magical fantasy land for all ages. Driving up to the beautiful Contemporary Hotel surrounded by the lush, emerald green lawns, perfectly manicured gardens, spring flowers, annuals and perennials, blooming profusely as though painted in place, found each of us aghast. We could not help but be amazed at the beauty and vivid colors all around us — the perfectly trimmed topiary trees shaped like Disney characters lining the drive, and the cleanliness was beyond any place we had seen.

Our rooms were beautiful, as everything we had seen so far was. We didn't take the time to unpack or settle in. We didn't want to waste a minute. We were like eight little children in Paradise, hurrying to catch a ride on the monorail coming through the hotel lobby, whisking us high above the theme park and swan-filled lakes and the Polynesian Hotel, giving a sun-streaked view of a wonderland on a spring day before coming to a gentle stop at the entrance to the Magic Kingdom.

The Road to Disney World

We spent three full days in this playground of sparkling beauty, standing in long lines for certain attractions, eating good food, and searching nervously for Susan, only 8, every time she got lost in the crowds. Phoebe had warned her before leaving home to stand perfectly still and not move from the spot if we ever got separated from her, and one of us would find her. Sure enough, this happened three times, and seven of us always found her standing very still, waiting. Danny and Bryant, Jr. bought ugly, rubber monster masks that covered their heads, either to scare us with or to get lost themselves. We spent long, lazy hours in the afternoons swimming in the hotel pool or lagoon, paddle boating, water skiing, relaxing before dinner, getting a second wind for "Main Street" all aglow every evening with thousands of shimmering lights, one more trip through the "Haunted House," and all of the spectacular, dazzling fireworks ending another day.

Anything after Disney World would be a disappointment, though we didn't realize this until we had started home. We had reservations for the last night of this trip in Jekyll Island, Georgia, about half-way back home, and it turned out to be a long, quiet ride. Allison and Bryant, Jr. were worn out from Disney World and slept nearly all of the way, making room for each other on the back seat of our car, snuggling pillows against the rear windows. None of us had ever been to this island, but Bryant had researched it, and with the Crouches following behind us, and after a few extra turns, not shown on our carefully marked eastern United States road map, we found our way to the motel on the Georgia coast where we were to spend the night.

Soon after we checked in, I answered a knock on the door connecting our adjoining rooms. There was Phoebe. With a puzzled look on her face, she asked, "Do your lights work? Ours were working when we came in, but now they're off. It's crazy! Susan turned the TV on and the lights went out. Check yours."

During our conversation, the children were running back and forth giggling. Bryant, Jr. had turned our lights on only to find that the TV would go off. Dan and Bryant were trying to analyze the problem and soon discovered that the light switches in one room controlled the lights or TV in the other room. Phoebe and I were disgusted.

"I don't know how we ended up in this dump. Phoebe, come look at this place. Shoot, we can't stay here."

"Our room looks the same way, 'Ruum.' Bobby pins on the floor. I don't think it's even been vacuumed. I wonder if they changed the sheets?"

Bryant was ill. He and Dan both said they were not going to try to find anything else at this hour. They had done the best they could, and we just had to put up with it. Bryant kept saying, "Oh, you girls, quit complaining; you've just been spoiled. It won't look so bad after we eat."

We left the motel to look for a place to have dinner. Bryant turned into the parking lot of the first restaurant we came to, and through the open car window, he yelled to Dan, "Is this okay?"

Phoebe answered for him, "It looks decent enough." We thought nothing of the number of people waiting, and took our place in the long line. Thirty minutes later, Bryant's whole countenance changed when suddenly he said, "Let's get out of here. It's just taking too long."

Like sheep following the shepherd, we turned and followed, as he ignored our grumbling. The next restaurant didn't appear to be as busy, and we were all seated in only about five minutes. We were delighted as they ushered us to a large round table next to a plate glass window overlooking the water where we could have a grand view of the sun setting. Our spirits lifted! We studied the menus left on the table by the hostess, clad in nautical dress complete with a sailor hat. Phoebe commented, "She's thin enough to be Olive Oyl."

The sun set, the basket of crackers on the table was empty, and we had still not seen our waitress. Bryant shoved his chair away from the table abruptly, stood up straight, and said, "We're not waiting another minute. We've been here twenty-five minutes, and we're leaving!"

Like sheep following the shepherd again, we rose and filed conspicuously out of the restaurant, wondering where we would go next. In the parking lot with the "herd" gathered around him, Jean asked, "Where now, oh mighty shepherd?"

"Jean, I'm doing the best I can. We would have been in that place all night. What do ya'll want to do?"

In unison, all four children yelled, "Eat!"

Bryant turned to Dan and said, "We'll follow you this time. See what you can find." His voice reflected his exhausted patience.

Dan drove a short distance, and we realized there was very little to choose from. Without hesitation, he made a short left turn, and brightly lit-up before us was a 7-Eleven convenient store. He got out of his car, and calmly announced to all of us, "There's food here; we can wait on ourselves."

With that, our "herd" of eight invaded the isles of the 7-Eleven, buying loaf bread, peanut butter and jelly, bananas, pimento cheese spread, potato chips, Oreo cookies, paper plates, napkins, and soft drinks for a ten p.m. "picnic" in our less than desirable and unattractive motel room.

As Phoebe and I spread sandwiches, she looked at me, and I knew exactly what she was thinking. "We got back to reality fast, didn't we? The Magic Kingdom, this ain't," she said.

"When this place was discovered, they didn't complete the name. It should be 'Jekyll-Hyde' instead of 'Jekyll'," I quipped.

We watched the sun rise the next morning through the windshield of our cars as we eagerly drove away from Jekyll Island shortly after 5:00 a.m. Everyone was up and ready to leave.

Chapter 49

Summer Days

School was out, and the first activity on the summer agenda was basketball camp for Dan, Jr. Our tall, lanky fourteen year old was looking forward to being with some of his teammates and to meeting some of the N.C. State basketball players who would be there to instruct them.

My first week free of car-pooling would be spent getting things ready for our beach trip to Emerald Isle with the Aldridges. Emerald Isle. Just saying the name brought beautiful pictures to mind. Wonder why they named it that? Would it really be that green? I couldn't wait. Going to the beach was still a novelty to me. The last time Dan and I had been to the beach for a whole week was on our honeymoon.

Jean and I had made out the menus deciding on who would bring what, so I was trying to check off the things on my list each day. By Friday, everything was ready except for the duffle bag of dirty clothes Dan, Jr. would bring home that afternoon. Of course, that presented no problem. I would have those things washed and put away or packed by bedtime.

The early morning drive to the coast took four and a half hours. As we drove through Kinston, we told Dan, Jr. and Susan this was "Aunt" Jean and "Uncle" Bryant's hometown. As we drove down Queen Street, I said, in my tour guide voice, "And on my right is the church they were married in, Queen Street Methodist."

The house we had rented was a typical beach house. Bedrooms and baths on either side of a large family room and kitchen. It was modestly furnished and clean. From the front deck, we enjoyed a view of the ocean; out our kitchen window, we could see Bogue Sound. Jean and I got the kitchen squared away while Dan and Bryant walked to the beach with the children. By the time they returned, we had lunch ready. After lunch, we enjoyed a time of relaxation and rest. It had been a busy morning! Susan fell asleep on the floor, so Jean and I stayed with her while the others went over to the sound to dig for clams. We would join them as soon as Susan

Summer Days

woke up. I told Jean I knew she hadn't slept a wink the night before because she was too excited.

When Susan woke up, she asked, "Where is everybody?"

"They walked over to the Sound," I answered, looking at her as she sat up. "What in the name of peace is that in your hair, Susan," I exclaimed.

"I don't know, Mama," she replied.

Upon further investigation, I discovered she had been chewing gum when she fell asleep. It had fallen out of her mouth and gotten in her curly locks. A wad of hair the size of a golf ball was entangled!

I looked at Jean and quipped, "Now, isn't this going to be fun?"

We took her in the kitchen where the light was better to assess the situation. Susan's hair was long and thick, and I shuddered at the thought of having this chunk of hair cut out over her left ear. Like a voice from heaven, an article I had chanced to read in the newspaper, only a few days before, came to mind. It was one of those "household hint" articles. In it was a letter from a woman telling how she saved her daughter's "beautiful long tresses" from being cut when she too had gotten chewing gum stuck in it. She used peanut butter! I took the Peter Pan jar down from the shelf and started working Susan's favorite sandwich spread through her hair. It worked beautifully, and in only a few minutes, an impending tragedy turned into a memory that ended happily.

Our week of relaxation and happy diversions was passing quickly. We went on a little excursion to Fort Macon one afternoon, but that was cut short by bad weather. It was the only time it rained that week! We found an ice cream shop on the way back to the house, so the afternoon wasn't a total loss.

Dan, Jr. had gotten stung by a jelly fish a couple of times. It was very painful for him and made all of us very apprehensive about swimming in the ocean. Even though Allison was a teenager now, she remained attentive to Susan. They were always able to find amusement in the simplest things. Jean and I never heard, "Mama, I don't have anything to do," from those two girls.

As we said our good-byes on Saturday morning, we were already looking forward to our next visit. We had made tentative plans to get together again soon.

* * *

The main conversation that summer with everyone shifted from the ending of the Viet Nam War and the U.S. prisoners to the Watergate investigation taking place in Washington, D.C. The idea that anyone would break into the National Democratic Headquarters was unbelievable to all, and as the news media attempted to unravel the events being presented, the whole story became more and more mysterious. High administration officials, conspiracy, burglary, "paybacks" brought about much speculation and intrigue. We kept a portable radio turned and perched carefully on the wooden bench beside a red, Pepsi filled, Igloo cooler anytime we sought a brief intermission to sunbathe or bass fish from our pier at Gaston Lake. Bryant and I wanted to hear all newscast and stay abreast of the unfolding Washington saga. Gradually, as facts and figures increased and the whole story became more scandalous, the fingers pointed toward the President of the United States and the very real possibility that he could be involved. It gave us a sick feeling in the pit of our stomachs, realizing the powers and control that these people have the advantage of and the trust and faith we placed in their integrity. The American public's confidence in our President and government weakened as one illegal charge after the other was revealed by the Senate Watergate Committee. Ideally, we continued to hold fast, defending the old-fashioned values and ideals of honesty and integrity, wanting desperately to believe the stream of denials coming from Richard Nixon.

* * *

This had been a very busy summer for both the Aldridges and us. Although I had adjusted, somewhat, to living in the country, I knew I really had not accepted it. One of our good friends in Burlington owned a real estate company and knew of my discontent. I had told her if she ever found a house we might be interested in to let me know. Well, to make a long story short, she did, and in a matter of a few weeks, we were scheduled to move August 31st.

As I drove to Rocky Mount the week before our move, I couldn't believe I was going at this time. However, I had everything ready for our move, and it would not be hard. Jean could help me with furniture placement and window dressing. Susan and I talked, as we drove along, about her new room, new school, and how much closer she would be to all of her friends in our new neighborhood.

We four girls were pretty much on our own those few days, unrushed, enjoying each other. Sitting by the pool at the club in the late afternoon, Jean and I watched Susan and Allison swim in the cool refreshing water. No visit to Rocky Mount would be complete without a trip to Bulluck's, our favorite furniture store, to touch and feel everything.

On the way back home, I had a million things spinning in my head, one of which was our trip to Williamsburg. Jean and I had made plans for what we now called our annual Williamsburg "get- away." With this move into a new house facing me, I didn't know how I would ever get ready to go. I just knew I would.

Chapter 50

Following Bryant's Instructions

Although we never liked the separation, we had grown accustomed to Bryant's being away for business meetings or hospital conventions quite frequently, so when he left on a Sunday afternoon in January for his drive to Washington, D.C. and the annual American Hospital meeting, it was nothing unusual. We knew he would come home on the following Wednesday, and our routine would return to normal. I never felt anxious or afraid now when we were left alone, unlike the days when our children were babies and little people. Allison and Bryant, Jr. were company to me, and we felt very safe keeping watch over one another.

Bryant always called to check on us every day, but the call I received from him two days after he left was unlike any other. Being the reserved individual that he was, I couldn't help but be surprised at the height of the excitement in his voice as I heard him explaining as fast as he could get it out.

"Jean, we've just been told that President Nixon is speaking to our group at ten o'clock in the morning. It was completely unscheduled, a last ditch effort on his part and his staff to get support from the healthcare community while he has a captive audience, I suppose. Anyway, it's the perfect opportunity for all of us to see the President! Now, I've already made reservations on a 6:45 flight out of Raleigh for you and the children to come to Washington. I'll meet you at National Airport tonight when you arrive."

"Oh, Bryant, you have got to be kidding," I blurted out.

"No, I'm not. You pick up your tickets at the Eastern Airlines counter in Raleigh. Now, go get ready. Bryant and Allison will love it! I love you, and I'll see you tonight."

He was gone, and I stood frozen. It was eleven a.m., and I began to collect myself and try to think straight. Allison's 4:00 piano lesson had to be cancelled, and I had to pack for the three of us and make sure

Following Bryant's Instructions

everything was ready to go when they came in from school. I flew about the house with nervous and giddy energy.

Allison and Bryant, Jr. came in from school on time as usual but had trouble believing me at first. "Mama, I don't believe that," was their very first reaction. I honestly had trouble convincing them until they saw the bags packed, but they also knew how their daddy liked to "kidnap" us for little surprise adventures. We didn't have time for getting excused from school, and I assured them that a trip of this nature was certainly a good reason to miss a day of school. By 4:00 p.m., we were on our way!

We arrived in Washington with the snow falling quietly, and our excitement mounted when we saw the glittering lights of the city, reflecting on the historical monuments and government buildings as we came in for the landing. Bryant was there to meet us, and we just stood and laughed in disbelief when we saw him at what we had just done!

It was a wonderful opportunity to build a unique memory, and we've always been glad we did. We had fun staying in the Washington Hilton. We watched from our windows as the Secret Service swarmed the hotel in preparation for the President's arrival. We went to the ballroom where Nixon was scheduled to speak, early enough to get front row seats, so our children wouldn't miss a thing. We don't remember what he spoke about, that didn't seem to matter. The first lady was there, another surprise and added attraction, dressed in a bright patriotic red coatdress, and from the front row, up so close, Nixon looked gentle and trustworthy. Surely, surely, he could not be guilty of the horrendous accusations so prevalent on his character at that time.

Twenty-four hours, we were home again, hardly missed, and it was business as usual, but we had that speck, that tiny little jewel we all need to help spread a luster of joy and interest on this business of living.

Pushing the last crumbs of coconut cream pie onto her fork to finish her desert, Phoebe listened intently, humoring me with her warmth of friendship, as I told her enthusiastically all the details of our Washington excursion. I knew she would want to know. We discussed our seeing the Watergate building, and neither of us could bring ourselves to believe the conflicting stories we were fed daily from the media. Phoebe and I were in Raleigh having lunch, our first meeting since Christmas, as our schedules grew tighter, and the days on our calendars became more and more crowded. We knew we would be lucky if we could get together any time during the next few months, so we found ourselves lingering longer than usual.

Chapter 51

Palm Sunday

This spring, the first of many that Dan and I hoped for in our new house, was packed with surprises. The yard was coming to life, and each week we discovered something new. The color of the azaleas was the first mystery solved. It was evident each one had been planted, by the original owners, with care and careful planning. The soft pink and snow white of their blossoms blended perfectly with the exterior of the house. Their beauty was enhanced by the various shades of green in the grass and trees surrounding them. Susan's red playhouse, nestled at the edge of the yard near the woods, made a nice finishing touch to the picture. I was so pleased the Aldridges would see it at its peak. They were coming for Palm Sunday weekend.

Preparations for the weekend kept me busy that first week in April. I wanted everything to be ready, so our time with Jean and Bryant, Allison, and Bryant, Jr. would be relaxed. That meant I had to have some help and cooperation from Dan and the children. That wasn't always so easy. As usual, I ended up feeling like the wicked witch, but things were ready when our friends arrived Saturday.

In this house, we had more room to spread out, so we weren't running into each other at every turn. The men occupied the family room, glued to the television. Our two boys, who had very little in common now, did enjoy an occasional game of pool in the rec room, while Susan drug out all of her Barbie doll mess to show Allison. Jean and I found peace and a measure of quietness in the living room or outside walking around the yard.

Fortunately, the weather was good. Jean commented on how lucky we always were with weather each time we planned to be together. A warm feeling of contentment welled up in me as we visited. Things were going so well for both of us and the future looked bright. We were truly blessed. That evening, we grilled steaks, dined leisurely and enjoyed the children's intermittent contribution to the conversation. Susan and Allison helped clear the table while Jean and I loaded the dishwasher. Next was Saturday

Palm Sunday

night baths and getting in bed at a respectable hour.

Sunday morning started early. Breakfast was served, "everybody for himself style." Things went remarkably well with eight people getting ready for church and trying to be on time. Of course, Dan and I had to be there thirty minutes early for choir, so we left Jean and Bryant to get the "troops" there on time. The choir's rendition of "The Holy City" went unusually well as did the rest of the service. It was a fitting prelude to Easter.

The Aldridges' visit was, as always, over too soon. As we said our good-byes, it seemed as though they had just arrived only moments before. It's always that way with loved ones.

Chapter 52

Adjusting to Changes

It never ceases to amaze me just how fast summer vacation comes after Easter. Maybe as children growing up, we are programmed to think this, always looking forward to another school year ending. Maybe, the aging process makes us realize it so intensely, but for whatever the reason we were into another summer. I was reminded of my mother saying to Bryant, Jr. and Allison when they were only toddlers, "If only I could put a book on your head and keep you from growing up." I understood more and more what she meant. I felt the same way now as I watched our children growing, changing. It was a wonderful summer, and I wanted Mema's book to put on this time, to keep it just the way it was, yet I knew it couldn't remain the same.

Bryant, Jr. was a rising senior in high school, already graduated to a summer job as an assistant in an orthopedic surgeon's office, broadening his education even more. We didn't know what the next summer would bring with him. The only thing we were sure of was that he would be at home for only one more year, and we wanted to enjoy every minute we had left with him.

The bickering and picking between him and his sister was done with affection now, more spontaneous laughter, as the sibling rivalry subsided, and they accepted each other as equals. Allison was no longer the chubby little girl maneuvering a unicycle down the sidewalk in front of our house. She was almost fourteen, blossoming into a willowy and graceful young lady, managing to handle even her mouthful of complicated braces and minute rubber bands with a girlish charm. Her big brother couldn't help but recognize this.

I knew also that it would be our last summer with Allison not working, because when she reached the age of fourteen, we expected her to learn the same things about work ethics that her brother had been exposed to; therefore, it was important for this reason, also, that we make the most of this summer's freedom. She and Bryant, Jr. had their usual camping

Adjusting to Changes

experience at Camp Don Lee (his last), and our weekends were spent skiing and sunning as much as possible at Lake Gaston. (We survived those years of not wanting to be with parents, as Allison and Bryant respected the fact that their father needed time away also and never made going to the lake on weekends a problem for us.)

We managed to have two visits with the Crouches — July fourth at the lake, and with planning ahead, a long weekend in August we'll never forget. It seemed, as fate would have it, our families were together to share another moment in history.

The months and weeks prior to August ninth had been spent in utter dismay while the American public was forced to realize the guilt being proven now almost daily from the continuous Watergate investigation. As hard as it was for many of us to believe, we gradually faced the fact that it was the most alarming event that had ever happened to our rich and powerful country. We waited in disbelief for the impeachment of the President of the United States. After so much time, the nightmare was there in reality — Nixon at his desk in the oval office, somber, confessing, grateful to the people who continued to support him, noting his years as a loyal public servant, and referring to his mother in an apologetic, broken voice.

Phoebe and Dan, and Bryant and I, and our four children, all sat stunned watching television, as the world did, that Friday in August, 1974, as the thirty-seventh President of the United States left the White House, the magnificence of the highest office held in the world, to bid farewell before boarding Air Force One and a home far away from the Washington scene. Pitiful, still with dignity, his head held high, with outstretched arms and fingers gesturing a "V" for victory sign, we watched our President climb the steps of the plane and disappear. As we shared the events of history portrayed before us over and over so vividly on television that weekend, it all seemed like a fictitious film straight out of Hollywood.

The transfer of power had been well planned, and by the time Nixon arrived at his destination, the American people had a new President, Gerald Ford, and we were assured that the government was once again in good hands.

Life goes on, and the warm water of Gaston Lake was a blessed distraction for all of us, trying hard to overcome the traumatic news that had been inevitable. We even got Susan up on water skis that weekend, something she never really mastered, and Phoebe and I made sure of definite plans for our September trip to Williamsburg.

Chapter 53

More Changes

Human nature is strange in many ways, yet very predictable in others. When things are going well, we are inclined to tip our hat to the Lord and say, "We're doin' fine, Lord, doin' great on our own. We'll stay in touch!" That's exactly what Dan and I were doing without realizing it. However, when the good Lord steps aside and allows His permissive will to enter, He can get your full attention in a hurry.

We had just enjoyed our finest Christmas ever, materially that is. Santa had been most generous. Each one of us had received far more than we needed or asked for. My mother later shared her feelings of joy to see "things going so well for us." "Yes, life is going so well for us, finally," I replied, "and I am grateful."

The day before Dan's birthday (which was three days after Christmas), his boss called to ask him if they could meet at the office that morning.

The plant was closed until the first of the week; however, Dan didn't think anything about this request. In fact, he was pleased, because he wanted to discuss some new ideas he had had about better production without any interruptions. The morning passed quickly. Mother, the children, and I had already finished lunch. I was standing at the kitchen sink when Dan drove in the garage. "That's typical," I said. "He arrives the minute I get the last dish washed!" Then my eye fell on all the boxes in the front and back seats of the car. "What in the world is going on, and why is he bringing home that picture that hung in his office?" I said right out loud. In the next glance, I saw Dan just sitting there in the car, not moving, looking at me in a way that alarmed me instantly.

I don't remember getting to the back door or opening it. I just remember opening the car door and saying, "Honey, what in the world is going on? What has happened?" This man I loved, who only a short three hours before, had walked out of the house confident, eager to present his ideas to his boss, was sitting before me looking pale, dejected, and beaten.

More Changes

He looked up at me, his blue eyes moist, and said, in a voice barely audible, "I've lost my job, Honey!"

He got out of the car. We just stood there holding each other silent. Beau, our Sheltie, was barking at a squirrel in the back yard. Music from Dan, Jr.'s stereo and Susan and Mother's laughter were coming through the open back door. I opened my mouth to say something but couldn't utter a word. Emotions began to erupt inside me like a volcano. My inner voice was screaming, "No, no, no! Not again, not again."

I looked up at Dan, "I'm sorry, Honey," he said. "I am so sorry."

"Why Dan? Why did he dismiss you like this, without any warning?" I said, regaining my voice while at the same time trying to remain calm.

He answered me with a tone of disbelief, still in his voice, "The industry is in another slump. He's the boss. He said his salary, mine, and the other managers were more than he could afford at this time, so he has to let me and the other fellows go in order to stay afloat."

He closed the car door, and we went inside.

Dan, Jr. came out of his room and passed through the family room on the way to the kitchen. He stopped in his tracks when he saw us sitting there. The expression on our faces made our carefree fifteen year old ask with concern in his voice, "What's wrong, Daddy?"

When Dan spoke, his voice sounded strained and tired, "Son, go ask your sister and grandmother to step in here, please."

"What's wrong, Daddy?" Dan, Jr. repeated, "Has someone died? What's happened?"

"Go get the others, please, Son. I'll tell you when they get in here."

I dreaded my mother having to know about this now. Why hadn't I taken her home yesterday like she wanted. No, I had to insist she stay for Dan's birthday tomorrow. Some birthday present he's just been handed. Dear Lord, what are we going to do?

On our way to Disney World last year, Jean and I had talked about this "affluent bubble" everyone seemed to be living in. We were happy to be there, yet at the same time felt a little uneasy wondering how long it would last. This secure feeling of plenty was almost too good to be true. Today, our bubble had popped! Next to my mother, I dreaded telling Jean the most, and I thought if Bryant comes out with this famous "It'll all work out" that I would scream! I knew he would be right, but I didn't want to face any changes. The spoiled child in me couldn't believe that this could work out, and I didn't want to hear it. I was satisfied with things the way they were. Why did this have to happen to us again?

Jean and Bryant were as stunned and shocked as we were. They were so sweet and tried to lift our spirits. After we hung up, I realized we had not wished them "Happy Anniversary." Their anniversary and Dan's birthday fall on the same day, and I had always remembered it. Bryant, bless his heart, hadn't said, "It'll all work out," either. Shame on me!

The time that followed was fairly normal. We were confident Dan would find work in three months before the severance pay ran out. It had taken us a few weeks to tell our friends finally that Dan was without work. We were having to work through all the feelings of failure, embarrassment, and fear. Instead of going to friends and loved ones for support, we withdrew. When something like this happens, everybody is concerned about your situation, but they don't know what to say or do. Deep down they are thinking, "I'm so glad that isn't us." I know because I have felt the same way. By the end of March, Dan had not heard from any of the resumés he had sent out.

Standing at our dining room window early one morning, I prayed, "Lord, surely you would not have given us this lovely house and all that we have simply to take it away. Please help us to stay here and keep what we have." At that moment, it dawned on me our faith was being tested for the first time in our lives. Everything we had was His to do with as He pleased. We were trying to hold on to what we thought were "our things." Instead of asking, "Lord, what would you have us do?" we had been, in essence, saying, "Lord, this is the way we want things to be."

Chapter 54

Graduation Day

Bryant, Jr.'s senior year in high school was quite eventful, filled with hours of practice and high school football games, scurrying to take new tests, meeting deadlines for college applications, and keeping the '63 Comet running back and forth across town to his girlfriend's home. He and Allison had convinced us that Allison needed to return to public school life before he graduated, so she was no longer at The Academy but adjusting and getting reacquainted with her public school friends in the ninth grade now. It had been a good move for her, and the financial relief for us was nice. It didn't take long before she was surrounded with her little shelter of friends they proudly referred to as "The Club" — "Bean," "Bones," "Al," "Sid," and "Boots" were their affectionate nicknames, always reminding me of my "Crowd" of friends during our high school days, and the silly girlish feelings we shared. It was fun being with your grown up children, seeing them come out of the twilight zone of adolescence and having them begin to recognize you as a real person. Sharing and communicating on an adult level now was "super" (as they would say).

Our world was, without exaggeration, on solid ground, and because of our basic positive attitudes, it was difficult for us to imagine Phoebe and Dan's predicament being quite so grim. We kept in touch, sharing the allocated amount of business they wanted to tell us; but as their waiting stretched out, feelings began to change.

Phoebe was no longer my cheerful, laughing friend. Instead, as her frustrations grew, she was bitter and resentful, complicated and tired of pretending, a personality I had never seen and one hard to penetrate. No amount of consoling or effort of support helped as she seemed to have given up hope, making it more difficult to reach her. We gave them space, the only thing we knew to do. No more plans of vacations or lunches in Raleigh or long distance phone calls, all this would have to wait.

Being the loyal and faithful Duke supporters that we were, there is nothing that pleased us more than when Bryant, Jr. was accepted and made the decision to attend Duke University. We never doubted that he would get accepted but deciding to attend was a really monumental decision for him. He tried hard to go elsewhere to save us the financial burden but was unable to give up the opportunity of attending his father's alma mater when the time came, and the peer pressure working on him to go to a state supported school lost its importance, and we were glad. He was truly ready for graduation by the end of the school year, as most young people are, ready to move on and face an entirely new challenge.

His graduation was different, though. I had anticipated much more pomp and circumstance, remembering naturally my own high school graduation. We had grand plans for the long awaited day. Mema helped me. We stood for hours at the kitchen sink, cleaning fresh shrimp for the buffet dinner all of the family were invited to before the ceremonies. We were delighted with acceptances from Bryant's brother and sister and their children, but our biggest surprise was the good news that the Crouches would join us for our first visit together since Dan's job misfortune. They came a day early, and Phoebe was able to help me with all of the final preparations. We loved working together, planning and arranging; and soon, as though nothing had ever happened, her mood relaxed, and I was relieved. She was there to share this busy and emotional day with us and to be a special part in what she knew was a very important occasion for our family and especially our precious son.

In spite of all the well laid plans to keep our evening orderly and on a schedule, our dinner guests arrived almost an hour late, and from then on we hurried and rushed but we managed barely to meet the deadline. The picture I had envisioned of leisure and a relaxed dinner watching my son enjoy his favorite foods, and people appreciating my efforts, turned out differently just as the graduation ceremony did. I was reminded once again that what may be important to me is not necessarily important to anyone else.

Bryant dropped us off at the entrance to the stadium in order for him to park the car and for us to rush in and find enough seats for all of our family to sit together. We climbed high up in the aisles until we reached not good but available seats. From this perch, we could see everything, the artificial grass-draped stage in the middle of the baseball field, lined with speakers' chairs and a podium, the graduates marching in slowly; then a lump filled my throat. I knew not to say a word.

I had never been to a graduation ceremony in a baseball stadium, and it had been a long time since I had attended any graduation. We tried to pay attention to the carefully planned ceremony taking place on the field, but as the circus-like atmosphere in the stands around us grew, the dignity of this occasion faded. Phoebe remarked to me, "We could sell popcorn in this crowd, and they wouldn't know the difference." The pomp that we remembered was gone, and times had obviously changed, but the sound of our son's name over the loud speaker, ringing in the night air, watching him appear on that stage briefly and knowing he had finished successfully this phase of his life, filled us with even more elevated pride and happiness.

When the excitement of the evening had settled and the kitchen door was locked after Bryant, Jr. came in from his "after graduation" party, Phoebe and I sat up alone into the wee hours of the morning talking and reminiscing. It was our first chance in quite a while to catch up, and it was certainly the quietest time of the day. Only the ever constant humming of the refrigerator disturbed the silence. She explained their fears and frustrations again about Dan's job situation, and I tried to understand the best I could, never having experienced stress of this nature. We knew it would work out; things always do, but at times like this, you wonder if you have the patience to endure. I was reminded of a quotation I had read somewhere saying, "Inch by inch, life's a cinch, but yard by yard, life is hard." We reached our usual conclusion that the best you can do is to take one day at a time — and sometimes only an hour.

Chapter 55

Emptying the Nest

I remember thinking that we had plenty of time to make all the preparations for Bryant, Jr. to leave for his first year in college. I took my time getting around to the task of labeling sheets and towels and concentrated more on the slower pace of summer, enjoying my sewing and yard work.

Allison went immediately after her Camp Don Lee session into her very first paying job at the hospital. She worked all the shifts and odd hours in the hospitality shop which cut into many Saturdays and Sundays and made it difficult for us to get to the lake as often as we would have liked. Along with learning to make milk shakes and selling sandwiches and candy bars, magazines and get well cards, and running the cash register, Allison quickly became very skilled at exercising patience and saw the true strength of silence. I'm sure she will never forget the day she came home from work angry because all day one of her co-workers kept referring to the flies that had come in through the front entrance as "Aldridge flies" — some resentful person taking out her frustrations, with unnecessary ugly comments about Mr. Aldridge, intentionally trying to hurt her. There is no better place than the public workforce to learn first-hand about the human spirit, and so she did.

We were well into the middle of July when Bryant, Jr. surprised us with the fact that he had been accepted as a walk-on for the Duke football team and had been spending hours after getting off work each day keeping up with the exercise schedule the coaches from Duke had sent to him. (It was the same as his daddy had done the summer before his freshman year at Duke.) We knew that Bryant, Jr. had grown to love football and were impressed that he would try so hard to go a step further with the sport. It takes a lot of time and effort to get yourself physically ready for college football practice, and he had done this all on his own.

With this announcement, the summer suddenly seemed to close in on us as he had to report to Duke the first of August, which gave us only a

Emptying the Nest

few weeks to get all of his belongings ready. He assured us all along, though, that he didn't need much as the team would be spending the first two weeks in a motel in order to be away from the dorms and the students still in summer school.

The time slipped by and the day came, a sunny hot day, and before we knew it, we were on our way to Durham. Bryant, Jr. had decided what he needed, and it seemed at first like all the other many trips we had made in that dirction. The grasses along the winding roadsides were brown and parched from the summer heat, but the rows of vegetable gardens beside the farm houses seemed still to be producing fresh vegetables. We chatted nervously and laughed as we passed the corner in Wake Forest we had named "Bryant's Corner." (We had stopped many times at that spot for Bryant, Jr. to overcome nausea after a bout with car sickness.)

Bryant, Jr. knew exactly where to go, and we followed his directions. It was all very exciting, parents meeting coaches, new recruits all trying to be very nonchalant about greeting each other for the first time. We excused ourselves in order to give our son the independence he needed saying we would catch up with him later in the cafeteria. The cool of the air-conditioned building was heavenly and a Diet Coke over ice was wonderful until I heard Bryant, Jr. saying, "Mama, I gotta go now. The team's meeting in a few minutes, and I've got to go." He had followed us in just that quickly, gave us a quick good-bye (the best kind), and took off like a kite on a breezy day, only we could not reel him back in. The lump in my throat choked me as it grew tighter. Bryant and I walked out of the great cafeteria hall hand in hand, each knowing the other could not say a word, overcome with a flood of emotions. Neither of us was prepared for this numbness. Oh, yes, we had all the grown-up feelings — this is what we wanted for him, and what he had worked so hard for, we were proud parents, but it didn't make the initial hurt go away.

I thought of my mother and wondered for the first time if she felt this way the day she left me at Peace College. I could almost feel my son's warm hands on the back of my neck as I remembered the Sunday morning in our church when he carefully fastened a silver necklace, holding a tiny Eagle Scout charm, around my neck the same day he received his Eagle Scout award. Could he possibly know the pride I felt on that certain Youth Sunday when he spoke before our church using the scripture (Romans 8:28) I recommended and one I hoped he would always live by?

Oh, the memories of your children are countless, cozy, and warm. I visualized the blue jays our family had watched in the spring, building their nest in the giant oak tree just outside our bedroom window, the brilliant blue male and his mate carefully and methodically placing each twig to form a safe little nest. It was only about six feet from our window and at eye level, the perfect location from which to watch daily. We waited almost as impatient as the female for her babies to be born, and one day we saw tiny little heads popping up and down with mouths wide open begging to be fed. Each day, we counted to make sure they were all there, safe and secure, bringing the neighborhood children in and up the stairs to our bedroom window to get a glimpse of the birds and nature at its best. One day after days of excitement watching the babies eat, Allison squealed, "Mama, come look. They're leaving the nest!" And sure enough, five baby blue jays had hopped out onto the old limb and were testing their wings. We looked for them after that for days, but they were finding their way about our yard, hiding under low growing shrubs and branches until they were sure they could fly and find their own nourishment. Then, one day, they were gone for sure, and the nest in the giant oak was empty.

Bryant, Jr. did not know how we felt, but some day maybe thirty years from now, on the day he takes one of his children off to college, he'll remember and know the feeling we had.

We had driven the distance from Durham to Rocky Mount in silence, both of us lost in our thoughts, oblivious to the eighteen wheel trucks, cars and RV's passing us, but the quietness had given us the strength we needed by now to look at each other and chuckle with the assurance that our son would be fine.

I couldn't tell Phoebe what she was in for, for she was hurting enough.

Chapter 56

The End of the Tunnel

That same summer of 1975 seemed longer and hotter than the year before. Dan tried selling insurance for a couple of months but soon realized that wasn't his calling. He traveled to different cities in North Carolina, Georgia, and Tennessee for job interviews. One of the most promising was in Lancaster, Pennsylvania. Dan came home excited and hopeful! It was the first company to show real interest in him in eight months. We tried not to get our hopes too high. They were to let him know something soon. In the meantime, I had gotten a job at an elementary school as a teacher assistant. The hours were the same as the children's, so I didn't feel like I was cheating them. I had not worked outside the home in sixteen years! When Jean and I met for lunch in Raleigh the first and last time that year, I told her how mixed my emotions were about having to go back to work. I didn't like it one bit, but it was what I could do to help.

By the middle of September, Dan finally heard about the job in Pennsylvania. Once again, he heard the all too familiar words "over qualified," which was a nice way to say your previous salary was too large and you are too old. It was another blow to the ego and made it harder to maintain hope and a positive attitude. We believed the scripture in I Corinthians that tells us He will not lay more on us than we can bear but will provide a way out. We tried not to "be anxious about anything." We repeated Philippians 4:19, "And my God shall meet all your needs according to his glorious riches in Christ Jesus," over and over to keep the ever-mounting fear in us from surfacing too often.

The first of October an interview in Raleigh sent our hopes sky high again. They told Dan he was one of the final two chosen out of three hundred applicants. They were very encouraging, even showed him his office. He came home on cloud nine. The Aldridges were coming for the weekend, and it looked like we would have something to celebrate. I even went out and bought steaks! As I left for work that Friday morning, I told

Dan I would call him from school to get the good news. We were so happy and grateful, so sure that this was what the good Lord wanted for us. I waited until I knew the mail had arrived to call Dan. When he answered I said, "Well, did you hear from them?" So sure I was going to hear a jubilant, "Yes, I got the job!" Instead, I heard, "Yes, they hired the other fellow. He was in another division, so they hired from within the company."

That night, I called Jean to ask them not to come. We were not going to be very good company I told her and hoped they understood. She assured me she did but thought we should not be alone. Depression causes an indescribable pain. It makes you want to sever all contact with the outside world. Our household was at its lowest ebb. I would lock myself in the bathroom and cry, "Lord, what do you want us to do?"

Sunday afternoon I was in the kitchen cleaning up the dishes after lunch. The sound of a car door closing made me look out the window. There in our driveway were Jean, Bryant, and Allison. I called to Dan in the family room, "The Aldridges are here." As we greeted each other at the back door, Jean said, in a joking tone, "We knew you might not let us in, but we came anyway!"

"Things might be bad, but not that bad," Dan chuckled. As we entered the family room, Bryant said, "Why don't we adults go in the living room where we can talk?"

It was a sunny fall afternoon. The sunshine was pushing its rays through the large front windows, and I remember thinking, "I love this room and the warm feeling it gives."

As soon as we were seated, Bryant began asking Dan if he had any more job prospects. Dan said at this point he had very few. Then, Bryant told him about an opening at Nash General that he might want to apply for. He didn't know how Dan might feel about his being his boss but felt they could cross that bridge later if Dan got the job. The four of us agreed nothing was worth putting our friendship in jeopardy. Bryant asked us to think it over and told Dan to let him know. I could not believe what I was hearing. The idea of our being together in the same town blew my mind!

The door to every job opportunity in the past nine months had closed in our face. Could this be the direction we were to take? After much prayer and pleas for guidance, Dan drove to Rocky Mount for an interview the following week. He was called back a second time, and they offered him the job.

So it was, that in November of 1975, Dan went to work at Nash General Hospital as the new Credit Collection Manager. Jean and Bryant graciously let him stay in their home until the children and I moved to

The End of the Tunnel

Rocky Mount on January 23, 1976.

It was like a dream. From the time Jean and I left Peace College, we had worked hard at keeping in touch and seeing each other whenever possible. Now the span of miles had been erased, and we were faced with a new element testing our friendship.

Thus began a whole new chapter in the Jean and Phoebe saga.

Chapter 57

Strengthening a Friendship

In establishing a new home for the Crouch family only a few short blocks away from us now, it meant also establishing a new realm in our life as friends. We were all aware that the friendship we had enjoyed and built through the years would be tested on a different level in the time to come. Bryant and Dan would be working as good and loyal friends side by side, day to day, creating a working relationship without favoritism that put our families at caution.

Our families were each others' families, and though we respected rights to privacy and living separate lives as we had always done, we knew how easy it would be to take each other for granted and possibly become neglectful. Separating business from our personal relationships was the task that lay before us. It meant honesty, open communication about our sensitivities, and consideration. It meant giving each other the space we needed to continue to grow, to relax, to have fun, and to enjoy each other when we could, but to hold fast to the anchor of friendship we were blessed with. It was important that pressures not be allowed to undermine this gift we valued so deeply.

(We had also promised Allene, Phoebe's mother, that we "wouldn't lay in each other's laps when Phoebe moved to Rocky Mount.")

Chapter 58

Home at Last

We lived in an apartment our first six months in Rocky Mount. Susan and Dan, Jr. were fascinated with apartment life, but Dan and I weren't. We thought we were through with that part of our lives. Guess "that's what we get for thinking," as my daddy used to say.

One afternoon in late February, I dropped by Jean's for a quick visit. The warmth of her family room felt good. I plopped down in the rocking chair near the fire place. "I love a rocking chair," I said, closing my eyes. "It's so relaxing, and right now it even makes this pain in my side feel a little better."

"What pain in your side?" Jean asked.

"Oh, I've had it for some time now, and according to my doctor in Burlington, it's just something I'll have to live with."

Jean's immediate response was, "That's ridiculous. You need to see another doctor."

Thanks to that particular conversation with Jean, I did see another doctor, and a few weeks later entered Nash General for an operation that made me feel like a new person. I sure was glad my "Ruum" encouraged me to get another opinion.

By June, we had found a suitable house, had moved in, and had gotten settled. It was a relief to get the boxes we had stored in Jean and Bryant's attic out of their way and unpacked.

Dan, Jr. had gotten a summer job at the hospital in the maintenance department. This filled his days, and dating and church activities filled his evenings.

Susan had met a best friend while we lived in the apartments. They were inseparable that summer. I knew what it was like to have a best friend. It pleased me to see these little girls enjoying each other and sharing their thoughts. One afternoon while they were enjoying a glass of iced tea in the kitchen, I overheard them talking. Susan was saying, "I was so glad to leave Burlington," caught my attention. She went on to tell how girls she thought were her friends made fun of her when her daddy lost his job. I couldn't believe my ears. She had never mentioned this to us. As I listened, I learned why. Her friend asked, "What did your folks say?" "I never told them. It would have hurt them too much," Susan answered. Wisdom in one so young touched me deeply.

That night, before she went to bed, I told her I had overheard their conversation and wanted to say thank you with a big hug and kiss.

It occurred to me that we were no longer visitors in Rocky Mount. We were home at last!

Chapter 59

Mema Failing

*I*t is so easy as you yield to the pressures on your own time and energy to forget often about the needs of the ones who are closest to you. I was well satisfied that my mother and my older brother, Sandy, were taken care of at this time. I knew that Sandy had moved to Raleigh, lonely, trying to recover from a failed marriage and the separation from his two young sons. In an attempt to relieve our mother from working and the responsibility of rearing a teenager, and taking care of a young person, he had convinced Mema to give up her job as a governess in Kinston and move to Raleigh with him. I was surprised and hoped that it would be the right move for both of them, but I could see the handwriting on the wall from the very beginning. Phoebe and I visited with them several times, and it was evident that Mema was not happy.

By the time we moved Bryant, Jr. home from his freshman year at Duke and he and Allison were settled into their summer jobs, Bryant and I had made the decision to move Mema back home to Kinston. She was showing the first signs of emphysema which we did not realize. We only knew she was sleepy all of the time and short winded, and the doctors continued to say she suffered from chronic bronchitis. The age of parents creeps up on you like darkness after a golden sunset and you search for light wanting to regain the glow.

Bryant and I went on an apartment hunt in Kinston early in June of 1976 and found what we thought to be the perfect little cottage for Mema. We moved her immediately the very next day, and she loved it. It was a tiny one-bedroom cottage situated in the back yard of a lovely home. Perfect! She would be fine.

Sandy was still searching and decided to take a job in Des Moines, Iowa. He saw this as an opportunity to travel, to see more of our beautiful country, and hopefully to find a new life.

Chapter 60

1976 — Celebrating the Bicentennial

We were ready in July for a nice trip as it had been quite an eventful and very emotional year, but all was well and we were taking time off together. Bryant, Jr. had to give up the idea of playing college football after injuring his back in spring practice, and we were thrilled to think he would take a trip with us that summer, giving us one more time of togetherness with just our family. Allison had graduated to the medical records department and was given time off for a brief vacation, and Bryant had a meeting in Philadelphia which coincided with the bicentennial celebration planned for our country, so it was a wonderful time to visit a city we had never seen. Another adventure, another memory etched! Independence Hall, the Declaration of Independence, the Liberty Bell, long walks along the historic streets of Philadelphia filled our days. We toured Lancaster County, Pennsylvania, and were moved by the simpleness, the absolute plainness, but the unique diligence of the Amish community of people, young and old tending the land. We were impressed with their quiet, private way of life, always turning their backs to avoid our taking pictures of them any time even when riding along the roads in their buggies.

We had saved one day at the end of the week to visit Washington, D.C., on our way home and spent the final night of our trip just outside of the city. The people of our country had apparently been frightened by the news media exaggerating on numbers leading up to the bicentennial celebrations. We were continually surprised at the small number of people, as we had been led to believe that the crowds everywhere would be tremendous during this time; so just to play it safe we tried to get early starts each day. On this particular warm July day, we wanted to see as much as possible but never dreamed that the small crowd we saw gathered in front of the brand new Science and Industry museum was there waiting for the official dedication ceremonies to begin, and our new President, Gerald Ford, would be the principal speaker. We joined the

1976—Celebrating the Bicentennial

crowd, thrilled at seeing and hearing another President and being a part of another moment in history. Our spirits were lifted even more when we entered the doors of the museum as they were opened for the first time, and Bryant, Jr. exclaimed, "Look, there's the Gemini Capsule we saw in Florida that time. It's the same one." And it was the same one, just as Bryant had predicted, here safely enclosed behind glass displayed in the entrance of this grand place for all the world to see. This time, however, no longer could we reach over and gently touch the heat shield as we had been allowed to do that day in Florida so many years ago.

We thought we were well on our way back to Rocky Mount after that busy day in Washington. We had absorbed about all we could in one day touring the Smithsonian. We were weary, hungry, and ready for the long ride home. After walking all day, we settled ourselves in the car for a welcome rest, longing for a cold soft drink before beginning our journey home. However, without our knowing it, Bryant had other plans. He drove as far away from Washington as possible leaving the heavy traffic behind before stopping for gas; and while we waited in the car, he was plotting his strategy.

"We're going to see if we can find Sonny Jurgenson. He lives only about a mile from here. Don't you think that would be fun?" he announced as he made himself comfortable in the driver's seat.

I said, "Oh Bryant, you're not serious!"

Bryant, Jr. and Allison chimed in, "You're kidding! Sonny Jurgenson. Oh, Daddy!"

We all were very aware of his Duke classmate and the famous Washington Redskin hero. It had been years since he had seen him, but we agreed that it would be fun just to see where he lived. With excellent directions from the service station attendant, Bryant drove directly to his home, and almost as though it had all been planned in advance, there walking in his front yard was Bryant's friend. Bryant, Jr. and Allison fell on the floor in the back seat of the car as if to escape from being embarrassed exclaiming, "I can't believe he's doing this. I just can't believe it. He's going to think we're crazy!" Their daddy parked the car, got out, called for Sonny, and the next sight we saw was two old friends shaking hands and reminiscing, laughing, and waving for us to get out and come in.

It was lovely, and I'm sure that Bryant, Jr. and Allison probably remember more about visiting with Sonny than anything else we did during that entire trip. He lived in a beautiful home overlooking the Potomac River, enclosed privately with perfectly manicured grounds. He had a giant screen television and a library of film capturing his days on the football field. It didn't take long for our children to be captivated with this friendly fellow, and their fear of being embarrassed was quickly erased. Bryant has an incredible gift of spontaneity that added unexpected excitement, joy, and adventure to our lives and often in the most simple way.

Chapter 61

A Lesson in Williamsburg

*I*t was good to have the Aldridges home. Everybody was back in the fold, and that's always a good feeling.

A couple of weeks later, during our regular morning walk, I told Jean I had to go that morning to fill out a job application. I had put it off long enough! "I'll ride over there with you," Jean said. "Wish you didn't have to go to work!"

"Wish I didn't have to either, but that's the breaks," I replied.

Later that morning, I picked Jean up and off we went to get this chore behind me. It didn't take long to fill out the necessary papers. As we walked back to the car, I told Jean I had stopped to talk to a friend of hers who offered to put in a good word for me.

By the end of the day, I had met two of Jean's teacher friends who quickly offered to give me a recommendation. The next day, I was asked to come in for an interview, and four days later I had the job. It isn't always what you know, but who you know. It's nice to have friends. My starting work the middle of August meant that Jean and I would have to change the date of our Williamsburg escape to the first of August rather than September as we had originally planned.

"What do you reckon we're in for, Ruum, staying in that boarding house?" I asked, as we approached the ferry landing on our way to Williamsburg.

"I don't know. Everybody says it's nice. It'll save us some money, and if we don't like it, we'll find something else."

Bryant, Jr. had been dating a young girl who was a student at The College of William and Mary. She was attending summer school and renting the attic apartment in a boarding house, and knowing that the owner rented rooms to tourists at a reasonable rate, she had suggested that we try it.

The house was easy to find across from the campus and was within walking distance of Merchants Square and the historic area.

As I parked the car in front of the house, Jean said, with relief in her voice, "Shoot, Phoebe, this is good. It's going to be fine."

"It's a beautiful old house. Looks well kept and clean," I said.

We unloaded our luggage and approached the entrance to this three story white colonial house. We were greeted by the owner, a tiny little widow with grey hair pulled back in a simple bun. She appeared cool in a faded pink cotton dress, and the ivory Cameo pin at her neckline caught our eyes immediately.

She led us to our room on the second floor and explained to us that we would be sharing the bathroom with a student living across the hall. After we closed the door to our room, we didn't know whether to laugh or cry.

"Phoebe, this place looks like a museum. Everything in here looks just like her."

"What are we going to do?" I said.

"I hate to hurt her feelings. Are we going to stay here?"

"Phoebe, she has surrounded herself with all her precious, tiny little things. I have never seen so many starched crocheted doilies. Every table top is covered with all that stuff."

"Look at this room, Jean, one single light bulb hanging from the ceiling. Can we sleep on that double bed? We'll die in here; it's so hot. We don't even have a fan."

"Well, it's clean, Ruum. We can stand it, and there's no way we are going to hurt that little lady's feelings," Jean explained.

We weathered our stay, lying motionless with our hands folded across our chest like a corpse in the double bed at night, praying for a breeze to come through the open windows. The nylon lace curtains never moved.

Each morning, we tried to get out the door before being stopped by the little old lady waiting for someone who would listen to her tell the history behind each of her little treasures.

On our way home, we agreed this was the most unusual Williamsburg trip yet! Unlike the convenient motel rooms we had had in the past, we were reminded of what it was like to be without air conditioning. We had skipped the Rum Cream pie and spoonbread at Christana Campbell's for simpler and less expensive meals at Morrison's Cafeteria. We spent more time than we had planned talking with our little old lady friend. She asked us to call her Miss Rose. She had treated us as guests in her home, and it made us feel good to think we had filled some of her lonely moments. That's what you do — you take the time to make someone else feel good, and it makes you feel good. Sometimes that's not your only reward. As Jean and I left, Miss Rose did not want to charge us one penny for our three night's stay. We finally made her accept a twenty dollar bill.

Chapter 62

A Nightmare in November

Watching Bryant, Jr. drive away in the little Comet station wagon to begin his sophomore year at Duke was no easier than leaving him as a freshman the year before. (I don't suppose I will ever get beyond the lump that fills my throat as I choke back tears every time I say good-bye to my children.) Allison was an active junior in high school, and Phoebe and I still were amazed that Dan, Jr., a senior, and Allison were actually attending the same school. Susan, just a seventh grader, was a reminder to us of our children's childhood days, as we watched the older ones becoming more and more grown up each day.

Phoebe's new job had changed her life, and the free time we had enjoyed together was now taken away. We saw less and less of each other, and we went our separate ways. Sometimes, we would go for a week or more and only have an occasional phone conversation, but we kept in touch enough to know what was going on in each other's lives. It was as though she didn't live in the same town at times. They were busy with their work and the new circle of friends they had made, and our families' schedules were very different, sending us off in opposite directions.

The fall was always a busy time with everyone gearing up for a new year. Bryant's meeting schedule was full, but we had the gorgeous golden autumn Saturdays to follow the Duke football team and to enjoy frequent visits with our college son. And before our eyes, we watched our daughter shed her braces and the awkwardness of adolescence, celebrate her sixteenth birthday, and blossom into a beautiful and poised young lady, and become our friend. She kept us occupied for many afternoons during this time following her tennis team, and we loved this activity, but we seemed to be constantly juggling dates on our calendars trying to accommodate to everything.

In early November, Bryant was scheduled to be the guest speaker for a hospital law seminar being held in Raleigh on the same day as the Duke-N.C. State football game. He decided that this would be a good opportunity

A Nightmare in November

to take his girls with him to a meeting. He never liked leaving us at home alone and enjoyed having the company when he had to be away. He made reservations for us at the motel where he was to speak bright and early on Saturday morning, and our plans were set to meet Bryant, Jr. for the game after the scheduled speech.

It was wonderful sneaking Allison away with just the two of us for a quiet dinner and evening together. Bryant was nervous about his speech as usual, so by nine o'clock we were settled in our comfortable room; he was in the bathroom working on his speech, and Allison and I were cuddled and warm in our beds watching "Dallas" on television.

The sudden sound of a telephone ringing can be so startling and unnerving, especially when you do not want to be disturbed. I jumped to grab the receiver when the telephone rang that night beside the bed hoping not to disturb Bryant studying in the bathroom. Naturally, the call was for him which didn't surprise us as we were accustomed to calls from the hospital at all hours wherever we might be. Strange, one of our good friends and a neighbor only wanted to speak to Bryant. Allison and I turned back to watch television, but the dead silence from the telephone told me something had happened. I saw the ghostly expression on Bryant's face and my heart began to pound as never before. "Oh, dear God, please, please don't let it be our boy. Please let him be all right," I prayed instantly. I looked at Bryant and asked, "Is it Bryant, Jr.? Has something happened to him?" Seeing my anguish, he covered the telephone receiver and said, "He's okay. It's our house. There's a fire." I said, "Oh, thank God, thank God, that's all."

Allison and I knew very shortly that our home had burned that evening, and we had to get up and leave immediately. We rode home to Rocky Mount, numb and trying to figure out every possible thing that could have happened. Did I leave the stove on? Did I leave the iron plugged in? I tried to be so careful. Phoebe and Dan had fed "Champ," our little Sheltie, and put him in the house for the night, and Allison kept crying softly, "Oh, Mama, Mama, Champ's in there. What about Champ!" I could only think, "Oh, Allison, oh Allison, thank God, you are with us."

The scene that greeted us as we turned into our neighborhood and onto our street was mass confusion. Near our house, the street had been blocked off stopping all traffic, but we were allowed to enter when the police recognized our car. Yellow reflective tape used by the police department circled the pine trees sequestering the yard and house to keep out the curious onlookers. Our neat white frame home still stood soundly, it seemed, in the light from the enormous flood lights illuminating the entire area like a fairground making it visible for all to see.

* * *

It was a night I will never forget. One that is engraved in my memory forever.

I told Jean I had been to dinner with a friend whose husband was attending the same meeting as Dan. Dan, Jr. had a date, so I was without a car. When we came home, I said, "Dan's car isn't here so that means your husband isn't home either. You might as well come in and visit for a while." As I unlocked the back door, I heard a siren. "I thought I smelled smoke," I remarked. "There go the fire trucks. Sounds like more than one, must be a big one."

Fifteen minutes later, our visit was interrupted by the phone ringing. I answered the phone. The voice on the other end said, "Phoebe, the Aldridge's house is on fire! Get here as fast as you can!"

We rushed for the car, and in a matter of minutes we were there. (Thank goodness she stayed to visit. Nothing happens by chance!)

As we turned the corner, I could see two fire engines, lights flashing, fire hose running everywhere. Smoke was boiling out of the back bedroom window, the firemen had just extinguished the flames. I was out of the car before it stopped and running toward the house. The police stopped me at the edge of the large crowd that had gathered. "Please let me through, please!" I pleaded. The fire chief, who was a member of our church, saw me and told them to let me pass.

I yelled, "Chief, their dog is inside. Did you get him out?"

"No," was his reply. Turning to one of the firemen, he said, "Go with her to get the dog."

We ran around back and through the garage. "You'll have to break in the door. I forgot the keys," I exclaimed! We were surprised to find the door already open. My hopes mounted for Champ's survival. Suddenly, I heard my daddy's voice out of the past saying, "Always crawl low to the floor. There'll be four inches of clear air there." Sure enough there was. I could see all the way through the kitchen, down the hall and into the entrance foyer. The fireman found little Champ. His mahogany coat covering his still body was untouched by the smoke that filled the house. His little nose was pressed against the crack under the door as he had desperately sought another breath of air. It was going to break Allison's heart, but all I could do was thank God none of them were in the house.

I went back to the front yard and told the chief we were too late to

A Nightmare in November

save the little dog. At that moment, I realized they were getting ready to enter the front door with the fire hose. Once again, my daddy's words came to mind: "There's a lot of unnecessary water damage if they turn that nozzle too soon." Without hesitation, I got behind the fireman holding the hose, grabbed his belt and said, "Don't turn that water on until I punch you in the back!" It did not occur to me until later what I had done, and it was even more amazing that the young fireman had acted exactly as I said.

Dan was standing in the front yard as I came out of the house. We waited there while the fireman did their job and brought everything under control. All we could do now was wait for Jean and Bryant to arrive. The large crowd dispersed and the ones left waiting were small groups of concerned neighbors and friends.

Someone said, "The Aldridges are here!" I turned to see their car coming to a stop at the edge of the boundary. As I started toward them, I was struck by the picture they made. Allison had leaned forward from the back seat, her face between Jean and Bryant. All three expressions were the same — calm but stunned. When I got closer, I could see Allison had been crying.

"Did they get Champ? Is he all right?" she called to me. I dreaded telling her he was gone.

* * *

Bryant and I moved quickly past our friends and up the front walk, stopping half way and stared into the open front door. Bryant immediately began talking to the fire chief, Allison's group of friends were there to comfort her, and I felt an arm holding me saying, "Mrs. "A," I'm so sorry." The head of the maintenance department from the hospital stood there and tried to comfort me, our dear and sweet friend.

I asked, "Dick, what in the world has happened?"

He answered as gently as possible, "Someone set your house on fire."

I asked in utter dismay, "Oh, Dick, why would anybody want to do this to us?"

Who could answer that question? He merely said, "I don't know. I just don't know. They broke in through the kitchen door and deliberately set it."

I stood looking through the front door, everything inside as black as the walls of a fireplace, the wallpaper in the foyer hanging burned and useless, and firemen, with their wet and muddy boots tracking water and soot in and out on our carpet. It was hard to believe the picture painted before me, but the relief I felt knowing we were together and that our children were safe was all I cared about. Everything else could be replaced. I was calm and so very thankful. All the way home from Raleigh, we kept remembering good friends who had lost three children in a house fire as they stood in their yard and watched their home burn to the ground unable to do a thing.

After a brief explanation from the fire chief, he took Bryant and Allison and me into the house to survey the damage, and it was bad. Seventy-five percent of our beautiful home and all its contents were gone.

There would have to be a thorough investigation in a case of arson. The SBI would have to be brought in with all of the suspicions that could possibly link this act of madness to the vicious accusations of mismanagement directed so many times at Bryant and the hospital. The fireman was holding a large flashlight showing us the guest room as he explained to us what would take place. Like a dream, I could only feel Allison's slender warm fingers squeezing my hand as we strained to see in the darkness the ashes and remains of our belongings. My sewing machine, where is my mother's sewing machine, I thought; it's gone, too.

Chapter 63

Better Not Bitter

*I*t's funny how the fire divided our lives. So much of what we do now is related to before the fire or after the fire. You reach for things that are no longer there, and you wonder if you had something before the fire or if it's just been misplaced.

The night after the fire, we spent with kind and generous neighbors, never sleeping but just lying in the bed in their guest room wondering what we would do or where to turn. Bryant kept saying, "It'll all work out. Don't worry. Try to sleep. It'll all work out."

Morning finally came and the nightmare was very much a reality. So many people came — Mema and my Aunt Selma, Nannie, and finally Bryant, Jr. It was a cold but bright Saturday, and we had gone to the house early. Someone gave me an old coat to wear into the house in order to save my good one, and Dan and Phoebe were right at our side. We couldn't do much, walk around waiting; the police would only let us in the house for necessary clothing which was of no use. Dan took the job of policing our driveway; and as I watched him approaching the sidewalk keeping curious people away, I saw Bryant, Jr. coming towards me smiling. He was tall and handsome, a beautiful sight, and I was so glad to see him, to touch him, and to know he was safe. He took me in his strong arms and held me and in his gentle consoling voice said, "Mama, it's all right. Now you can redecorate. Just think, you can make it even better."

God literally sends to you those you need. That very day a wonderful contractor friend called offering to help get us back into our home as soon as possible, our paint contractor did the same, and our blessed high school friend and decorator was there as soon as he heard. I looked at him and asked while standing in the blackened rooms he had so carefully helped me plan and decorate originally, "Robert, what are we going to do?" His reply to me was simply, "Don't worry. I've just finished a job like this in Kinston," and he went on to explain to us exactly what to do. I only had to make one telephone call to take care of the furniture, and he would help with the

For All The World To See

rest as we needed him. More relief!

On Sunday, we moved to the Crouch's to live until we could make other arrangements. It was a very uncomplicated move. We only had the clothes we were wearing and a set of night clothes, toiletries, and a pair of shoes. We certainly didn't need much room. We tried to relax with Phoebe and Dan, but it was hard to discuss anything other than the evidence surrounding our unnecessary disaster. Someone had taken a crowbar and tried to raise windows all around our house, finally breaking the door knob completely off of the kitchen door and entering the house successfully. The person then went into our guest room, ripped the pages from a treasured book that had been written and autographed to us personally by a high school friend, one who had spent eight years in prison in Viet Nam, and this book described his ordeal. With the pages from this book, the intruder fashioned a torch twisting the pages together tightly and created a lasting flame. He then went from room to room setting the draperies in our guest room and study on fire, unlocked and walked out the front door and left our home to burn and our helpless pet to suffocate. We wondered how anyone could be so despicable.

The old saying of "when it rains it pours" was surely what seemed to be our lot that weekend. My mother seemed fine the day before, but the call from my aunt that same Sunday afternoon told me differently. The shock of the fire, nerves, and her general poor health had made Mema deathly ill, so we had no other choice but to go immediately to Kinston and get her settled in the hospital and pray that she would be all right. Emphysema can be a crippling disease, and the lack of oxygen causing one to hallucinate is frightening. She was suffering so, but once again the doctors assured us that she would improve.

The week following the fire was busy beyond our imagination. The first order of business we had decided was to take Allison to Raleigh shopping for new school clothes. We needed something to wear other than what we had been in for the last three days, and leaving town was a good remedy for our sadness. Not only did we buy her clothes, but we treated her to a huge plush teddy bear she named "Punkin." She had lost along with Champ all of her collection of dolls and stuffed animals in the fire, and she was trying to be so strong.

Doors kept opening! We learned on our return from Raleigh that we had an apartment available to us, offered by a good friend. We rented it the next day, and following more advice and directions from concerned friends, we were able to rent all of the furniture we needed to furnish a three bedroom apartment comfortably and have it delivered. By Friday afternoon, we had established a temporary new home, a much needed haven for our family.

We had seen the bad, the mean, and the good, and the good far outweighed the bad. This had been one of those opportunities where you find out who your friends are. It had turned into a good natured joke guessing how much weight we would gain because our friends had taken such thoughtful care of feeding us every night with delicious full course dinners and trying to help meet our needs.

Only two days after settling into the apartment, our neighbors surprised us with an old-fashioned "pounding." I didn't know what a pounding was, but our friends were well educated on the subject. They showered us generously with food and linens, an iron and ironing board, small appliances, and house plants, so the cold of the apartment was quickly transformed and furnished from the warmth of our friends. We were truly overwhelmed, and the love and concern kept pouring in.

The next afternoon, I answered the door bell and was greeted by three gentlemen from the maintenance department of the hospital delivering to us several appliance size cardboard boxes bearing gifts. The loyal and caring employees at Nash General had sent us a pounding that brought tears to our eyes. I needed help just going through the layers of packages.

Allison called Phoebe and I heard her saying, "Mama said for you to come see what's sitting in our living room; you're not going to believe it. Bring Susan."

They were there in only a few minutes, and we could hardly wait to see their faces. Phoebe walked through the door and her first remark was, "Have mercy, Ruum, what is it? What now? Good Lord, ya'll have been pounded again!"

With that the four of us fell on the floor laughing and releasing the tension of the last few days. We began opening the gifts that revealed loving kindness from genuine salt of the earth people. Blankets, linens, gift certificates, coffee, canned goods right off their pantry shelves, pots and pans, kitchen utensils, toothbrushes and toothpaste, various amounts of money in unsigned envelopes, and six books of S&H green stamps bound with a rubber band touched our hearts. It made us so happy we were laughing and crying at the same time. No one could see such a display of unselfish generosity without being moved. The only problem we had after that was finding a place to store forty-five pounds of sugar, thirty pounds of coffee, twenty-five pounds of flour, ten jars of peanut butter, and enough canned goods to last us for a year.

Mema was well enough by the end of the week to come home from the hospital. I had just enough time to pack all of our pounding away before going to bring her to live with us in the apartment while she recuperated.

* * *

The police and SBI investigation of arson prevented us from being able to begin any clean up for two weeks. Looking at the whole of what had to be done was too overwhelming, so the four of us started with one room at a time. We emptied all the drawers into large plastic trash bags. After we labeled each bag, we put them aside. Jean and I tried to count articles of clothing as we went, but Dan and Bryant wouldn't take the time to do this, so we gave up and started dumping everything like they did. The insurance company wanted an inventory of everything in the house. After each drawer, shelf, box, and closet was unloaded, we had to go through each bag to determine if anything could be used, counting and itemizing as we went.

The most interesting clean up attempt we tried was cleaning the silver! Someone had told Jean to line the bathtub with aluminum foil and add Spic and Span to the water, then dip each piece of silver. We brought all their silver to our house, and after washing the black, oily film off each piece, we followed these directions. It worked! The silver looked like new. I was telling one of the teachers at school the next day what we had done. She said, "No wonder it worked! It removed a thin layer of the silver!" Oh well, live and learn. Jean and I decided it was worth a layer of silver as long as we didn't have to clean all of it.

Every week night for six weeks was the same. After school, I would check with Jean to see what time we would meet to dig through the ruins. We worked with surgical masks on and wore the same clothes every night. If we worked longer than thirty or forty-five minutes at a time, our eyes would burn and our head ached. Standing in the front yard breathing in the cold fresh December night air, sipping coffee or hot chocolate one of us had brought in a thermos, was heaven. The surrounding houses with lighted candles in each window, decorated for Christmas looking warm and cozy, were a sharp contrast to the dank, dark house behind us.

Endless loads of wash yielded very few items that could ever be used again. The last thing we did was strip the drapes and cornices from the windows. The furniture had been hauled away to be refinished, the carpet was gone and all contents were removed. Now, Jean and Bryant could turn it over to the contractors. The worst was over. The rebuilding could begin.

> *"I can do everything through him who gives me strength."*
> Philippians 4:11-13 NIV

Chapter 64

The Spirit of Christmas

Almost everyone can remember a special holiday or Christmas that stands out in his or her mind more than any other. It may be the one spent at a grandmother's house, stuffing yourself with sweet pickles and pecan pie, or maybe the year you found the shiny red wagon under the tree, or the Madame Alexander doll. It could be the time you remember watching a snow falling like a miracle outside your bedroom window as you enjoyed the warmth of your home filled with the sounds of carols and spicy smells of Christmas. Some will even remember the peeping buds of yellow forsythia rushing spring on a Christmas day during an unusually warm southern winter. I will always remember the Christmas our family celebrated in 1976 as a bright and shining star among the galaxy of holidays we have been blessed with.

Mema was well again and still with us in the apartment we rented after the fire. Bryant, Jr. was home from Duke for the holidays, and our thoughtful neighbors had given us a precious Sheltie puppy for Christmas. It was not easy having a puppy to train at that time, but he brought so much new life and joy into our home that we didn't mind. He filled the void and eased the ache in our hearts after the fire, and we named him Star.

Put to test, I doubt if any one of us could list the tangible material things we received that Christmas, but I am confident that we would all recall more than anything grateful hearts, joy and happiness, and a rebirth of thankfulness and appreciation for our values, giving us strength and peace. Again, home is truly where the heart is, and that Christmas ours was in a cozy apartment we'll never forget. It has been said that suffering builds character, and I will add that character relieves suffering.

Chapter 65

Nannie

The holidays passed; and with each day in the new year, we watched the progress of reconstruction on our house with excitement. The visible signs of the fire were cleared and began to fade as new materials replaced the damaged, and I worked diligently every day with our dear friend and decorator to create an entirely different look for our home. The SBI investigation continued throughout: new leads, conferences, high hopes (but nearly always in vain). We wondered if this awful mystery would ever be solved.

The experience had taken such an emotional toll on our mothers. Mema had bounced back and seemed to be doing well back at her home in Kinston, and Nannie tried hard to figure out a way to solve it all. She was ready to give up her last dime on private detectives to help track down the party guilty of such a vicious attack on her son. She finally gave up her life with the worry.

The call came in March of 1977, only weeks from her being able to see our world put back together. She had been with us the day before, surveying the new of our home, happy for us, still full of questions but more anxious than we realized. Now she was gone.

Allison and I were at home alone in our apartment when I heard J.P.'s voice, "Nannie has died of a massive heart attack." It was beyond our belief, this loss now of one we loved and needed so much. It was difficult to comfort our beautiful sixteen year old sobbing with a broken heart from more tragic news. We located Bryant at his meeting, and I called Phoebe and Dan. In only a few minutes, we were on our way to Kinston where Nannie had lived since Pappy's death, grief stricken, to plan our mother and grandmother's funeral.

We have missed Nannie; her soft, silver hair and her quiet, gentle manner, her wise advice in times of need, the hot caramel cakes held together with toothpicks, and even the coffee can she discreetly placed her cigarette ashes in. (She thoughtfully kept it covered with a plastic lid to keep the stale cigarette odor out of our house.) She left us priceless memories and died in a way she would have wished. Always thinking of others, but independent, her final days would have been miserable if she had been dependent on anyone to care for her through an extended illness. Knowing her and accepting God's plan for our lives helped, but the lonely, longing for her presence took a long, long time to subside. She missed sharing so much of our lives.

Chapter 66

Dan, Jr. and Wingate

It did not seem possible that Dan, Jr.'s high school graduation was only a few days away. He would be graduating on June 3rd, his eighteenth birthday. Kitty and Dad Crouch were coming to help us celebrate.

After graduation, it felt good to be out of school, to sleep past six o'clock in the morning and not to have to be on any set schedule. Jean and I met for our morning walks whenever we could. These were the only moments we had together most of the time. We were in opposite directions these days. With me working, our lifestyles were different now. These eight weeks I had off would enable us to catch up and hopefully see more of each other. We put our Williamsburg trip on the calendar right away so nothing would happen to those days in July.

Trips to the beach, mountains, and Lake Lure dotted our summer. The time for me to start work again and Dan, Jr. to leave for Wingate was speeding toward me.

Although Jean had told me what it felt like to take your first born off to college, I had to experience it for myself. When the day for us to embark on this new journey arrived, we were ready. Daniel and his girlfriend rode in the little blue Toyota. Susan, Dan, and I were in the larger car. Wingate is a small Baptist junior college located not far from Charlotte, N.C. After a quick lunch at one of the local fast food establishments, we drove to the campus to get Daniel settled in his dorm. This, much to my dismay, went rather quickly, and suddenly we were at the moment I had suppressed for days. Deep within me, I felt the dam getting ready to burst. "Oh, please, dear Lord, don't let me embarrass Dan, Jr. by blubbering all over him," I prayed. He walked us back to the cars. Dan and Susan rode in one car, and Daniel's girlfriend and I were in the other.

As he leaned in my window for a quick kiss, he patted my arm and said, with a twinkle in his eye, "I love you, Mom. Be careful driving home."

The picture of him in my rear view mirror, as we drove away, was one of an excited, confident young man.

Chapter 67

The Changing Roles of Parenting

I watched her leaving that morning, Allison, rushing, excited, so ready to begin her final year at senior high.

She yelled as she went out the back door, "Bye, Mama."

She smiled happily, and we waved. She was off, and I wondered how time could have passed so fast. It seemed like only yesterday that I was a senior in high school myself. I peered out the kitchen window through the pine trees and dogwoods, craning to watch the car carrying our grown up daughter until it disappeared completely out of sight, but she never knew. I stood staring at the dogwoods seeing a tinge of red already showing on the tips of the leaves, and like a magnet I went up the stairs and into Allison's room, drawn to the dogwood tree outside her window. I sat on the side of her bed very melancholy and gazed at the sprawling branches stretching from window to window like a huge umbrella. Looking down into the top of a tree gave me a whole different perspective, a much closer view of all the details, and I was glad that we had saved Allison's dogwood tree.

It had been a major production during the construction of our house. The little dogwood tree kept getting knocked over, and Bryant and Bryant, Jr. built a barricade around it with scrap lumber for protection. Now, it was a huge beautiful tree that bloomed profusely each spring, and we delighted in looking down on the flowers from Allison's room. I was so very glad she would be at home for another year. I couldn't imagine what it would be like without her, and I didn't want to think about it. I smoothed the covers on her bed and put that depressing thought out of my mind and said a silent prayer, "Oh, God, fill our home with the laughter of youth this year, and keep it free of pain."

We had moved back into our home in May of 1977 only a few weeks after Nannie's death, and even though the mystery of our fire was still unsolved — and we will probably never know who committed such a hideous act of madness — our spirits were high as we celebrated and christened our beautiful new home with our loved ones that summer. The

Crouches were finally able to get on with their lives, free of Aldridge worries, and it was good we could all think of something else.

So much had happened during the year leading up to September of 1977. We had a new President. Jimmy Carter, our southern statesman, had taken over these reigns in January. Elvis Presley died in April after a tumultuous life of wealth, fame, fast living, and drugs. He surely had to be the symbol of the rock 'n roll generation and will probably always remain the most famous of his kind in history. We were so wrapped up sometimes in our own worlds that we hardly had a chance to discuss the world events happening all around us.

That winter was no better for Mema. Her health kept deteriorating; and while Allison's senior year progressed with tennis, piano, yearbook staff editor, and Tim (her beau at that time), I ran back and forth to Kinston caring for Mema who was in and out of the hospital.

I didn't like having her sick. I wanted her well and whole. I wanted her like it used to be when we shopped and had fun. I wanted her to take care of me. I didn't want her to be old and for me to be forced to make all of the decisions by myself. Where was my brother? If only he could come and help me with her. No one could convince her that cigarettes harmed her, and it was frustrating. She would get better, start smoking, and get sick again. By the time Allison's graduation from high school came that spring, I had made the decision that we would move Mema to Rocky Mount where we could care for her daily. (She was waiting for me to take over, and I saw a reversal in roles coming to pass, one that was inevitable.)

Allison, like her brother, had worked hard achieving and had gained admission to Duke University, also. With this accomplishment behind her, we spent much of that summer planning and dreaming of the college days that lay ahead for her. I knew that only a miracle would bring her a college roommate and friend like I had been given, and we talked often of how wonderful that would be. Bryant, Jr. teased her constantly about whom she might get; and when her roommate assignment came, we didn't know what to think but were anxious to check her out. Of all the far away places that students come from to go to Duke University, Allison's new roommate was from Graham, N.C., only thirty miles from Durham. All of her visions of visiting a roommate in exotic lands very quickly disappeared. By the middle of July, they had corresponded enough and made arrangements for our first meeting.

We have wondered so often how it all happened, but there was the miracle. Meeting in front of the stately Duke Chapel, we knew immediately that Duke had made a near perfect match. Two mothers, two

The Changing Roles of Parenting

daughters, two families with much in common, granted a gift of friendship we learned to cherish. This doesn't happen to many people.

With all of these questions answered, Allison settled back into her summer job as a teller at one of our local banks, and I concentrated on Mema. We found her an apartment available in August, and with the ever present help of Phoebe and friends, we painted furniture frantically and prepared Mema for her move to Rocky Mount. Anything was fine with her, so the day we moved her into her little home, Phoebe and I had it in perfect order — curtains all hung, cabinets arranged, pictures and furniture in place, even geraniums on the front stoop. My mother was like a little girl in a brand new doll house. We had given her a fresh new outlook on life.

Mema was happy and well, and before we knew it, Bryant, Jr. and Allison were ready to leave for school. Bryant, Jr. was still driving the little '63 Comet, and being an old hand at college life and a rising senior at Duke, he packed his car with what he needed without help from anyone while Allison and Bryant and I scurried around making sure Allison had everything she wanted loaded into our car. We were proud of our children and happy that we could give them an opportunity like this.

The ride to Durham was much the same. It seemed we had made this trip through Spring Hope and Bunn and Wake Forest a million times. Only today, I could think of nothing else but the empty nest we would return to and giving up my baby. We had become so close, such good friends.

The day was extremely hot, and we found Allison's dorm room on the third floor almost unbearable. The two fathers unloaded and lugged their daughters' gear up the three flights of steps and went to Roses and bought window fans and miles of extension cords. (Bryant, fearing for their safety, carefully explained to Allison and her roommate, Shawn, how each electrical appliance took turns on the extension cords.) Shawn's mother and father were a jovial pair and kept joking about the strings of beads hanging as a door to the closet like a French whorehouse. We laughed and had fun getting our girls settled. Bryant, Jr. met us for an early dinner, and afterwards in the parking lot outside the dormitory, we knew it was time to let our girls go. We cried and laughed and cried and laughed, hugged and kissed, and waved good-bye, and Bryant and I drove home to our empty nest.

We had a trip to California planned to attend the American Hospital meeting early in September, and it proved to be a great distraction from Allison's absence from us, coming at just the right time. Bryant and I had never been to California, and we were really looking forward to seeing the west coast — a well deserved trip after the events of the previous year, we felt.

Chapter 68

Sandy

My mother had always been a good one for surprises, and the call from her on Friday afternoon before we were to leave for California in 1978 really put me into a state of shock. She was on her way to the airport in Raleigh to pick up my brother, Sandy. He was coming home from Iowa to visit Mema for a week, and we had not seen him for nearly two years. Mema had never been one to show much excitement, but I could feel the elation in her voice as I sank with disappointment, realizing we would be leaving the next morning, away for Sandy's entire visit.

They came by that night about ten o'clock, and we had a hurried visit, touring our newly decorated home, catching up on his and our activities during the time he had been away, packing all we could into an hour's visit.

He adored traveling and was thrilled that we were on our way to the west coast, and his final words to us before saying good-bye again were, "Go to San Francisco, try to see the Big Sur, and you will surely see God's handiwork."

The long flight early the next day was actually relaxing. We were ready to get away. It was a comforting feeling knowing that Mema had the most prized visitor she could have wished for staying with her while we were away; our children were safe and busy in school; and we longed for a vacation.

* * *

While leaving for work that morning, I noted with joy the air had a hint of coolness in it. A drop in temperature couldn't come fast enough for me. The first thing I did when I arrived at school was open every window to let this heavenly morning air in.

"It's a beautiful day in North Carolina," I said to myself. "Hope it's this nice in California for Jean and Bryant."

The children arrived with their usual energy and excitement. I took the lunch report and passed out morning work folders while their teacher started circle time. The day was underway and going well.

Our morning was interrupted by the office secretary's voice on the intercom, "Mrs. Crouch."

"Yes," I answered.

"Please come to the office. You have a phone call."

I looked at my co-worker and said, "What in the world could this be."

My heart skipped a beat when I answered the phone and heard Dan's voice. "Hi, honey."

"What's wrong?" I asked not really wanting to know.

"It's Sandy. They brought him in a little while ago. He's had a heart attack. I'm afraid he's gone." I could not believe what I was hearing as he continued. "I've been with Mema. I left her long enough to call you. I'll wait until you get here to tell her."

"I'm on my way!"

Driving to the hospital, I tried to sort out what Dan had said. Did he say a heart attack? Sandy was so young, only 47 years old. Had Jean mentioned his being sick? No. I would have remembered that.

When I arrived, I was taken to the room where Mema and Dan were waiting. The room was small and white, devoid of color. When Mema saw me, I think she knew what Dan was going to say. All I could do was take her in my arms and hold her while Dan repeated what he had told me on the phone.

As we drove back to her apartment, we didn't say much. It was about eight o'clock in California. Jean didn't know about her brother yet, but she would know we were taking care of Mema. God's timing is so perfect. What if Mema were still living in Kinston? What if we were still living in Burlington...what if Sandy had been in Iowa?

Mema did not feel comfortable going back to her apartment, so I took her to Jean's house where we waited until Aunt Selma arrived. Later that afternoon, I went back over to Mema's apartment to clean and put things in order.

* * *

A telephone call from home, awakening us at eight o'clock in the morning in Anaheim, California, on the second day of our vacation, had to be more bad news. And so it was. The shock and dismay I felt as I listened to Bryant relay the message to me about Sandy's death weakened me. Just

Sandy

the day before, we had taken his advice and flown on a mini adventure up to San Francisco for the day. I had seen what he referred to as some of God's handiwork, and I would never get to tell him. My thoughts then immediately went to Mema as Bryant worked out return flights home as soon as possible. The best we could do was early afternoon, so we went to the airport and waited for hours as though that would get us home faster. There was nothing else to do. The glamour of California and rest vanished while we waited heart-broken in the hum of the Los Angeles airport.

The closest flight we could get was to Greensboro. We arrived at two in the morning, rented a car, and drove to Raleigh to pick up our own car, only to find upon arrival that Bryant had forgotten to turn the lights off when he left it, and the battery was dead. With the help of the attendant on duty, we managed to get started again around four o'clock and arrived safely in Rocky Mount at five. We slipped quietly into the house praying for a few hours of rest before facing the next day. I could not face another thing. (Maybe it was all a dream anyway.)

Eight o'clock in the morning came quickly, and Mother was waiting for me to take over. She was calm and passive, shaken beyond belief. Whatever needed to be done was fine with her, so Bryant and I set out to make all of the final arrangements. We had become familiar with the procedures, and the funeral director was a good friend.

The next day, we said good-bye to my brilliant and beloved brother, something I never thought I would have to do. Although he was away most of my life, he was a part of me and always came home. Now, I could not bear the thought of his not coming home again. His passion for learning had broadened all of our horizons. He created in me an appreciation for music and history and the value of our family heritage. He gave me a keen awareness of a much broader world and the finer things in life. He worked hard for his education, and sometimes it was difficult for us to communicate because he was very intelligent, but that bond of love for brother and sister was always present. While completing his doctorate in musicology at Columbia University, he worked as an editor for Columbia Encyclopedia and did free-lance editing, later assuming the position as editor of the University of South Carolina Press. (Phoebe and I could use his expertise right now, and when I think of his poetry and short stories, his unfinished book manuscripts and symphonies of music in my attic, I know that no one will appreciate our efforts like he would have.) His short life is over, free of pain, never having accomplished the enormous dream that, I am confident, was ever present in his magical and tender heart.

We carried Sandy to Kinston and buried him at the spot he had carefully selected, ironically only days before he moved to Iowa, under the low sprawling branches of North Carolina pines in a quiet secluded area near his grandparents. He had reserved the plot beside him for Mema.

The Homeland
J. Sandy Peake

These plains! these rolling hills! this blessed land!
It took two centuries to make this land; Two thousand years will be
required to ruin this evidence of men and homely lives. The gins, the
houses - hovels, mansions - barns,
the stores, the signboards, churches, water-tanks;
All, all are touched with spendour at this time:
The sun, surrendering to the queen of night, Recedes into the West; the
silent music
Of the evening, his recessional:
The soundless beat of blackbirds' wings resounds,
And not a twitter as they fly toward East; Imaginary echoes of a bell;
The fiery splash of color in the West; And purple clouds and misted light
above. As shadows gather, deepen in far woods,
As the swift and black steps of night march on,
My mind rests calm and still, but, oh! my soul,
My spirit, inner being, flutters fast
And keeps in time with air-like streams of light,
Light moving, sparkling, flashing, shattering!
I feel it: every breeze, and each blown tree; The moving grasses, the softly
whispered song Of this my country - heritage and duty.
Oh, yes! I feel it in the pit of my stomach A powerful and urgent driving
force
That brings my love for every shaded path Across the fields and every
bridge and stream!
It's ever like this: man must be at home: When sunshine leaves the hill,
some charm is gone;
The same if night is passed without a moon; What is a bell without its
swinging clapper? A man away from home is out of place -
He wilts, as though some captive fish on land,
And dies, if not outright, then in his soul; His voice falters and he stops his
song,

His feet unsure upon the unknown streets; He changes to a mere machine
at work. But put him back within his habitat
And coursing joy will vitalize the man; His work becomes his play; again
he sings The swelling song of Nature - happiness. And so am I when I am
gone from here: The sun without his sky, the mighty tree Without a root,

For All The World To See

the leaf without a limb;
I've felt it in far city streets at night When every bus is whinning through the dark, Its windows lined with ghostly phantasm faces,
And oh! how small and pent-up I became: Like an ant who tries to climb a sand-pit wall;
Like to an owlet caged and teased with lights;
Like to a thrush who's lost his song of freedom;
Far away from home I've felt no song,
But melancholy ruled my heart and mind, The lamb and lion of every soul's demesne. As though an ant, I tried to hide away From all the unknown stares of unseen eyes; As though an owl, I tried to fly away; And when, a thrush, I lost my singing heart, I howled: a beast who bellows at the moon; A beast who bellows, crying rage at pain, I limped my way back home - my love and master.
The moment when I saw from far away
The varied tapestry of rolling plain Caused praise and melody to flood my brain; The days I spent reposed in pasture-grass Have, like a medicine, congealed my wounds And made me whole - an animated body Supple to the wishes of the wind.
Home! Home! I'll sing you hallelujahs loud And Benedicti sweet, within my heart;
Your virtues I'll extol unto all men;
No other name than thine shall be so loved, So treasured up, so tender on my lips! I'll versify each common clod of soil
And orchestrate Te Deums to the corn; I'll love and serve the endless, flowing streams
Of lowly men and blooded lineage;
I'll worship at your altars in the wood And dance ballets symbolic on the malls; Your every mood and tone shall be to me Ecstatic music - acme of this life -
My lullaby at dreaming that last dream:

Your whisper, voiced as wind, shall send me hence
To sit beyond the door of sorrowed sleep; And even there will waft the wildest wings Of my home's flying soul.
Yet not with me
And my death shall young song cease to be sung,
For I am not the only one who loves;
Oh, no! The countless millions yet unborn The embryonic hope of all mankind -

Sandy

Shall tread your paths and drink your loveliness:
Your unbegotten children follow me
To kneel to you in green cathedral-aisles.
I know not how they'll use you, nor what song will shape their lips: if it be sharp war-cries,
And if they battle on your curving breast, The bomb-pits will reveal to hungry eyes Forgotten glories of your history;
If songs of planting and of harvesting Swell through their throats, and if with hallowed hearts
They furrow down your belly, bared to plow, Then even will their shares turn up some shard,
Some fragmentary beauty of your past.
No matter how their adoration is,
You'll but remind them of their bounden chore;
To build, to strengthen, glorify thy name. No, love, my home, don't think I sing your dupe;
Though now I sing at day's last filtered light,
Though now I chant you praise in sunset's flame,
I sing not of your own descending sun; It's just that twilight's majesty is best.

Chapter 69

Another Milestone

After the shock of my brother's death, we were able to settle back into what we believed to be a pretty ordinary pattern of life. My mother enjoyed fairly good health now, after finally giving up her cigarette habit; and with a freshman and senior in college, just keeping in touch kept us occupied. We were thankful for the ordinary.

We had been in Wallace Wade stadium many many times during the past twenty seven years watching more football games than I could count, and on this day we were back sitting in the horseshoe end of the stadium, not on the sidelines or the fifty yard line, but in reserved seats to see our son receive his diploma from Duke University.

It too was a different scene, but one we were beginning to adjust to. There were grey caps and gowns slipped on over cut off blue jeans and bare chests, thongs for shoes, confetti throwing, champagne bottle caps popping, graduates celebrating in the craziest ways, each in his own way. They reserved respect and attention for the speakers and dignity for the procession, but they were bursting from an elevation of pride and accomplishment.

Duke students are well known for their ingenious tricks, and today the engineering students topped them all. Unknown to the speakers and audience was a wire stretched across the field, high in the air, reaching from a press box located on the east side of the field to a press box on the west. With perfect timing and precision and in almost slow motion, these zany students had rigged a sign half the width of the stadium, had run it out on the invisible wire, stopping it just behind the speaker's platform to create (what they thought was) the perfect backdrop for the graduation ceremony. The audience roared with laughter, the speakers didn't know what was going on. Their speeches were not that funny, but the gigantic "Go to hell, Carolina" banner displayed behind them was!

It was a brilliant sunny afternoon, the trees circling the stadium were

Another Milestone

weighted with the spring shades of green leaves, our hearts were overflowing with love and pride, and it was Mother's Day, 1979. I said to myself, "Oh, Bryant, Jr., what a wonderful gift, and what a glorious way to celebrate being your mother."

Allison and Bryant, Jr. came home for the summer again, faithful to their summer jobs and grateful for them. They had learned to appreciate the nest egg they accumulated during those months, and we were relieved each year when they announced to us they were coming home. We continued to bask in the ordinary weekends at Lake Gaston, charcoal steaks, and home-churned ice cream, bass fishing on the end of the pier, and heavenly barbecued chicken cookouts with Jesse, Bryant's brother, and his family. Jesse grilled and basted chicken in his own vinegar sauce, Millie baked fresh Vidalia onions, and our families enjoyed a feast on wooden picnic tables under the huge oak trees. We watched Millie and Jesse's daughters, Millicent and Sally Anne, grow to be vivacious teenagers. It seemed each year that they grew older, but we didn't.

We had known for several years Bryant, Jr.'s desire to become a lawyer and can remember the day and the peak of our happiness when he was accepted to the law school at Wake Forest University. He worked long and hard to achieve that goal but still had not become too independent to need his father and mother's help in setting up an apartment. He knew exactly how to make us feel needed. Allison returned to Duke in September, seasoned and ready for college life away from her big brother, and we moved Bryant, Jr. to Wake Forest to begin his long awaited journey through law school.

Chapter 70

A Strong Constitution

The journey we traveled with Allison and Bryant, Jr. through their college years was extremely satisfying. Our reward was being able to see them develop into intelligent, self-confident adults, possessing the courage to believe in themselves without losing the ability to be mindful of others. Just as they had brought us joy as children, they continued to as young adults. We shared the birthdays and holidays, exams, and frustrations; we rode high on the hills and deep into the valleys, and we shared our lives.

During this journey, we saw some of the scientific advantages coming from the space age — a progressing world of unbounded computers, complex electronics, improved and sharper television, and a food preservation process beneficial to everyone. With the development of cellular telephones and satellites, we were granted instant world communication. More and more women left the home and entered the workforce, creating the need for day care centers to nourish their offspring. The signs of affluence from easy credit was evident in all directions. It was difficult at times to comprehend this rapidly changing world.

This road of complacency was interrupted in November of 1980 by a sudden relapse in Mema's health. Our children were home to celebrate Bryant's birthday. Mema was not feeling quite up to par, so she was more than glad to spend the night with us, near her grandchildren and in the security of her family. We were all awakened in the early morning hours with the familiar sounds coming from our guest room of her frantically gasping for breath. Bryant, Jr. was the first one at her side. Realizing the acute problem, he lifted her up in bed to clear her air passage and talked her into breathing slowly, releasing the panic. It was truly a frightening experience, a helpless, weakening feeling of distress. With the aid of prompt assistance from the emergency medical technicians whom Bryant had called immediately, Mema was soon with oxygen. We admitted her to

A Strong Constitution

Nash General Hospital again into the constant care of our hospital family.

For the next three months, we hovered over her day and night. Sharing a vigilance, Bryant, Phoebe, Dan, Allison, Bryant, Jr. and I could only wait as her lungs weakened, and her condition deteriorated slowly each day. She was frail, confused and almost lifeless. Her shallow breathing barely moved the covers warming her gentle body. She was beyond seeing the flowers and cards decorating the window sill and table tops in the quiet sterile hospital room.

On February 2, I was given the only choice left after a critical day of placing Mother on a respirator for breathing. We were warned that she might never again be taken off that machine. (I remember the picture in my mind of the horrible polio epidemic when I was a teenager and how all of these polio victims were living in iron lungs.) I could not give her up, nor was I ready to accept this as a last resort. Instead, I asked to have her transferred to Duke Hospital for what I prayed would be a miracle. Just as most families, you try to do what is best, holding on to any thread of hope.

I drove to and from Duke Hospital, zombie-like, every day after that for conferences with her new physicians, thrilled to find my mother sitting in a chair, feeling, as the doctor described her, "as well as she can ever be," only three days after her admittance. They had taken her off all her medication, stabilized the level of oxygen, and though weak she was comfortable but thinking she was fine. She remained at Duke for two weeks. We then transferred her back to Nash General for two more weeks of stabilization and monitoring.

Her doctors at Duke had told us she couldn't possibly live more than two months, so I made arrangements for my Aunt Mary to come live in with Mother during that time. On March 3, she was back in her apartment pulling behind her from room to room twenty feet of plastic cannula connected to an oxygen tank, her lifeline. She thought of nothing but recuperating while we waited silently for the doctors' prognosis. Two and a half months later, my aunt announced to me that she had to return home; and with spunk in her voice, Mema informed me that she could take care of herself if we would only stop doting on her.

I was petrified to leave her, but Bryant convinced me that we needed to give her the opportunity to try, so Mother took over. With daily attention and care, she regained more strength and courage, determined not to die but to live. The trauma subsided and our thoughts turned to a wedding.

Chapter 71

Our First Wedding

We had known for nearly five months of our son's plans to be married.

That particular weekend visit was a pleasant one for us all after getting a slight reprieve from Mema's illness. Allison and Bryant, Jr. were both at home to check on their grandmother, and Bryant decided that the timing was right for a quick adventure.

"We all need some seafood, and there's no better place for fried shrimp and hush puppies than Tony's at Morehead," he declared that Saturday at breakfast.

It was the first time just the four of us had been together in quite a while. Maybe we were ready for some adventures, maybe some space. Our college students were accommodating, falling for their daddy's suggestion hook, line, and sinker.

Like a great escape, we drove through downtown Kinston past all of the landmarks we were familiar with, on to New Bern counting the many church steeples and towers as we passed over the Trent River bridge, through the busy section of Havelock and Cherry Point filled on a Saturday morning with the hustle and bustle of marine life, crew cuts and fast little cars. The stroll from our parked car along the waterfront at Morehead City showed signs of an early spring at the coast. The fishermen, scrubbing and hosing down their boats, a few tourists clad in warm sweatshirts, sea gulls dipping and diving and hovering, waiting to be fed, and the smell of the salt air and frying seafood on this cool day made each of us long for summer.

The ride after our lunch along the ocean from Atlantic Beach to Emerald Isle brought back many memories of vacations here. Bryant had a pipe dream of owning property at the beach some day, and we soon realized he had an ulterior motive for bringing us to the picturesque point on the end of this island that afternoon. He parked the car just off the road, careful not to get too far into the sand; and for almost an hour we

Our First Wedding

walked over a beautiful lot he dreamed of buying, over the high dunes and through the tall sea grasses onto the beach along the breaking ocean rushing and foaming at our feet.

Nobody wanted to leave (the feeling we always shared while visiting the seashore), but the day was growing shorter, and the practical thing to do was to get started for home. Our tennis shoes were wet from the surf and our feet were getting cold, but our hearts were warm and full of love as we climbed back over the sand dunes to our car. The heater felt good, and Allison and Bryant, Jr. began dreading the ride back to school the next day, so we were anxious to try to get back to Rocky Mount before too late.

Bryant and I never really rested until we heard from Allison and Bryant, Jr. on Sunday nights after they returned to school, giving us a safe and sound report. The sound of their voices was always sweet relief. Bryant, Jr.'s call came around ten o'clock with a safe report, but he had saved the news of wanting to get married until he called. He had spent the entire weekend at home without telling us (that must have been why he came), so we realized how difficult it was for him to break this news to us. It came as a total shock and certainly one we were not prepared for. This was so unlike Bryant, Jr. with his considerate manner and analytical thinking; it left us speechless.

Our first approach was to meet and discuss their plans in the manner our family was accustomed to doing. It was agreed that we would meet him and his fianceé for dinner the next night in Durham, half way for each of us from Winston-Salem. We could include Allison and share the surprise news with her.

"If you've come to tell us we can't do it, it won't do any good," was Bryant, Jr.'s greeting immediately when he saw us in the restaurant that night. So unlike the son we knew, on guard, so bold, so abrupt. We realized at that moment the influence this young girl had on our only son's life.

"Son, we've come to hear your plans. Let's sit down and enjoy each other," Bryant responded, hoping for an avenue of warmth and better communication.

We listened to their opinions and their plans. They seemed to think the timing was right even though he had another year before completing law school. They had decided on a date.

Bryant, Jr. and his fianceé were married on an extremely hot and humid day in August of 1981. It was a lovely wedding, in the impressive and majestic Gothic style Duke Chapel, towering above all other structures on the campus of Duke University. Our hometown minister and friend came from Rocky Mount to officiate, making it even more personal for us.

For All The World To See

There were pretty bridesmaids and handsome groomsmen, sweet smelling summer flowers, and thrilling, moving, vibrating music from the Flentrop organ echoing in this great hall of worship. Mema was there, carefully placed with Phoebe and Dan, sitting proudly in her wheelchair at the very front of the outer isle, a miracle in itself, her being able to come.

I thought to myself, choking back tears as I watched alone from my assigned seat on the front pew, my handsome son winking down at me telling me with his crystal blue eyes not to cry — What young girl would not be thrilled to be handed on her wedding day this package: an abundance of God's richest blessings, a husband who loved her, a family with open hearts and proud of a strong heritage, good health and security, and an extended family of loyal and supportive friends surrounding her? Not all are so fortunate.

The setting was perfect, the day blissful and harmonious and filled with rich emotion. We believed that God had blessed us with someone who was happy to be a part of our family.

Destinies
Like warp and woof all destinies
Are woven fast,
Link'd in sympathy like the
keys of an organ vast;
Pluck one thread, and the web
ye mar;
Break but one
Of a thousand keys, and the
paining jar Through all will run.

– John Greenleaf Whittier

Chapter 72

Allene

Mothers don't get sick, or at least that's what I thought when I was little. It gave me a safe feeling and chased away the fear of ever losing mine. However, age happens to all of us, and changes everything.

When Dan and I moved east, it put me closer to Jean, but farther away from my mother. This made it difficult to see her often. She was not a seasoned traveler, which meant it was like pulling hens' teeth to get her to Rocky Mount. Now, she would never make the trip again. Mother had always enjoyed good health, but since the summer of 1980 she had been fighting cancer. Now, as I drove toward Asheville, almost two years later, I was grateful for this Easter vacation to be with her. There was no way for me to be prepared for what I found when I arrived at the little house on Clairmont Avenue. Her sister, Audrie, who had been staying with her, told me on the phone the week before that she was not doing well, but I never dreamed she was this bad. She looked so frail that I was afraid to hug her. A white terry cloth turban covered what was left of her beautiful natural curly hair. I wanted to scream. My precious mother's life being stolen by this hateful disease that shows no mercy. I was sickened by the thought of watching another loved one die because of it.

Each day that week, she grew weaker, but we laughed and visited like we always had. I hung a basket of hanging geraniums on the porch outside her bedroom window and she enjoyed seeing them.

One afternoon, just before she dropped off to sleep, she looked at me and said, "You know what I miss?"

"No, Mama, what?"

"I miss my birds. You've been feeding them, haven't you?"

"Yes, Mama, they've been fed," I answered.

While she was sleeping, I moved one of her bird feeders to the front yard. She was so thrilled when she woke up, but not one dumb bird showed up that afternoon. Guess I confused them by moving their food supply.

For All The World To See

Early the next morning, I found some of Mama's corn bread she kept stored in an old JFG coffee can to feed her feathered friends and made a trail of it to the feeder's new location. "If they don't follow that they are really dumb," I said to myself. "That stuff's good enough to make their tongues slap their brains out eating it." When I told Mama what I had done, and my thoughts while I did it, she laughed till she cried. It worked though, for by mid-morning we had birds!

One week later, Mama was gone. While I waited at her house that evening for friends and family to arrive, I walked around the house looking at things the way she had left them. Pictures of my daddy, of Dan and me, of Susan and Dan, Jr. were everywhere. She could not have looked anywhere in any direction without one of us smiling back at her. In her bedroom, there hung a picture of me in a white cap and gown holding a diploma. It was high school graduation. I felt warm tears roll down my face as I thought about Susan graduating from senior high in two months. Her senior year had been fun for all of us. She had been a cheerleader since junior high, which meant Dan and I had spent many hours on bleachers around the area. In the past two years, her cheerleading squad had won a number of trophies in competitions, and this year the Rocky Mount Senior High basketball team won the 4-A championship.

Susan had a happy spirit that was infectious. She never went through a moody, withdrawn phase like some teenagers. She listened to us and never acted intimidated or threatened by our advice. Sometimes after we talked something over, she would hug me and say, "I love you, Mama. Best friends forever."

Not until this moment, looking at this picture of myself, had I allowed myself to think about our nest being empty soon. Mother had been thrilled when I called her in February to tell her Susan was going to be a Peace girl, too. In the course of our conversation, she had said, "Maybe she will find her Jean."

On April 21, 1982, Allene Elizabeth Ray Fair was laid to rest. It was a sunny spring day, the kind she loved.

Dan, Jr. looked very handsome in his Marine dress uniform. After three years of college, he had decided to join the Marine Corps. It was a good move for him because he was uncertain about a profession.

That night after everything was over, Susan and Daniel were visiting in the living room while Jean, Bryant, Dan, and I sat around Mama's dining room table drinking a cup of decaf.

I looked at Jean and said, "What am I going to do with all the stuff in this house? I don't know where to begin."

"Ruum, why don't we all go back home tomorrow? You need to get away from all this for awhile. Take a week at home to think, and then you and I will come back and clear this house out."

I took her advice.

Chapter 73

You Gotta Let It Go

Jean and I were actually looking forward to the six hour drive to Asheville that Monday morning. We had not been away by ourselves like this for a long, long time. As we passed the hospital on our way out of town I said, "Good-bye, Dan and Bryant," and we laughed about how we had tried not to act too excited about leaving. We turned off US 64 onto Highway 98. The countryside was very green. Cattle grazing in the morning sunlight gave us a feeling of calm. Just outside of Bunn, I asked Jean with a serious tone in my voice, "Shall we take the Bunn by-pass or go the business route?"

"By all means, let's take the by-pass. We don't want to hit the morning rush," Jean quipped.

(The by-pass was a two-tenths of a mile dirt road short cut which enabled us to miss the left hand turn at the small farming community's crossroads.)

Then she said, "We're acting like a couple of fools."

On through Wake Forest, past the old college campus where Dan spent a year, Durham, Burlington, Greensboro, we were oblivious to the world outside the car. We decided to have lunch in Winston-Salem. The break gave us new energy. We were good for three more hours.

As we approached Hickory, I told Jean to get ready to see the mountains. In the blink of an eye, there they were rising before us in all their majesty. We were almost there.

The familiar driveway felt strange as I drove up and parked the car. Mama wasn't standing at the kitchen window watching for us. She didn't run out the back door with outstretched arms, laughing, hugging, kissing. The lump in my throat felt like it was the size of a grapefruit. Jean sensed what I was feeling and sat quietly with me for a moment.

When our moist eyes met, she said, "Now, Ruum, we can't do this all week. Allene wouldn't like that."

Suddenly, the reality of why we were here hit us.

You Gotta Let It Go

The afternoon sun streamed through the large kitchen window just as it always had. Mama's African violets still sat on the wide window sill. Everything looked the same. Jean and I began opening drapes, windows, and the front door — anything that let in light and fresh air. In no time at all, we were settled in, ready to evaluate the situation. The decision was made to start upstairs and work down. The attic, our first goal, was small, but we soon learned it held an amazing amount of things Mama deemed important enough to keep.

"Look at this, Ruum," Jean said with amusement in her voice. "These suit boxes are full of tissue paper. Can you believe that?"

"Yes, I believe it. Over here, I've found over thirty hat boxes. She has saved every hat she bought for the last twenty years it looks like."

"The handwriting on this box is mine," Jean said, surprised. "It's your wedding dress," she continued as she opened the box.

There, wrapped in black and navy blue tissue paper, lay the chantilly lace gown Jean and I had worn as young brides.

The next morning, I found Jean cleaning out the refrigerator. With two eggs, bits of vegetables and cheese, she made the best omelet I have ever tasted. A steaming cup of coffee made it perfect. We could not allow ourselves the luxury of lingering too long, tempting as it was. There was much to be done.

Dan and Bryant called daily to check on us and our progress. It was always good to hear from them and how things were in Rocky Mount.

Each day, the light at the end of the tunnel grew brighter. We worked constantly, packing, taping, and labeling boxes and dividing everything into three categories: keep it, throw it away, and take it to the Salvation Army.

The kitchen was saved for last. "How many meals do you suppose my mother cooked in this little kitchen?" I asked Jean as we stood pondering our next move.

"Now, wouldn't Allene be proud of us for using all that tissue paper she saved to pack her dishes," Jean said lightheartedly trying to ease the pain of this depressing task.

We packed the last box we had gotten at the liquor store. All week long we had worked through her things. Teasing comments, like "well, Allene, if you aren't the prissy one with all these fancy evening clothes" made by Jean when we emptied her closets, helped get us through each day. In three and a half days, we had managed to pack-up, give, or throw away all the worldly possessions my parents had accumulated in a lifetime.

Friday morning before we left, I walked through the house for a last minute check. Each room looked stripped and bare. Last night, I had found a box pushed back in the dark corner of a closet. Inside it were pictures, letters from Daniel and Susan, Mother's Day and birthday cards from us, a few letters from me, and one from Dan written a few weeks after we were married. Across the top of this box my mother had written, "Precious Memories." For me, the feeling of home in this place was now only precious memories.

How dear to this heart
are the scenes of
my childhood,
When fond recollection presents them to view:
The orchard, the meadow, the deep-tangled wildwood,
And every lov'd spot which my infancy knew.

—Woodworth

Chapter 74

That Last Year

Her little grey Ford Pinto station wagon was loaded to over-flowing with clothes and shoes, boxes of books, and the yellow metal file cabinet, the faithful portable typewriter, a small television set, and bright yellow, green, and royal blue polka dot pillows she planned to use for decorating her room as well as the compact refrigerator she had inherited from her brother. The 1978 station wagon was probably not the car she might have wanted for her twentieth birthday, but she never let us know, and it was what we could afford at the time. The '63 Comet had been retired to our driveway in Rocky Mount, and Allison needed safer transportation. She had her little car packed carefully, ready to leave for her senior year at Duke. Allison had been there just long enough to appreciate fully being a college student and that carefree stage in her life, so the realization of finishing and the anticipation of parting saddened her.

She and Shawn, her cute roommate for three years, were taking single rooms as seniors but on the same hall. They had become wonderful and loyal friends just as we had all hoped, but they decided to venture out and give each other some privacy during their final year. Allison had to report to school a week early to help with freshman orientation and she was anxious to get her own private room in order; so she gathered all of the things a college student needed for comfortable living in a dormitory during those days.

Of course, Bryant and I were not satisfied with sending her off alone to get set up. She needed us there to help unload, and her daddy had to install the window fan and make sure all of the extension cords were connected properly. She couldn't possibly get her curtains hung and place all of those decorator pillows without her mother's help. Allison was a gentle and perceptive daughter; and knowing that this was our last chance to fix up her dormitory room, she assured us of her constant need for our help, conscious more of our needs than hers.

She continued through the year with absolute enthusiasm just as she had begun it, studying to complete her degree in elementary education, practice teaching, working at a part-time on-campus job, and participating in sorority and university activities. Maybe like her grandmother, Allison enjoyed a surprise. At Thanksgiving, it was announced on the national news that she had been selected to participate in the National Maid of Cotton Selection in Memphis, Tennessee. There were only fifteen young women selected from the United States to compete for this title as a spokesperson for the National Cotton Council. It was a surprise to everyone! Even Phoebe heard the news on television, and it had been hard to keep this from her, but this was the way the cotton council handled the selection announcement.

We had one month to put together a complete all cotton wardrobe for the competition. The rest of the arrangements were made and sent to us by the cotton council.

We celebrated Christmas four weeks later with the Crouches and Mema. It was the very first year without having our son at home on Christmas morning and a hard adjustment, but the excitement of our expense paid trip to Memphis with Allison and our call from Bryant, Jr. early Christmas morning helped.

Bryant and I accepted the fact that our twenty-fifth wedding anniversary three days after Christmas would be celebrated at another time. There was too much going on. We were to leave for Memphis on December 27, and being with Allison was certainly more important than an anniversary. We would be together anyway, and that was important in itself.

I can remember the slipping in and out of the house preparing for the trip, but I was unaware of our home filling with family and friends for a surprise anniversary party Allison and Bryant, Jr. had planned for us the night of December 26. I think they even caught me in hair curlers. (I never could understand how they accomplished this, but I feel sure that Mema and Phoebe were in on the plot.)

That trip to Memphis was but another bright memory we had the privilege of sharing with our daughter, Allison. We enjoyed the glamour of the occasion, mingling with celebrities at the elegant dinner dances and meeting families from all over the United States. Memphis is a lovely city, the largest in Tennessee, and stretches along the east bank of the Mississippi River. We were treated with a panoramic view of this flowing and active river from our hotel window. Lunches and fashion shows at the historic Peabody Hotel, watching their famous ducks parade from the

That Last Year

elevator to the fountain and pool located in the center of the grand lobby, shopping along Beale Street, and touring the cotton market gave us a great glimpse of the city's heritage. We watched proudly the final evening of the selection as Allison spoke with intelligence, grace and charm of her feelings and rewards from teaching handicapped children. She spoke to an audience of fifteen hundred people from the magnificent old stage of the now restored and famous Orpheum Theatre. Winning would have meant giving up school for a full year of travel throughout the world to help promote the cotton industry, so as much as we saw the extraordinary opportunity, we were frightened at the thought. At the end of the evening, she was declared the runner-up, not quite the top, but oh what a mountain she had climbed.

We couldn't leave Memphis without a visit to Elvis Presley's home, Graceland, and the detour by there on our way to the airport the next day was well worth the effort. It was quite remarkable to find the varied and unusual signs of hero worship so evident even then. Fresh flowers, pictures, gifts, notes, and letters laid on his grave as well as wreaths from fan clubs all over the United States. It was interesting for us to see one there from Tarboro, N.C., so close to our home town of Rocky Mount.

We had absorbed it all and painted a memory like the many colors of oil on a canvas. We returned to North Carolina and home, but we never fly over the Mississippi River without a sudden flash of that joy we shared in Memphis.

We found Mema continuing to do well, for which we were all grateful. She was still able to care for herself and keep up with her many medications, thanks to a chart Phoebe helped me plot out showing the hours of the day and the specific medications she checked off. It was always amusing to watch how skillfully she maneuvered around her tiny apartment always hooked to her lifeline of oxygen, and it was satisfying for me to see her still proud and dignified.

We had all worried about Phoebe's mother, Allene, whose health failed so quickly. Phoebe had been so much help to me always with Mema, but there was little we could do for Allene. Everyday, we had prayed for a miracle hoping she would improve and live free from suffering. We knew this was another stage in our lives of watching our parents age and possibly become ill. So many of our friends were feeling the same pain.

The warmth of spring was finally ushered in with jonquils and azaleas, green grass, and Boston ferns in hanging baskets appearing gradually on front and side proches. Soon came May Day, and Susan Crouch's eighteenth birthday. (Could that be? Phoebe and I were only eighteen when we first met. I wondered if our daughters might someday be close enough to their college roommates to see each other's children reach that age.) For our family, the most spectacular spring event would be more graduations.

Again, it was Mother's Day when we gathered with hundreds of happy parents to participate in another Duke graduation exercise. The sun was shining brightly, and it was another very warm and humid day in Durham. Different today from Bryant, Jr.'s graduation held in the football stadium, Allison's was set up on the quadrangle of East Campus with hundreds of chairs on the lawn surrounded by the Georgian architecture. What could possibly make a more precious and lasting gift for a mother on Mother's Day than to see her children receive a college diploma? It was another beautiful day in our repertoire of happy days as Allison graciously accepted her degree, and we knew in our hearts that we had helped make it possible for both of our children to have a priceless gift that no one could ever take away.

Our celebrating was not over. In another week, we were on our way to Wake Forest University to see our son receive his law degree. It was a glorious time for our family — more caps and gowns and inspirational speeches, more pride and joy for deserving young people. They had once again achieved an important goal.

Chapter 75

The World's Fair

It was hard getting back to a normal routine again. For five weeks, I had been on an emotional roller coaster.

Dan and I were having dinner with Jean and Bryant at a local restaurant the week after my return to work. They had been telling us about Allison and Bryant, Jr.'s graduations. I had just said, "It is good to talk about a happy occasion for a change," when Bryant changed the subject by saying, "I think it is time for the four of us to take a few days off to relax and have some fun!"

"Oh no! What wonderful venture do you have in mind for us this time?" I said laughing.

"Well, as you know, the 1982 World's Fair opened the first of this month in Knoxville, Tennessee. I think it would be a shame for us to be this close and not go. What do you think?"

Two weeks later, we were on our way to Knoxville. We tried to do some homework on what to see by reading information sent to us by our nephew who was in the tour bus business in Asheville. "Energy Turns the World" was the fair's theme.

There were exhibits from twenty three countries, numerous corporations, and several states. China had a special museum filled with treasures, including two-ton bricks from the Great Wall. The Egyptian pavilion had a chariot belonging to Pharaoh Ramses II, and the Japanese, not to be outdone, had robots greeting their visitors and speaking in various languages. The United States pavilion was the largest at the fair. It was a six story structure built over a man-made lake in the middle of the fairgrounds. Inside were many different examples of energy, from wood burning to a solar collector that powered the building's air conditioning and hot water system. The theater had a movie screen seven stories high which was ranked as the world's largest. However, the most outstanding structure on the fairgrounds was the 266-foot sun sphere. Its exterior glass elevators carried us to observation decks, and in the sphere on top, covered with glass that had been tinted with 24-karat gold dust, there was a two-story restaurant.

A friend of Jean and Bryant's had given them four passes to the V.I.P. restaurant at the top of the sun sphere. Sunday afternoon, we returned to our rooms early to dress for dinner. Truly, the best was yet to come. From the moment we stepped off the elevator into the plush entrance to the restaurant, we were treated like royalty. Our personal waiter, a student at the University of Tennessee, was one of nine young men chosen for this job and was specially trained to serve the celebrities who were expected to attend the fair. We dined in elegance at a table perfectly set with fine linens complete with crystal knife rest. As we watched the sun set over the pavilions, the fading day light transformed the fairgrounds into a sea of color flashing and blinking below us.

The five course epicurean dinner was ended dramatically three hours later by our waiter creating an arc of flame from cup to cup with the Irish coffee. As we drank the exotic blend, we were fascinated by the Federal Express laser beam show piercing the dark evening sky.

We were brought down from our mountain top into the valley quickly upon our return home. Jean was met with the news that Mema's condition had worsened again. Allison had admitted her to the hospital that afternoon.

Once again after being away for pleasure, Jean came home to another trauma.

Chapter 76

Paddling About

Time passed, Mema stabilized and was able to go home from the hospital but only for two weeks before we had to take her back. With this last hospitalization, we were faced with a decision we had hoped to avoid, but there seemed to be no alternative. We were told that she could no longer live alone. She would need twenty-four hour monitoring and supervision for administering her medications, and it was crucial that her oxygen level be kept exact at all hours.

There is a certain amount of denial that goes along with making the decision to place your mother into a nursing home. Right up until the very last minute, you keep believing that there has to be another way, this won't really happen, she'll be okay and won't have to live out her days like that. It's a heart wrenching realization of life, of the shortness of time, of holding on, of guilt and love, and of finally knowing that you're doing the best you can and glad you're able to be there for one who desperately depends on you. We had to make it right.

Bryant spent several days making contacts, and because of his position he was familiar with the procedures and acquainted with the administrators at the local nursing homes. We visited several, and I still could not imagine my mother living in these places, dark and crowded, smelling of different odors from hall to hall. After only a few days of investigating, Bryant called and I could deny no longer. A bed became available for Mema, and we needed to go immediately to see it and make the final decision. Although it was not what we wanted to do, we knew it was right, and an answer to our prayers.

The nursing home was located only one mile from our house, attractive, light and cheery (as they go), and the perfect double room near the nurses' station. Mother's bed was next to a large picture window with a view of a small garden and a bird feeder. We had been told that we could bring in small personal items, and my mind literally raced with ideas to make it as comfortable as possible. The decision was made. This was to be

Mema's new home.

Breaking the news to her was our next difficult task. Even though we had carefully prepared her for this possibility, she didn't want to accept it, was hurt and angry, but tried to understand. This is not an easy move for anybody. I could only hope that in time she would be happy. I knew she would be safe and well taken care of, so we began the next day bringing into her new home the overstuffed swivel rocker, television, clothing, and personal items we decided she needed for comfort. We provided floral sheets like home, hung her favorite pictures, her sewing box for mending, and a floor lamp for reading and crocheting. She had every convenience and was surrounded with as much familiarity as possible. The next afternoon, we carried her to her new home.

Soon, the days turned into weeks and the weeks into months, and with my daily twice-a-day visits and little afternoon excursions, Mema's condition improved and her attitude began to change. Her sisters and friends came, Phoebe and Dan came, Allison was there everyday, and she enjoyed the constant attention. It was obvious we had not "put her away" but had given her a safe haven. I learned to live with the criticism coming from those who didn't understand and tolerated their different ideas for her care. She adjusted. We all adjusted. She had the love and support of a family and good friends, and with God's help this little corner in our lives grew brighter. With this security, Mema soon became the queen of the nursing home; she was the contented, safe little spirit paddling about in her very own wheelchair visiting her neighbors from room to room and spreading cheer which was returned to her threefold.

Chapter 77

A Step Back in Time

It is possible that each of us will have the opportunity to attend a graduation of some kind more than once if we live long enough. Most would agree that they are basically the same. The same, that is, until you are a parent, and it is your child who rises to accept the diploma. For a few brief moments, it becomes very special and exciting. So it was with us again when Susan received her high school diploma on June 11, 1982. The preceding week she had been the recipient of the Most Valuable Cheerleader award — another proud moment for us on awards day. The ceremonies ended, and high school days were a thing of the past in our family. There had been the gathering of family and friends, gifts, and picture taking. All that was left were the tearful good-byes. Young girls promising never to forget each other and to stay in touch always. As I watched and snapped more pictures, thoughts of high school friends I had felt this same way about crossed my mind for the first time in years. Where in the world are they today, I wondered? The cycle never changes, only the names and faces.

Susan was happy to have had her big brother home for her graduation. His new duty station in Charleston, S.C., didn't allow him to get home often.

1981 seemed to be the best year Daniel could have chosen to join the Marine Corps. Our newly elected President Ronald Reagan was in his second year of office now. He had made patriotism popular again, and our country had a more positive attitude toward the men and women serving in the military. President Reagan was very personable and very well liked. Where else but in America could a former movie star become President?

On March 30, 1981, our country was shocked as once again we listened to television bulletin reports that our President had been shot. "How could this be happening again?" we were all asking.

As President Reagan had walked to his car, six shots were fired. One of the bullets hit him in the chest. Three other men were wounded, also.

For All The World To See

Fortunately, there was a hospital nearby where he received immediate treatment. It was reported that he said, "I hope you're all Republicans," to the surgeons who operated on him. John Henkley, Jr., the man who committed this terrible act, was found not guilty by reason of insanity on all charges after a year and a half of examinations and trial.

Only ten weeks after Susan's high school graduation, the little AMC Spirit with her at the wheel rolled out of our driveway. Her large Raggedy Ann doll sat in the rear window smiling back at us as we followed behind her.

Susan had been assigned a second floor room in Main to be shared with two other girls. The moment I saw it, I realized it had been the infirmary when Jean and I were at Peace. I told Susan that Jean had been in this room many times to have her sore throat painted with Merthiolate. What a madhouse that room was for a few hours. Three moms decorating their own daughter's corner, three dads moving furniture and hanging curtain rods, and three excited girls unpacking suitcases and boxes. Dan and I were the last to leave. Everything was hung, unpacked, and put in place in Susan's corner of the room. The white muslin curtains tied back with yellow, green, and blue ribbon hung at the large windows. On her bed, we had put the bright yellow bedspread and placed cross stitch pillows I had made around Raggedy Ann. It looked exactly as we had pictured.

It was time for us to leave. Susan walked with us to our car. The time I had been dreading for weeks finally came. We made our good-byes brief. As we waited for a break in the traffic to exit the parking lot, I watched our beautiful daughter walk up the long brick walk leading back to her dorm. She turned to wave and blow kisses until we were out of sight. Was this the way my mother felt so long ago? Yes, I'm sure it was. I cried all the way home.

Chapter 78

Rewards

Another summer had passed almost before we knew it. I was amused as I thought about the question that people, mostly younger women, asked of me frequently, "What do you do with all of your free time now that your children are no longer at home?" It seemed that as I grew older time passed faster and our concerns were bigger and more far reaching. Free time was a premium. We had spent this entire summer taking care of Mema's needs. It was a time in our lives, another stage of awareness, and what sometimes begins as an insurmountable problem, with patience, usually ends on a high note, and this unusual summer had.

Bryant, Jr. had taken the bar exam. He announced to us, too, that we were to be grandparents the next spring. (This came as a big surprise. Bryant and I wondered if we were ready for that phase in our lives.) He and his wife had moved to Greenville in August where he was to begin a law practice, and Allison had readied herself for another year of schooling. Before her graduation from Duke, she was accepted into graduate school at the University of North Carolina where she planned to obtain a master's degree in special education. Her love and compassion for handicapped children had ultimately directed her toward this goal.

Every family needs a pick-up truck for life. If only we had known how many moves we would make and how many times we would move our children, we surely would have invested in a pick-up truck. We have probably paid enough in U-Haul rental fees to pay for one, but we wouldn't have had it any other way. Helping our children move and seeing them settled happily was always a comfort and a joy to us. So, soon after helping Bryant, Jr. get established in their apartment in Greenville, we proceeded to move Allison to Chapel Hill. She had been fortunate in finding an apartment to share with two of her friends. They had already furnished it with pretty white wicker, big fluffy bright Chintz cushions, and all of the accessories to make it warm and homey. She only needed furnishings for

For All The World To See

her bedroom, so the parents of her friends certainly lightened our load.

Another new experience began for Allison, and we returned once again to our empty nest. After four years, we had grown accustomed to the peace and quietness of our home, and with each year we appreciated this serenity more and more.

It was Phoebe and Dan's turn now to face an empty nest. They had taken Susan away to college, Phoebe was back at work, and I knew the ache she carried with her each day missing her daughter. I understood and she knew it, so many afternoons after she finished work we consoled each other. She always knew where to find me, nearly every afternoon in Mema's room at the nursing home. We soon found this to be a good retreat, a place to slow down and be still with no feelings of guilt for doing so. We gathered for our visits with her to laugh and cheer each other, all the time watching in amazement as Mother sat in a cross-legged position, Indian style, in the middle of her bed, making room for me to sit on the foot and giving up her rocker to Phoebe. We listened and grew from Mema's little words of wisdom, sharing our life with her and reminisced about our days at Peace College. We promised Mema that someday we would return together and stroll through the halls so familiar and significant to us. Eventually, our biggest decision after visiting with Mema was where Dan and Bryant could take us for dinner — hidden benefits of the empty nest syndrome.

Allison continued to bring fun and excitement into our lives, and with each new surprise and experience that we shared, we became closer and closer. Surely, one of God's richest rewards is that of a close and understanding relationship with your children. She was home for the weekend to celebrate her twenty-second birthday that September and also to get our advice on entering the Miss Rocky Mount Scholarship Pageant (the possibility of another bright adventure she brought to our attention). After lengthy discussions of the pros and cons and days of telephone calls and apprehension, we were convinced that it would be a nice opportunity for scholarship monies and a maturing experience. She had signed a professional modeling contract after graduating from Duke, so she was not camera shy and enjoyed the challenge of public speaking, all important attributes if she should win the title. She now would be faced with the challenge of balancing her time as a full time graduate student, a part-time model, and a beauty pageant contestant.

And in six short weeks, in her steady and confident manner, she did exactly that, fulfilling every requirement and obligation. We pulled together a wardrobe for each required appearance, high heeled shoes, bathing suits, perfectly matching accessories, and glittering gowns for her stage appearance. She practiced and honed her piano skills, and in early November in time for pageant night, she was poised and relaxed, prepared, and ready.

The high school auditorium where the pageant was being held was humming with an incessant buzz when we arrived, filling gradually with families, friends, well wishers, and press. We took our seats on the reserved front row next to the long runway surrounded close by with family and with Phoebe and Dan directly behind us, and Phoebe keeping her Kodak Disc camera clicking as fast as the tiny disc film would revolve. Shawn and her parents were there from Graham as a surprise for Allison.

The curtain finally rose, and the show began. For the next three hours, we watched twelve lovely young women do their best appearing in bathing suits, evening gowns, and performing their chosen talent, each one trying hard to be the winner. The entertainment was over, the questions answered, and the electrifying moment finally came, and there was no question about it. Appearing in the borrowed red shimmering pageant gown with tiny spaghetti straps over her bare shoulders, her long hair piled high on her head with glittering rhinestone earrings, Allison was the true winner. Miss Rocky Mount 1982-83, graceful and elegant, her cheerful blue eyes sparkling as she looked down at us, accepted her crown.

The excitement subsided, and we had visions of the Miss North Carolina competition. We left the auditorium and walked into the cold November night air and blindly into the world of pageant people.

We went straight to the nursing home. It was very late, but we knew Mema was waiting.

Chapter 79

Out of the Fold

The four of us decided to spend a quiet New Year's Eve together. Dan and I joined Jean and Bryant at their house for dinner. We watched one of the many televised football games while we relaxed by the fire and recalled special moments of the holidays. When the game ended, Bryant switched to the channel carrying the Time Square celebration in New York. A new year was moments away. We watched the huge ball begin its descent. The last seconds of 1982 were ticking away. When 1983 flashed on the screen, a deafening roar rose from the sea of humanity gathered there. Another year had begun. We toasted each other with wishes of love, good health, and many more years of being together.

Dan and I had enjoyed having our children all to ourselves for the holidays. We were free to talk, laugh, discuss any topic, do spur of the moment things, just sit and read, or watch television. Daniel had wanted to bring his new girlfriend home, but we had said no. However, it did not take long to realize he was more serious about her than we thought. This led to many probing conversations about her and her family. Much to our dismay, we soon concluded that our influence on Daniel's decision was a big fat zero. We could have talked until we were blue in the face, but his mind was made up. The night he returned to Charleston, he confessed to us that his Christmas gift to her had been an engagement ring. They planned to marry in May.

I informed Jean of the wedding plans during one of our after school visits that following week. She was as full of questions as I had been. Unfortunately, we were still in the dark about the whole situation. "Dan, Jr. and his bride-to-be are coming for a visit near the end of January. Maybe we will know more then," I told her.

The weekend visit came and went well. Dan, Jr. and his betrothed seemed to be at ease. On Sunday, we drove to Raleigh for Susan to meet her future sister-in-law. On the way home, I noticed that our young couple in the back seat had suddenly gotten very quiet. The atmosphere had changed. When we arrived home, Dan, Jr. said they wanted to go for a ride around town. "Don't be gone too long because I'll have supper ready soon," I requested. One hour later, they returned. Dan, Jr. walked into the family room, turned the television off, and asked us to listen to what he had to say without interruption. We could not imagine what had happened or what he was going to say. They've called the wedding off, I thought. That would be wonderful! She is so young, only nineteen. I was nineteen, but that was different. A million thoughts were racing through my mind in a matter of seconds, but I never came close to what our son nervously blurted out!

"Mama, Daddy, we are married! We were married this past Wednesday afternoon."

The whole weekend had been a charade. We had been taken in by their game of deception. It hurt us deeply not to be included, to be left out, but it was done and nothing would be gained by expressing those feelings at this time.

> *"Oh my son's my son till he gets him a wife,*
> *But my daughter's my daughter all her life."*

— Denah Maria Mulock Crath

Chapter 80

Taylor

We woke that morning to spring's beginning. Although the calendar said it was spring, there was still a lingering chill in the air and especially in the mornings. A turtleneck and sweater, maybe a cardigan, would still feel good, I told myself as I began hurrying to dress for the day. I couldn't call Phoebe at school; her principal didn't like that. Dan would just have to tell her where we were. Bryant was on his way home from work, and I was pacing the floor wondering when he would arrive. The bed was made, the kitchen was in order, and the strewn newspapers from the evening before and breakfast had all been picked up. There was nothing left to do but wait.

Bryant, Jr. had called after eleven o'clock to say they were on their way to the hospital. His sweet voice was total excitement and wonder.

"Mama, there's no need for you to rush over here; it could be hours. We're fine, but if you can come, that would be great."

I assured him without hesitation that we would be there as soon as we could get ready.

I was overcome by a sudden rushing wave of excitement and could barely speak as I heard him say, "I love you, Mama. You and Daddy be careful."

There was no way we weren't going to be there.

I heard the car door slam shut in the garage. Bryant was home, coming through the back door as I came down the stairs. He knew I was about to burst with so many emotions. We hugged and could only smile. "Grandparents! You'll need a coat," he said.

We rode through Rocky Mount so thankful to get across the train tracks that divided the town in half without having to stop for a long Amtrak passenger train likely to pass through at this hour of the day. We breathed a sigh of relief as we left the city streets behind and watched the narrow highway to Greenville rise before us. We were on our way to be with our son and to await the birth of our first grandchild. It all came back like a flash — that morning our son was born on New Year's Day. We were so young; the labor pains, Mema, wheeling me into the emergency room from the car, dressed in that beige flowered corduroy maternity top, so much relief, so much wonder, and now our first born waiting as we did for their first born. I stared into the enormous clear blue sky and prayed silently, "Oh, God, please be with us all, take care of our children, and please let our baby be all right."

We made the left turn in the little town of Pinetops past the junk store on the left. I wondered how some places and things just never seem to change. I was always curious about all of that old junk lining the sidewalk in front of that place. What seemed to be utterly ridiculous to me was surely someone else's treasures. One day Phoebe and I will come exploring and go in there, I thought. Bryant drove right by the service station, one of his favorite stops for ole timey hand-dipped ice cream without even a mention of food. It occurred to me that we had not eaten lunch, but that could wait. We didn't have far to go now.

Soon, the sight of the hospital was before us, surrounded by an expanse of parking lots filled, it seemed, to capacity with every type of car imaginable. Bryant stopped before a gate to retrieve his parking pass. The electronic box spit out a ticket, the large arm of the gate flew open, and we could finally park.

Bryant was familiar with Greenville's hospital, so within seconds we made our way to the labor and delivery section. We found our little couple walking the halls, waiting, and we were not too late. Mother Nature was taking her time. We all walked and waited. The afternoon sun fell and the large windows of the hospital revealed the glow of street lights as the dark of evening crept through. Bryant was almost ravenous by now, so we decided to have dinner in the hospital cafeteria, and after that we joined other anxious parents and expectant fathers in the waiting room.

Bryant, Jr. came out of the labor room periodically to give us progress reports, but by eleven o'clock he insisted that we go to their apartment and wait for his call there. We didn't want to leave but he thought it best, and we were there to please him. It had been a long day, and a little rest would seem good.

We had not come prepared to spend the night and expected to be called at any moment, so we stretched out fully clothed on the twin beds in the little nursery prepared and ready for the new baby. Sleep was out of the question, but rest for weary bones was nice. I thought about the beds Bryant and I were lying on, solid pecan beds we had bought for Bryant, Jr. when he was only four years old, his beds that he had grown up on. We could have lost them in that awful fire. Now, he would have a child to grow up in them, and someday find himself sitting on the side of these same beds reading to his own or maybe soothing growing pains in little feet and legs in the middle of the night with rubbing alcohol, just as we had once done for him. Yes, I was glad he had his furniture and hoped he could someday pass it on with another legacy of sweet memories.

Pleasant thoughts had nearly lulled me to sleep when the phone rang. Only an hour had passed, and this time Bryant said it was for real. Again, my heart began to pound, and I fought tears of joy.

Within a matter of minutes, we were back at the hospital anxiously waiting and filled with joyous expectation. Bryant, Jr. was in the delivery room assisting with the delivery, so our reports of progress came now from nurses on duty. This was all very new and strange to us, this thing of fathers being present in the delivery room. We were from the old, old school where an idea of that nature wasn't even thought of. I learned soon what a valuable experience of sharing it is, though.

The big double doors from the delivery suite swung open, and Bryant, Jr. came toward us, unshaven and weary, but smiling as we had never seen before.

"It's a little boy," he said walking into our arms, "and he's perfect." He stepped back and looked down at me and with the love and tenderness a mother never forgets and said, "Mama, I don't know how you did it. It's incredible."

For as long as I live, I will never forget the moment and the expression on his face. How wonderful! He had thought of his own birth and his mother as he watched the birth of his son. My eyes filled with tears. Thank you, God, oh thank you for my son.

We were laughing, blinking back tears of pure joy as we waited to see our new baby, and Bryant, Jr. was right. The new mother was fine, and their son was beautiful with big eyes and a precious little head covered with brown hair, and we were his grandparents. It didn't matter, Grandma, Granny, Nannie, Mema, Grandpa, Granddaddy, we didn't care, whatever he wanted to call us would forever be music to our ears, just as his name would be Bryant Taylor Aldridge, III, and we called him Taylor. (Nannie's maiden name, she would have liked that.)

March 22, 1983, a glorious day, and I experienced happiness, elation beyond description. We returned to Rocky Mount that morning and planned a celebration that same evening with Phoebe and Dan, dinner and a trip to Greenville to show off proudly our little miracle.

Youth was gone. We were in love with a tiny little boy, and we knew instantly that we were ready to be Taylor's grandparents.

Chapter 81

Competing in Raleigh

Above and beyond all other titles, the one she held that spring as Aunt Allison was by far her favorite. Little Taylor had become the apple of her eye. It's amazing how our hearts seem to grow bigger as we make room for new people to love. With all of her duties, being a full time student and representing the City of Rocky Mount, along with practicing the piano in preparation for the Miss North Carolina contest in July, she always found time for Taylor.

It gave all of us great pleasure knowing he was close enough for us to share in his growing and development. The first time Mema saw her only great grandson was an indelible moment for us. Bryant and I were baby-sitting when he was only three weeks' old. Nervously, we brought him home with us to spend one night. Phoebe came over the next morning bright and early to play with our littlest angel, and Allison went to bring Mema for a visit, a very special visit that Saturday morning. She was able to leave her oxygen for brief periods of time now, and she was comfortable doing so. Allison helped her into the house, and Mema settled into the rust colored Lawson chair she always sat in. I remember bringing Taylor in and placing him in her lap. At the first sight of him, she wept in her gentle way and began to describe to us his every tiny miraculous little feature. We watched as she held her great grandson in awe until we were all crying, finally erupting into cheers of laughter. This was a moment in time for which we were all grateful, for many never see or feel such an extraordinary moment.

Taylor was a sweet distraction, but the Miss North Carolina competition loomed before us, and the biggest burden fell on Allison. She had searched through the many boxes of music I still had stowed away in the attic, the music that once belonged to her Uncle Sandy, and finally she came up with what we thought to be the perfect piece for her talent competition and what certainly suited her personality. She selected an excerpt from the Third Movement of Rachmaninoff's Concerto No. 2,

Competing in Raleigh

beautiful, melodic, and flowing-only too long. She was convinced it could be done, and with the help of a very talented friend and piano teacher, they worked out a condensed and lovely arrangement. She learned it and practiced and practiced and practiced, perfecting her talent. She finally mastered the work and could bring chills to us as we listened to her touch the keys of the piano. Her eleven years of piano study now brought her much pleasure.

Not to be forgotten during this time was the all important wardrobe fit for a queen. She knew exactly what style pageant gown she wanted — white lace sprinkled with pearls and sequins, high neckline, long pointed sleeves, and straight with a slit above the knee. I found the lace and a dressmaker in Raleigh who helped us design and make such a gown. During the three months it took her to finish the gown, Allison and I found the other pieces to complete her wardrobe — a royal blue suit for her interview with the judges (perfect with her eyes), bright and cheerful dresses for daytime, cute play clothes for practice sessions, my handmade magenta moire' taffeta sundress with chic bubble skirt for the opening introduction on stage, extra gowns for finale, just the right rich purple swim suit, and fuchsia silk organza with a wide white satin heavily sequined belt accentuating her tiny waistline for the talent performance.

This all continued along much like a dream. Each unique piece of the puzzle progressively falling into place, and we moved forward with confidence following instructions as though we knew what we were doing. I wished a thousand times that Phoebe could be with me scouting all over for this and that, helping me make decisions, and keeping me company. She would have enjoyed it so much. How we looked forward to the day she could quit work, but for now we were satisfied with what we had. Our children were happy and well, Mema was doing beautifully after organizing a Resident's Council of which she was immediately named chairman (a wonderful idea making the residents of the nursing home who were still able to communicate feel needed), and we had reservations for the Crouches and the Aldridges to spend the week of the Miss North Carolina Pageant together at the Radisson Hotel in downtown Raleigh. We looked forward to a wonderful and exciting vacation.

Early in the week, our home began to fill with bouquets of fresh flowers and balloons, gifts, cards, and letters. The whole town wished Allison well. We had not expected all of this and found the thoughtfulness of our friends and the citizens of our city very touching. Arrival day, the last Sunday in June, she was ready for this dream to become a reality. Phoebe and Susan and I were ready also, plenty of film, plenty of Kleenex, and excited! Bryant and Dan were not as demonstrative but very helpful. We needed two cars for wardrobe, so the Crouches would bring half and we could bring half. Our men loaded the cars at our direction, careful not to wrinkle any garment, each one stuffed with yards and yards of pure white tissue paper. Allison appeared in a brightly flowered pique dress, her face a picture of charm framed by a hot pink wide-brimmed straw hat looking as crisp and fresh as the pristine hours of a spring day, and we began our journey to fantasyland.

Peace College opened it doors to all of the contestants for residence during that week-long stay. We arrived to find its grand and serene little campus swarming with lovely young women, groomed to perfection, being led around by pageant directors and pageant people, each one thinking he or she could produce the winner. We had met some of these people earlier in the year when Allison made appearances at various local pageants and realized they were true professionals, full time pageant people (dubbed in just by Phoebe and me as "PP's").

We were allowed to help her get unpacked and settled and attend the afternoon photographic session for the press. Again, Phoebe's handy little disc camera clicked merrily. The glamour and fun for us had begun, but Allison was off-limits after that, only to be visited briefly after each evening performance. With the rigorous schedule they had for the week, it was difficult even to reach her by telephone. This nearly drove us crazy as all of our news came through the local director from Rocky Mount who was with Allison each day.

After days of anxious anticipation, now dressed in our cocktail dresses and glitz, like blithesome spirits, Phoebe and Susan and I found our way through the isles of Memorial Auditorium, followed by Bryant and Dan, and took our reserved seats as near the stage as possible. All around were family and friends — our own private cheering section — and then the world of pageant people. Like the many small worlds of different people who make up our universe — doctors, lawyers, politicians, circus people — we found ourselves in the midst of this different little world. Some of these people came year after year, followed the pageant circuit all winter and spring, knew the talents and statistics of each contestant, and how often different ones had competed. It was serious business to them, and we knew we were definitely the novices.

At last, the house lights dimmed, the orchestra's overture slowed to a pause, the gigantic curtains parted, all eyes were on the brightly spotted stage, and the long awaited show began.

Phoebe squeezed my arm and whispered, "Oh, Ruum!"

For a long and interesting evening, we watched a continuous parade of lovely young ladies dance and twirl, tap, speak, and sing their way into our hearts, for they were all doing their very best. We were thoroughly entertained and mesmerized by the poise and sophistication of Allison as she made her evening gown appearance in the glittering white Alencon lace gown. She was certainly our favorite.

Visiting with her afterwards was too brief. So many people, hugs and kisses, greetings, flowers, cameras flashing, and excitement! She was radiant and calm. Her physical beauty was unequaled only by her inner beauty, as she had proven time and time again. We had to leave her, and the pride and happiness we all shared kept us awake very late.

The next night, we fancied ourselves again and made way for our seats. It was the night of her talent, and we were all nervous. The parade progressed and eventually before us on the huge stage was our beautiful daughter in a single spot light seated at the grand piano. She smiled at the judges and slowly turned her attention to the black and white ivory keys. Her slender and nimble fingers began to play the concerto so familiar now to us. Her music was thrilling and flawless, bringing the audience to thunderous applause just before the end of her playing, promptly causing her to draw a complete blank in concentration. She was unaccustomed to an interruption such as this; and for an instant the piano was quiet, but for those who knew it, it was too long. She never stopped completely but gained her composure and played to the end without hesitation. She was very aware of what she had done, stood, and accepted graciously a standing ovation. My heart pounded, I felt Bryant's warm and strong hand squeezing mine. This was not the end of the world, and Allison had learned long ago how to deal with disappointment.

Afterwards, the disappointment was there, but she greeted all of her well wishers with the same enthusiasm and charm as before. She wanted to go with us and play and have fun knowing that her chances for the title now were foiled. Talent counted fifty percent, and we perceived that the judges were looking for an entertainer.

We spent two more days of vacation in Raleigh and two more nights of pageant. Each night, the show was the same, giving every group of ladies their chance at the different phases of competition. Each night, Allison and all of the young women appeared as pretty as ever, never giving up hope, and finally the long and complicated road came to an end. At the stroke of eleven o'clock on Saturday night, the winner was at last announced, and we did not hear our favorite's name. There was only one title holder, but there were no losers. Every young lady appearing could be applauded. The title would only last for a year and then be relinquished, but the crown of knowledge gained from competition and discipline, the growth in self-confidence and poise, and a higher level of tolerance and maturity could last a lifetime.

Chapter 82

Attractions of Home

With the pageant circuit and some much needed rest behind, Allison was able now to concentrate on the teaching career that lay ahead for her. Somehow, she found the time and doubled-up on her studies during the year and had completed successfully the requirements for her Master's degree in Special Education, much sooner than we expected. She was ready to begin working with the special children whom she had grown so much to care for and to love.

After weeks of anxiously waiting for results from job applications, she accepted a teaching position in Atlanta, Georgia; and reluctantly, we made plans for her to move. She longed for a position she had applied for in Rocky Mount, but no word came. The days slipped by, the new school year approached rapidly, and we all gave up hope of her being at home with us. The very thought of 1,000 miles separating us filled me with an overwhelming sadness. Selfishly, I wanted her near to share her world, her company, the bond we held so dear.

We had never been very good at fooling each other, but on this occasion we tried. The move to Atlanta would be wonderful, and she was really fortunate to get the job; our trip down together would be fun and exciting; we would find a great apartment for her, get her all settled; and I would fly back home and leave her in Atlanta alone. No matter, every thought was positive. We pulled her belongings together and loaded once again the little Pinto station wagon to the brim with clothing and necessary treasures, teaching materials, and her trusty lemon yellow two drawer metal file cabinet. By early afternoon, the only thing left to do was go to see Mema to say good-bye and run by the Crouch's for another good-bye. We planned to leave early the next day for our nine-hour drive to Atlanta.

It had been a hot and sultry August day as we trekked back and forth through the house helping Allison pack, and we welcomed the end of that chore to freshen up and cool off. I remember being at the kitchen counter pouring us a glass of iced tea, and thinking of the time and how we had to hurry to beat Mema's dinner tray to her room at Guardian Care. We always tried to get there to help her with her evening meal. I saw through the kitchen window Phoebe's blue car turning into our drive just as the telephone began to ring. We didn't need the telephone interrupting our already busy schedule, but Allison answered the call as I greeted Phoebe at the back door. She saw the packed car and gave me a look of despair.

We could hear Allison in the background. "Yes, this is she. Yes, sir, yes sir." Silence. "Yes, sir. That will be fine. Thank you, sir. I'll be in touch with you. Good-bye." Phoebe and I stood quietly in the kitchen waiting for the brief conversation Allison had on the telephone to end. She carefully placed the receiver back into its cradle on the wall and looked at us. We saw her puzzled expression change to joy, and she said happily, "They want me to teach in Rocky Mount!"

As we had done so many times before, we wondered what to do but soon realized that the most difficult task would be calling Atlanta and opening up the position Allison had taken to some other hungry young teacher out there waiting for just such a telephone call. Allison called at 9 AM the following morning.

And in the next week, she readied a classroom for the beginning of a new school year, the beginning of a new career adventure, anxious to pass on some of what she had received; and Bryant and I, for the first time in twenty years, sent a teacher into the classroom instead of a student.

We said good-bye to the summer of 1983 after a long, relaxing Labor Day weekend at the lake. The aroma of Jesse's red pepper, butter and vinegar chicken barbecuing on the huge oil drum grill, making everyone hungry long before time to eat, golden corn on the cob, Millie's baked Vidalia onions, the sound of motor boats with sun tanned skiers bouncing and gliding over the water getting in their last long ride for the summer, and our precious five and a half month old grandson, Taylor, a pure delight to all, watching the bustling activity from his private playpen on the pier — all created another happy and real picture for us; good times you don't want to end, a time you want to hold onto, a picture some people can only dream about. It was a secure and satisfying feeling having our families together, happy, healthy, and settled.

September is always a new and fresh start. (I've often wondered why the actual beginning of the new year begins in January when our lives, from the earliest days of school, are programmed to start a new year in September.) I always tried, after being lazy all summer, to begin again my

Attractions of Home

neglected exercise program. My early morning walks after Labor Day held telltale signs of another season approaching fast. The curling leaves of the dogwood trees, borders of orange and yellow marigolds beginning to turn brown, drying grass tired from the blistering summer sun, the last few remaining heavy pink and white blossoms on the crepe myrtle trees, and the puffy grey and white clouds gradually covering the blue of the sky, ushering in a cold front, easily changed my thoughts to shorter days and tighter schedules. Everyone had a routine to meet.

Before the giant orange pumpkins lying in the farmer's field had turned to Jack-O-Lanterns, and the chilly autumn days had run us inside for our afternoon visits, we knew the names of practically all of Allison's new students. Another world was revealed to us when she introduced them one by one through stories of their capabilities and daily school activities, a moving and fascinating world far beyond our own of the mentally handicapped and learning disabled. Allison would come into the nursing home after school nearly every day and find Phoebe and me chattering away in Mema's room waiting for her to join us. The twinkle that always came into Mema's eyes, when Allison entered her room and perched herself happily and comfortably on the foot of Mema's little bed, was that of a proud and satisfied grandmother. Our conversations went immediately to the varied and interesting stories of school days. As part of our important afternoon routine, Allison and Phoebe helped to carry us all away from the walls and halls of a nursing home with happy and sometimes sad tales of their activities, creating our own little private forum as we listened and shared our thoughts and learned from Mema's wise and gentle words on each subject. This was time well spent, valuable time; time that we have never forgotten.

Allison continued to grow and learn, as we all did, from her grandmother's experience and guidance, and the stories of those less fortunate than we brought home to us a constant reminder of the abundance of our blessings — good health; bright and sharp minds; safe, warm, comfortable homes; and the never-ending love of our families. And in the midst of what we already had, God had added another dimension to our family, Taylor, a perfectly healthy little child who made us even more grateful for the wondrous world we sometimes took for granted.

Family gatherings were always important and happy events. The only disappointing factor now was Mema's not being able to join us, so we brought our times of togetherness to her through the many photographs and candid snapshots we took. November 20, 1983, was no different. Our cameras were clicking overtime, for the sun shone brilliantly; we were dressed in our Sunday best, and every face was aglow with joy. We had driven over to Greenville with Allison and Phoebe and Dan to join in the celebration of Taylor's baptism. It was a beautiful and emotional day for everyone as we met Bryant, Jr. and his little family outside the church. Taylor was dressed in his father's christening clothes which added to our pride and emotions on that lovely day. Touching his tiny feet, covered with the aged and now yellowed soft leather shoes, brought another wave of nostalgia to me as I was still able to picture in my mind the day we made these same sacred vows promising to rear our little Bryant as a Christian. Now Bryant, Jr. stood holding his son tenderly as this sacrament was administered, pledging the same. Like father, like son, pass it on, and be proud of the portrait you are painting, I thought, as I was impressed again with this awesome responsibility.

It had been a remarkable day. Two sets of grandparents, (a third adopted set in the Crouches) an aunt and an uncle—all doting on this special child—a new home for the family to enjoy, a bountiful picnic, and smiles and laughter made this a true day of thanksgiving and celebration. I thought of my mother and the stories we would have to tell her, of Mema and how she would have enjoyed this day with us, and I hoped that all of the pictures would be good so that she could not only feel the beauty of our day but also see a small portion of it.

Chapter 83

A Corner Darkening

"It'll be here before you know it!" I had listened to my mother say this to me so many times when I became impatient; and now as I reached the half century mark, her words continued to echo in my ears, for it seemed again that before we knew it Thanksgiving was behind us and we had celebrated Taylor's very first Christmas. It was an exhilarating Christmas, having a little child in our home, seeing the joy in the eyes of a baby and playing with children's toys again.

It was during this visit that Bryant, Jr. laid out for us the details of their plans for a skiing trip to Vermont in January. My first thoughts were of icy, snow covered roads and fifteen hours of driving with their little angel sitting in his car seat, but Bryant had it all mapped out and was confident there would be no problems.

We naturally began to worry. (Do parents ever stop worrying about their children's safety and well being? I think not.) And as the cold days of January grew shorter and darker, I knew that their trip would be here before we knew it, but at least it would get behind us.

The day they traveled I busied myself with the usual household chores knowing that an occupied mind is the best way to pass time fast, but being very careful to keep a close check on the news and weather in the northeast every few hours. Bryant was at home with me when the long awaited telephone call finally came. They had arrived safely, and as though he could see the relief on our faces, Bryant, Jr. said, "You can stop worrying now, Mama." We could hear the gaiety in the background, and for the first time I could picture them in the safety of their friend's home, the snow on the mountains and the beauty of Vermont, and Bryant happily skiing with his good friend. After giving Allison the relieving news, I called Phoebe because I knew she had been worrying, also.

Only two days passed before Bryant, Jr. called to give us an update on their skiing adventure. He had been able to ski only once, everybody was fine, but he was flat on his back with the recurring back problem that had been so chronic since his football days. He was lying on his friend's floor in excruciating pain unable to move, but having had the problem before he knew how to take care of himself. Now we had something to worry about. Our biggest concern was how to get him home and cared for as soon as possible.

Bryant, at home, checked out every means of transportation available. We called Bryant, Jr. in Vermont and kept in constant communication with him on his condition and discussed all possible arrangements. After nearly a week, Bryant, Jr. made the decision to start home. He felt sure that he could make it back to North Carolina propped up in the back seat of their car, and he could depend on his little wife's driving.

And so the waiting began again. We knew exactly when they left Vermont to start home. He had given us the route they would take and would be in touch, and many hours later our prayers were answered. The sight of their light blue Cutlass turning into our driveway was nothing compared to the sight of Bryant, Jr.'s blue eyes, blood-shot and tired looking up at us as his daddy helped him from the car. They were all fine, exhausted, ready for much needed rest, and our son was hurting.

The next day, our good friend and orthopedic surgeon admitted him to Nash General Hospital where he had back surgery the following day, but he was secure and at home with those who loved him. Successfully, he was relieved of the awful disc pain and began a slow recovery. I happily became the full time baby sitter for our grandson, freeing his mother to spend all of her time at the hospital with Bryant, Jr., taking care of his needs or to run the many necessary errands she had at that hectic time. After a full week of hospitalization and good progress, he was released to recuperate further at our home in Rocky Mount which pleased us greatly. Seeing our son gain his strength back and having his family with us for a few more days gave us a sense of security and made us very happy.

Bryant, Jr. was relaxed and seemed to be more comfortable with each day that passed, and because I was so preoccupied with meals and Mema and Taylor and my usual responsibilities, I was unaware of the mounting tension within his wife during those few days. The strain and awkwardness of the past several weeks had apparently been too much for her to cope with, leading eventually to an unpleasant outburst directed at me. Her perceptions were very real to her making it difficult to reach any logical conclusion. I decided to dismiss the emotional eruption as that of a tired and confused young mother ready to go home. I tried not to take her words personally. Although this little corner of our lives had been scarred,

A Corner Darkening

the tension seemed to ease in the next few months with no visible signs of hostility. With special care and exercise, Bryant, Jr. recovered from his back surgery and soon was able to return to his normal routine.

We not only celebrated Taylor's first birthday that spring as adoring and happy grandparents, but on April 21, 1984, Good Friday, we also celebrated the glorious news of a dear friend's being given a second chance to live with the miraculous aid of a heart transplant. Allison's college roommate's parents had become very close friends with us since Allison and Shawn's college days. We were all aware of Shawn's father living with a severely damaged heart from several heart attacks. We also knew that a transplant was his only hope for survival.

Seeing him in the hospital only a week after his incredible operation was a humbling experience for us all. Bryant and Allison and I drove to Richmond to visit the family, never dreaming of seeing him. We soon learned from the nurses on duty that our friend could see us in the waiting room; so with proper instructions and clad in hospital masks, gloves, and robes, we made our way to find our friends. As we entered the waiting room, we were greeted with his outstretched arms and his sweet voice: "Where have you been? I've been looking everywhere for you. Come over here and give me a hug. I want to touch you." With tender hugs and smiling faces beneath our paper masks and eyes brimming with tears, we praised God for life and this miracle which had all been made possible by another human being's heart, the constant rhythm giving a new life to this gentle and courageous man. This is awesome. This will bring you to your knees.

Funny, coming home from Richmond that afternoon, the odorous ride past Roanoke Rapids and the cotton mill there wasn't as offensive as usual. This trip gave new light somehow to the lustrous green leaves on the trees, the mixed wild flowers along the roadside, and the remarkable robin's-egg blue of the sky — all mighty reminders of the beauty of life and what we have to be thankful for.

Chapter 84

Brandon

The news that we were to become grandparents was received with mixed emotions. The first year of Dan, Jr's. marriage had been stormy and unsettled. The military can be very hard on a young couple just getting started. Our son had told us the Marine Corps reminded the men that if they had wanted them to have a family they would have issued them one. Nevertheless, we were elated at the thought of having a grandchild, though apprehensive about the relationship. When I shared our news with Jean, we both hoped that being parents would be the binding factor they needed.

A child does not ask to be born, though, and should never have to carry the burden of being the mender of a troubled relationship. The baby was due the end of July while one of the ever dreaded "floats" loomed on the horizon for the new father-to-be. We were hoping the baby would arrive before Dan, Jr. left, but it was not meant to be. "C" Company would leave in the early morning hours of July 26th for a six-month tour of duty in the Mediterranean.

On the evening of the 25th, Dan, Jr. called to say good-bye. His voice was filled with emotion. His heart was aching at the thought of missing his first child's arrival and the precious early months of its life. Once again, he asked, "Mama and Daddy, please take good care of my little family for me." We talked as long as we could find things to say and then the awful time came to say good-bye.

That weekend, Dan drove me to Jacksonville to begin the vigil. The week began with the exciting realization that we would become grandparents very soon. The doctors were contemplating inducing labor, but her labor began naturally Monday evening and I took my daughter-in-law to the Naval Hospital at Camp LeJeune around 9:30 p.m.

There is absolutely no way to describe the feelings I had waiting for our first grandchild to be born. Jean had described to me the feelings you have, but until you actually live it there is no way to comprehend it. My daughter-in-law had asked a close friend to be in the delivery room with her, and the friend was keeping me posted on what was happening moment by moment.

After a long delay in reports, around 2:45 in the morning, I felt I had better check for myself. I crept down the hall behind the labor rooms reserved for fathers. Recognizing my daughter-in-law's voice and hearing the excitement of the team assisting her, I could picture in my mind what was going on and began to feel a part of the impending birth! At 3:30 a.m., someone said, "Get her to the delivery room!" Four minutes later I heard the gusty cry of our baby, and a voice saying, "Look at that boy!" Dan, Jr.'s prayers had been answered. He had a son. Christopher Brandon Crouch had arrived in this world at 3:34 a.m., July 31, 1984. I was bursting with joy as I returned to the waiting room. Twenty-two minutes later, I was holding our grandson. His mother's first words to me were, "He looks just like Daniel!" He really did look just like his daddy did at birth. It is an awesome feeling to hold your child's child. He was so sweet and precious. All I could do as I held him and looked down into that innocent little face was to weep tears of joy and thanksgiving. He was perfectly formed and developed in every way. I silently prayed, "Lord, thank you. We are so grateful. Lay your hand on Brandon. Bless him and lead him in the way everlasting." My emotions were drained. With Brandon and his mother in the capable hands of the hospital staff, I went in search for a cup of coffee and waited for Dan to arrive. As dawn broke, I made my first telephone call, as a grandmother, to Brandon's Aunt Susan. Later that morning, my second call was to Jean. When she answered the phone, I said, "Now I understand what you have been saying for the past sixteen months. I have a grandson, too!"

Chapter 85

Feelings Disturbed

"There comes Phoebe," Mema said as we watched her car pull into the circular driveway at the nursing home. She took great pride in recognizing all of the cars coming and going. The air was still warm enough for her to sit on the porch in late September, so she had paddled her wheelchair with little short steps down the hall and out into the porch to enjoy the beginning days of another autumn and all of its earthy colors. Her very favorite place was on the porch where she could watch the traffic and speak with every visitor approaching the entrance.

Phoebe joined us and took her seat beside me, pulling up a white wrought iron arm chair. This was about all it took to make Mother happy each day. Such a small thing just knowing we were coming and having us there with her. Phoebe began talking about school, and Mema immediately asked if I had heard from Allison as she wrapped the quilted afghan tightly around her knees and legs, feeling the breeze of the late afternoon.

As the summer slipped by, Allison's teaching job in Rocky Mount was so indefinite that by August she had decided to make another career move, and her new work in teaching and modeling had carried her three hours away from us. She, like her brother, had made the decision to move and luckily both were now living in the same town near each other. Bryant and his family were settled in another town, another apartment, and a new job. Allison was settled, also, ready to be on her own, and we were back to our empty nest.

Mema missed Allison's regular visits each day now, so I tried to have news of her activities ready. We passed the time with stories of our grandchildren, Phoebe about Brandon, me about Taylor, and Mema about Allison and Bryant, Jr. (She seldom mentioned her other two grandsons. This was painful to her because she knew very little about them.) Phoebe and I would listen intently to her dreams of having the porch at Guardian

Feelings Disturbed

Care enclosed so the patients could enjoy this area even in the cold of winter. She had great plans for attempting to complete such a project.

Soon, the cold and darker days had driven us inside where our thoughts turned to fall festivals, Thanksgiving activities, and before we knew it — Christmas. Anticipation of the holidays, seeing family and friends, remembering days gone by, good food and rich deserts, only allowed at Christmas, and especially the precious children's choirs, singing carols in the halls outside her door each day, filled our senses with excitement and kept Mema entertained. Knowing that our children would be coming home gave us a rush of pleasure as we prepared for the season.

* * *

Brandon and his mom arrived a few days before Christmas for a visit. Jean and I made plans for our families to get together. They had to attend their traditional Aldridge family dinner in Kinston on Sunday, the day before Christmas Eve, and planned to come by our house when they returned. As usual, they were running late. When I heard car doors closing, I ran to the back door to see if they had arrived. "It's them," I called and opened the door to let them in. The minute I looked at Jean my mood of utter delight changed to one of concern for her. Her face was as white as a sheet, and her expression was one of distress. Her greeting was a weak, "Sorry, we're late." Her voice sounded tired and strained. She's sick, I thought. As we hugged I asked, "Are you all right? You're as white as a ghost."

She said, "I'll tell you about it later."

Our two little grandsons were the center of attention. Taylor was adorable and had grown so much since we last saw him. Jean and Bryant had not seen Brandon since their visit to Jacksonville when he was born. While everyone exchanged hugs and wished each other a Merry Christmas, I kept my eye on Jean. In all of our years of knowing each other, I had never seen her look like this. As soon as I could, without being too obvious, I said, "Jean, come back here and let me show you something. Y'all excuse us for a minute." She stood and followed me from the living room down the hall to my bedroom. When I had her alone, I said, "Now. What in the name of peace is wrong with you?"

"You wouldn't believe it if I told you. Yes, you would believe it." Jean answered. "Remember the outburst that occurred Thanksgiving over the 'See and Say' toy?

"Yes."

"Well, yesterday was twice as bad. When words are not enough, how can you relate to someone who loses complete control and would physically attack you?"

"I have no earthly idea," I said to Jean.

"Phoebe, we've never known such unnecessary anger."

At that moment, Susan and Allison couldn't stand it any longer and appeared at the bedroom door with puzzled looks on their faces. "Mama, what are y'all doing back here?" Susan asked.

"I'll explain it later; we've got to get back to the others."

I hugged Allison, understanding now the sadness in her eyes and her quiet manner.

The disturbing events of the previous day did not alter our plans for Christmas Eve. Brandon and his mother and Bryant, Jr. and his family left early that morning to continue their Christmas plans with their other grandparents.

Going to the Methodist Church for the communion service with the Aldridges had become a tradition. Afterwards, we met at Jean and Bryant's house to have dinner and exchange gifts. Susan and Allison's frivolous and foolish humor made all of us feel lighthearted and festive. At dinner, the six of us joined hands around the table with heads bowed as Bryant thanked God for our abundant blessings. In each heart, there was a special prayer raised, asking for the love that came down at Christmas to descend on us and each member of our family.

* * *

What would I have done without Phoebe during this time, my faithful friend and steady shelter. The closeness of our families had been the cement of our lives, and now to know of the divisiveness that had entered our home frightened me and broke my heart. I was fortunate to have a loyal friend to turn to. I could only share these events with her and Mema now, and we groped hopelessly for a solution. Mema's advice, always in her gentle wisdom, was to keep the peace, apparently the simple and practical philosophy of her generation. I can see her sitting Indian-style on her bed shaking her head, telling me, "Jean, just keep the peace. Do whatever it takes to get along. Anything else is just not worth it."

So we took my mother's advice, but a wall continued to be built, a wall already so ably begun. In retrospect, it seemed to have been so cunningly plotted that our family was unaware of the capable experience of its builder.

Chapter 86

Mema

*R*ecently, I stood and listened to a young woman describing her uncomfortable feelings after working voluntarily with old people in a hospital for a short period of time. This was just not her thing she said: "I hated it! They make all these awful noises and want to touch you, and they can't talk so you can understand what they're saying. Old people are just not my thing. I prefer being with the babies." As I listened to her animated analogy of her experience, I found my mind drifting peacefully back to my own uneasy feelings when I first faced similar circumstances.

Those days of entering a nursing home for the first time and adjusting to seeing the many conditions of the sick and elderly were priceless lessons for me. What frightened me in the beginning soon became a gratifying experience. There were so many of these old people reaching out with gnarled hands for just a pat on the shoulder, often with squawking voices trying desperately to speak to you, a few asleep in wheelchairs tied there to prevent them from falling, or some just rocking quietly and waiting for a friendly smile to brighten their day. It took very little to bring them a moment of happiness to show them you cared, and the reward was far greater than the time spent.

My mother's grateful spirit and healthy attitude certainly helped mine. She, being chairman of the Patient Advisory Council, had the responsibility of presenting to her council weekly a new idea for creating a more pleasant atmosphere within these walls. With a cheerful and persuasive ability, she usually could accomplish whatever different activities she planned. We remember the Easter parade in 1985, so simple yet so grand.

Family members were always included in holiday parties at the nursing home, usually held in the early afternoon with fruit punch and ice cream and cookies. Sons and daughters, sisters and brothers, or friends of patients arrived and were greeted with Mema's Easter Parade. With the help of the staff, all of the patients who were able to walk with aid or ride in their wheelchairs were assembled and paraded the halls to the strains of Irving Berlin's "Easter Parade," each one decked in an Easter bonnet suitable for Fifth Avenue. The mood of the holiday weekend had been set.

Moods can quickly change, for within less than twenty-four hours of the sweetness of the Easter parade, the taste of chocolate Easter eggs and flowering red and yellow tulips, we received the tragic news of my nephew's death. My brother's youngest son, on his twenty-first birthday, was vacationing from school, performing the sport he loved the most, mountain climbing. In repelling from the mountain, he failed to fasten one vital hook causing the fall and ultimately his young death.

We carried this awful heartbreaking news to Mema the morning after her parade. She had loved Christian and his older brother but always from afar. They were still her flesh and blood and the remaining link to her only son. Now Christian was gone, and the dream of ever knowing him could never be realized.

For the next several weeks, Mema grieved in her own quiet way, fighting back tears with every reminder of her grandson's, and ultimately a reminder of her own son's, early death. Her enthusiasm began to lag, and we soon realized that the combination of her already fragile health and bearing this grief had weakened her further, prompting an unscheduled visit to her doctor. After examinations and x-rays that showed the development of a spot on her lungs, we determined the need for a second qualified opinion.

We made arrangements to take Mother back to Duke Hospital on June 10, 1985. After treatment at Duke, we soon learned that the spot on her lung was definitely cancer. With her condition already weakened from emphysema, it was not possible to consider surgery or any other course of treatment.

During the following two weeks, she remained at Duke for monitoring and observation. Phoebe joined me for my daily trips to Durham during this time, and with every day that passed we were grateful to see Mother's improvement. Gradually, she regained her strength and some of her old stamina and pride. Before her return to Rocky Mount and Guardian Care, she swore us to secrecy, making us promise not to reveal her malignancy to anyone. "For whatever days I have left, I want things to be as normal as possible without any feelings of sympathy or pity for me," she told each of us.

Chapter 87

Breathing Time

Jean and I sat in her back yard drinking a glass of lemonade. Mema was home now and doing well. Life was almost back to normal. Whatever that was?

I watched a squirrel scamper across the lawn. He paused for a moment to look us over (or so it seemed), found us to be harmless, and continued on his way. He sprang to the nearest tree and began his assent. "Have you ever noticed that squirrels go head first everywhere they go?" I asked Jean.

"No. I haven't ever noticed that, 'Ruum'."

"Well, they do, as far as I know. Whether up or down, they go head first. Just thought I would share that fascinating observation with you."

"Thanks! It's fascinating all right!"

The breeze was gentle and pleasantly cool for the first week in July. The real heat of summer would be upon us soon. I dreaded the humidity. It was a peaceful moment. They had been far and few between lately, so we were savoring every minute of this one.

I don't recall how the subject came up, but we began talking about feelings folks have that pop out when they least expect them to. I began to spout off about one I had, as a for instance.

"It is so good to be out of school. I'm tired of working. Even though my working conditions are good, I have this feeling of resentment that is just below the surface all the time. I'm just like my mama was. She always kept things like that to herself in order 'to keep the peace,' as she would say. Now and then, I casually mention the fact that I sure do look forward to the day I can quit work. Dan always replies, 'Me too, honey.' Instead of coming right out and telling him how I really feel, I get miffed because he never says what I hope he'll say. He's supposed to say something like, 'Well, honey, you don't have to work if you don't want to.' He might even could say, 'I don't want you working anymore. Why don't you hand in your resignation?' Poor man. He, like most husbands, flunked mind reading."

Breathing Time

"Boy! That feeling sure popped out, didn't it? Now, I feel guilty! I guess you've noticed I'm the world's best travel agent for guilt trips!" I said.

Jean had been listening quietly.

"You got that right! Know what we need to do? We need to get out of town for two or three days to relax and do as we please!" Jean said.

In unison we said, "Williamsburg"!

A few days later, we were on our way. The cares of the world began to melt away with each mile that brought us closer to the place that had become our haven for rest and relaxation. We stepped back in time and embraced the pleasant feeling that lovely place offers anyone who chooses to enter. We slept late and ate when we felt like it. On this trip, shopping was secondary to strolling up and down streets in the historic area. We preferred sitting on an available bench to "people watch" and sip a Coke. We talked and shared our views and feelings on various topics. The cobwebs cleared, and the restoration was a success.

We returned to reality, rested, rejuvenated, ready to face the ordinary or not-so-ordinary days ahead.

Chapter 88

Surprise Ending

Brandon walked around in amazement as children and adults began to descend on his yard. Each carried a box beautifully wrapped and all for him. His mom was busy preparing food; Dan, Jr. was in charge of crowd control and games. It was a busy place, but everyone seemed content. For his first birthday, there were two cakes! I had brought one, and his mom had made one. There was no doubt they would be eaten. I hoped we would have enough. When there is a party, people seem to come from every direction, especially if the yards run together like they do on a military base.

After what seemed like hours, but was only an hour and a half, it was all over! We began clean-up detail. I was helping my daughter-in-law in the kitchen.

"As soon as we finish all this, I'll get Brandon cleaned up and ready for bed so you won't have that to do," I told her.

"No, don't bother," she said. "I'm driving to Charleston tonight, and I'll do that when I get there."

"You're leaving for Charleston tonight?"

"Yes."

"Don't you think it's too late for you to be getting on the highway by yourself with that baby? Can't you wait until in the morning?"

"No. My parents are having a party for Brandon tomorrow, and I need to be there to help. It's only four hours away. We'll be fine."

Four weeks later, we learned that her departure on Brandon's birthday was the beginning of her permanent separation from our son.

Daniel loved his little boy and wanted desperately to provide a stable, loving home for him. In spite of this, he and his wife could not reconcile their differences, and the marriage ended in divorce after three turbulent years.

Chapter 89

The Day Hospital

The ecstasy of this September morning was just what we had hoped for. As we awakened, we were greeted by a beautiful sunny day and the sweet sounds of our little grandson playing and calling for "B" and "Bubba," names he had dubbed us with in his childlike jargon. Our children were at home to celebrate with us the brand new Day Hospital opening later that day, and we could not have planned for a more perfect morning. The temperature was in the seventies and wonderful for the outside ribbon cutting, dedication ceremony, and luncheon that we had planned for dignitaries and out-of-town guests. Bryant was expecting a large crowd for the activities and wanted everything to be right as usual. Now at least the weather worry was over, and our excitement quickened as we prepared ourselves for the memorable event.

For years, Bryant had dreamed about and visualized this new concept in outpatient services, not just an outpatient clinic or surgery center, but a unique and ideal comprehensive ambulatory care center. He envisioned an open mall effect building giving the advantages of more economical construction and easy expansion, and creating an enticing, relaxed, and comfortable atmosphere for patients in a usually unfriendly environment.

With the rapid changes in technology and seeking new ideas for cost containment, Bryant convinced his board of directors that his concept of a Day Hospital was a more functional and cost efficient approach to ambulatory outpatient needs. After two years of construction, this dream, just as his dream for an all private room hospital, was a reality, standing ready to serve the public in an unparalleled way.

This day of celebrated accomplishment was complete. The many colored leaves of autumn floating down in the distance created a picturesque background for the hospital as the doors were opened September 21, 1985. With satisfaction, we saw the great public acceptance of this new facility standing solitary and independent, yet connected to

Nash General Hospital by a single corridor.

Chapter 90

Millie and Jesse

We really didn't want to go out that night. Even though it was a party we looked forward to, it had been a cold and rainy day, and the evening appeared to be getting even worse. The Christmas party season was in full swing by December 12, and on a dreary night like this, we felt we could skip one party and stay at home by a glowing fire. After wrestling with the decision for nearly an hour, however, we dressed in Christmas garb and found our way through the rain to the warmth of a beautiful and festive holiday gathering. Candles flickered, poinsettias abounded, and the aroma of bayberry and pine mingled with the rich and spicy smells of Christmas created an inviting atmosphere.

Making the effort to go out was sometimes difficult, but we knew it was always worth it. This was the evening of my garden club's annual Christmas buffet to entertain our husbands, a party with company we enjoyed and one we wanted to support.

Bryant drove into the wide circular driveway taking me directly to the front entrance enabling me to dash inside, leaving him the task of parking and making his way back to the house under the big black umbrella, dodging icy puddles of water along the way. I had worn a red Angora sweater splashed with a diamond of red sequins highlighting the left shoulder. The warmth of the wool and soft Angora was cozy and welcomed by my chilled-to-the-bone feeling as we gathered around the grand piano for Christmas songs and merriment. It was good that we had come. Bryant found dinner instinctively, knowing that I had prepared no food at home, and soon we were distracted completely from the frightful December weather.

The sheeting rain changed to a fine mist as we drove home later, bringing into focus the Christmas wreaths and boxwood garlands and single candle-lit windows decorating many homes along our way. The wet iridescent streets mirrored a profusion of brightly colored lights reminding me to get extra replacement light bulbs for decorating our tree during the upcoming weekend. A wave of excitement came over me as I thought of Allison coming home the next day to help us decorate our Christmas tree and make plans for the traditional family dinner now only one week away. There was much to be done, but tomorrow would take care of that.

We were home at last, safe and warm, free from the misty night air, and ready for a delicious night's sleep. Bryant switched on the television to the eleven o'clock nightly news as we readied ourselves for bed, and we were relieved to hear the weather report saying the rain would end but that it would be extremely cold.

At eleven fifteen, the telephone rang, and I thought, oh no, not tonight, what in the world? Bryant stood motionless and staring blankly with the receiver at his ear. Minutes passed before he spoke. Finally in a ghost-like tone, he uttered, "We'll be right there." He looked at me from across the room and said in shock and disbelief, "Jesse and Millie have been killed in an automobile accident. We have to go now to Roanoke Rapids."

He was trying so hard to keep his composure, but I saw his eyes well up with tears. We embraced, seeking the comfort and priceless security of each other's arms. We clung to each other, crying, and I felt his warm strong body trembling with grief. We knew what we had to do but had no idea of what awaited us. In another moment, he was on the telephone calling his sister as I dressed. He dressed and I immediately called Phoebe and Dan. After explaining the few details we had to her, I turned our home and Rocky Mount responsibilities over to them.

The rain was gone now, but the roads were still wet as we made our way up I-95 toward Roanoke Rapids. The usual steady stream of approaching headlights had lessened at this hour which brought some relief, and Bryant began to talk.

Jesse had accompanied Millie out into the county after dinner to observe a class in one of the high schools. Millie taught at the local community college and was responsible for certain continuing education classes in the county, and because of the weather that night Jesse didn't want her out alone. Millie was driving and on the way back to Roanoke Rapids, she rounded a curve at the top of a slight hill; and before reaching the bottom, she plowed into an eighteen-wheel flatbed trailer which was stretched, with no lights or reflectors, across her lane of the highway killing them instantly. A driver had been backing his truck loaded with bales of heavy steel cable across the highway in total darkness in an attempt to park the rig in his own driveway. The cab of the truck was in the opposite lane with its bright headlights facing Millie, and she had to have thought she was approaching an oncoming truck. Her attention was automatically drawn to the lights being flashed frantically by the driver; and unaware of the impending danger, she drove the station wagon into and under the bed of the trailer without ever touching the brakes. She and Jesse never knew what happened.

In but a flash, the courses of all our lives had changed. Jesse and Millie were gone, and the important thing now was their daughters, comforting them, loving them, and taking care of their needs. Sally Ann and Millicent, these precious girls, nineteen and twenty-three years old, young women but still their parents' babies, were thrust into this horrible senseless tragedy because of one incompetent human's mistake.

The miles of concrete ribbon that stretched out before us finally pulled us into the city limits of Roanoke Rapids and on to Millicent's apartment. She was there waiting with friends — quietly, shocked, devastated. We were told that a close friend had gone to Raleigh to bring Sally Ann home from college and would arrive in another hour or so. We waited together in despair and numb until dawn broke; and with the light of a new day, we began the process of making final arrangements.

Bryant left early with the funeral director to select gravesites for his dearly beloved brother and sister-in-law. I called our children and Phoebe while Millicent and Sally Ann waited with concerned and supportive friends for family to arrive. As the hours passed, we were strengthened by the bond of family and the compassion of friends as each of us groped for some understanding of this hideous tragedy.

The following day on a bleak hillside, we stood together beside coffins draped with American beauty red roses. With broken hearts, numb from disbelief, and in the piercing frigid wind, we said our final good-byes to Jesse and Millie.

Chapter 91

Painful Departures

As we ushered in another new year, the tragedy of Jesse and Millie's deaths still engulfed us. It was hard to believe that these lives so dear had been abruptly snatched from our presence.

On the afternoon of January 28, 1986, Jean and I visited Mema, and we discussed the events that had taken place in the morning hours of that day.

As though our personal grief were not enough, our country was dealt a crushing blow that plunged us all into mourning for families we had never met or ever would have known.

The launching of spaceships had become so commonplace to us that we seldom remembered them until they were mentioned on the evening news. The space attempt on this day, however, was unique and historical because for the first time in the history of our space program, a civilian, Christa McAuliffe, a 37 year old school teacher from Concord, New Hampshire, would be aboard. Thousands of school children across America were watching as the Challenger, sleek and gleaming against the blue of the sky, rose at 11:38 a.m. from its launching pad and began the climb into space. Seventy-four seconds into the flight, millions watched in horror as it erupted into a giant fireball and disintegrated before our eyes! Seven lives extinguished in a split second.

(Today we are reminded of that tragic moment in our nation's history each time we stroll the boardwalk in Beaufort, N.C., and pause before the permanent memorial marker for Michael Smith which has been placed there by the citizens of his home town, to honor him, the courageous pilot of the Challenger Spacecraft.)

* * *

During the days that followed this latest tragedy, we tried to come to grips with the sadness surrounding our own lives, remaining aware of the

Painful Departures

similar suffering among the families of the heroic astronauts. Mother kept reminding us that very few tragic things that happen in life are actually the end of the world, even though at the time it may seem like it. More important than the significance of the event is truly how we are able to cope. Life does go on. People resume their daily activities everyday, going to work and school, grocery shopping, mowing grass, cleaning, and caring for others. Diligently seeking comfort, we soon realize that God's gift of time is a wonderful healer; we learn to accept this philosophy; and with strength and renewed faith, we are able to cope with the next happening more positively and spiritually.

Mema was asleep in her little blue swivel rocker when I entered her room in the afternoons now. I had become oriented to seeing her more active and mobile during her three years at Guardian Care, often having to walk the halls in an attempt to locate her. Now, though, I found myself hurrying over each day to make sure she was well. She was in a semi-private room, and her roommate had died, so I consoled myself by saying that Mema was catching up on her sleep and enjoying the quietness of a single room, as I squelched the dreaded inevitable fear within me.

Sensing my presence in the room would usually awaken her, but she no longer could offer Phoebe her chair or sit on her bed, Indian-style, in an animated way. Phoebe and I sat on the side of her bed and listened to her interpret her dreams, unable at times to separate them from reality. She dreamed of hearing a siren and of looking out the window and seeing an ambulance taking Millie and Jesse to the hospital. She believed that she had seen the bright lights flashing and tried to convince us that they were not dead. As her oxygen level would increase, her mind became less confused, and we could speak more of reality. Waking or sleeping, she was obsessed with Bryant's loss and the welfare of our nieces, Millicent and Sally Ann. We convinced her daily that they were well and their needs were being attended to. The bond between us grew stronger and dearer, comforting all of us.

Every errand that I ran took me past the nursing home. Now with each errand, I found myself anxiously turning into the circular driveway of her home, compelled to stop to check on Mother, praying to see improvement, only to see her energy slipping away. Along with the breast cancer and emphysema, the doctors now suspected a debilitating muscular disease, which she was never aware of, making it necessary once again for immediate hospitalization.

She was happy to be going to Nash General, satisfied that she would get well and begin to feel better. On a cold February morning she waved good-bye to her little feeble friends and departed from the nursing home by ambulance, confident of her recovery. We marveled at her confidence and serenity, her love and appreciation for those caring for her; and one week later, she looked up at me all knowingly and whispered, "Jean, we knew this was coming." My throat caught, and I could feel my eyes prick with tears as I clutched her frail hand and leaned to press my trembling lips on her soft warm forehead. All the care in the world could not make her better. Her suffering increased, relieved only by medication and the constant love of her family. With us at her bedside, Bryant, Jr. looked down at her and said tenderly, "Mema, we love you," and her final words were, "I love you, too." Then with tiny puffs of breathe, she slipped away into a peaceful and comatose sleep. In less than two days, on February 23, she left us sad and broken-hearted but grateful for her legacy of patience and unselfishness, her sincere wisdom, her love, and her profound dignity.

I miss thee, my mother, when
young health has fled.
And I sink in the languor
of pain,
Where, where is the arm that once pillowed my head,
And the ear that once heard
me complain?
Other hands may support me, gentle accents may fall -
For the fond and the true are still mine:
I've a blessing for each; I am grateful to all, -
But whose care can be soothing as thine?

—Eliza Cook

Chapter 92

Love is Magical

Tom came into our lives as a real surprise the spring before Mema died; and during those months as we spent more time with him, we could understand Allison's falling head over heels in love with this young gentleman. A North Carolina Tarheel, he was handsome, suave, extremely thoughtful and successful in the furniture industry; and as destiny would have it, they met in an unusual way.

Tom needed a receptionist to work in his company's furniture showroom during the upcoming furniture market, and Allison was sent by the modeling agency she represented as a possibility to cover the job. Tom later said, "She looked like a sixteen year old, rushing into my office at 5:00, dressed in jeans and a sweater, so casual, explaining that she was coming in from school. I didn't really care where she was coming from. I just needed a receptionist, and I thought she probably didn't have enough sense to answer the phone. I really hired her as a last resort for the next day, angry at the agency for sending over someone so young."

Allison was not what he had expected when she arrived to work. She was intelligent, articulate, and very competent; and so their friendship began and a genuine case of love flourished. We approached this new relationship with apprehension, as always, not because of Tom but because as parents we try to weigh the good and bad, wanting the very best for our children. There was a slight age difference here that worried us, and Allison was engaged already, but she was convinced that she had never felt this way and understood now what we had tried so often to tell her about knowing when you are really in love. She eventually broke her engagement, and from then on it was only Tom.

The week following Mema's death, Phoebe was there to help me adjust to sitting by the fire in our den on these cold afternoons instead of being at Mother's bedside as we had done together for so long. It seemed strange, this feeling of being the elder generation in our families now. We had suddenly lost the splendid privilege of being daughters, and the extraordinary responsibility of being the senior mothers and grandmothers now rested on our shoulders. Thankfully, we still had each other and could draw from that strength. We wanted to pass on to our children the values and wisdom that were such priceless gifts to us from our own mothers, contributing to the stability of our lives. We only hoped we could do it as well.

Once again, our generous and faithful friends had supplied our needs with another bounty of wonderful food during this time of grief, and Phoebe and Dan and Bryant and I enjoyed feasting nightly from rich goodies we would never have prepared for ourselves. By the week's end, we had hardly made a dent in our supply. Allison and Tom were coming back for the weekend, and there would still be plenty left for all of us without having to cook. Just the thought of Allison's coming home so soon lifted my spirits.

The idea of staying at home appealed to us that weekend certainly more than going to a wedding party. We had been obligated to this function for quite some time, however, so the decision was made to go as planned on Saturday night with the hope that a happy outing would be good for all. Allison was radiant as usual to us, but probably Tom being in attendance added to her glow. Bryant and I went in our own car leaving the young people free to stay with their friends as long as they wished. We had had a long week and wanted to make this an early evening.

The party served as a pleasant distraction. We were back in the real world with happy oblivious young people and attentive friends, with music appealing only to the young and blaring loudly from huge amplifiers strategically located on either side of the dance floor. It was nearly midnight when we slipped away from the party ready for home and quietness. We were delighted to find Allison and Tom waiting there for us. A few more short minutes together with them before bedtime would be nice. Bryant settled wearily into his comfortable big yellow chair in the den, loosened his tie, and plopped his feet onto the ottoman. Tom started the conversation, and we listened intently as he described nervously but with certainty of how much he loved our daughter. Cold chills came over me. I knew now why the chilled bottle of Dom Perignon sat stately on the coffee table and where his polite soft voice was leading us just as Allison came into the room carrying four champagne glasses.

"I want to marry Allison with your permission. She has accepted," I heard Tom saying. My immediate thoughts went to Mema. Only one week gone, and she was so right. Life does go on, and with all our grief, we were given this timely happiness to dwell on.

Love is Magical

Tom continued; he answered our parental questions with satisfaction. The tears I shed were those of joy, mingled with grief still and motherly emotion. Bryant consented; and our future son-in-law popped the cork on the champagne, and we began together to make plans for our daughter's wedding.

She wanted a formal wedding, simple elegance she called it, in her home church where she grew up, with our minister, a service of worship shared with friends and those she loved. On Sunday after church, Allison and Tom checked the calendar with our minister before they left town and their date was set. We had five months until July 26, 1986 — enough time to meet our deadlines and get Tom through the summer furniture markets.

Planning a wedding, I had been told by so many, is a real burden, disappointments and misunderstandings, headaches and sleepless nights, but this experience for us was unlike what we anticipated. The joys of sharing this happy time with a daughter were invaluable and precious. Allison assumed her bridal responsibilities; we worked and directed our plans with excitement, loving every minute of this joyous, once in a lifetime, opportunity together. Our only problem was the two hours that separated us from spending every precious minute together.

The decision was made by her to use the Alencon lace gown she had used for her appearance in the Miss North Carolina Pageant, leaving me with the task of transforming it into a wedding gown. (We were still good at making do, and there was a certain sentiment attached to this beautiful dress.) So with visions of how it could be done, I found the courage to tackle our daughter's huge request. The wedding gown was the first order of business. Phoebe, giving me moral support, decided to take a day off from work on the day I had set aside for cutting and designing. The pattern I selected to work from was actually the cathedral train attached to Phoebe's wedding dress. I remember her gasping and exclaiming, "You're braver than I am," as I cut apart the back of Allison's beautiful gown and spread it open on the living room floor. From there, we placed the huge train over crisp new white satin, pinning, measuring and figuring, getting it into perfect position before cutting more. My anxiety lessened as I worked, replaced by excitement and determined confidence to help fulfill Allison's wishes. For the next six weeks, the dress and all of its parts found a home on the dining room table, stretching in any direction it needed for completion. I spent quiet hours stitching lace and tiny seed pearls and iridescent sequins into this labor of love. Allison's pure delight was all the reward I needed for my creation. Finally, it was finished and hung to wait out the remaining days for the special day, and we methodically checked off our responsibilities week by week as time flew by bringing us to the moment of Allison and Tom's dream.

We were greeted with a day brightened with sunshine and predictions of the temperature reaching into the high nineties. All of our plans and details were now in someone else's hands. We needed only to depend on these selected professionals and set out to enjoy every minute of this hallowed day. The wedding brunch that morning was a happy way to begin with special friends in a near antebellum setting. All of Allison and Tom's families were there with Taylor swinging merrily in the white wicker front porch swing, charming the guests and breaking any signs of wedding day jitters.

Allison and I sneaked in enough time before returning home to dress for the wedding to make a quick run by the country club to view her wedding cake, worried that it might wilt in the heat of the day. A few quiet moments alone. We spoke very little, only glances, reading each other's thoughts, protecting ourselves from a flood of emotion. All that we wanted to say to each other had been said, only she had not finished.

Unnoticed, she had carefully and thoughtfully slipped into our room at some time during the morning and left for Bryant and me a priceless gift. Upon returning home, we found on our dressers a special book of poems each with its own personal inscriptions from Allison. I lifted my book, opened its cover, and began to read, "Mom, as I begin my role as Tom's wife, I can only hope and pray everyday that I will have the unique happiness of becoming as wonderful a wife and mother, etc., etc., etc. ..." I could read no further at that point; the tears fell. I went to hold my daughter and told myself, "From this moment on, I have to count candles!"

It was just as Allison wanted — an all white wedding, flowers, candlelight, bridesmaids in white crisp handkerchief linen, Susan Crouch as her precious maid of honor, melodic harp and organ music she selected, serene and reverent. As I sat waiting for our bride to enter the familiar sanctuary, I knew she would be pleased to see this lovely myriad of ideas unfold before us, adding to her dream. Groomsmen, bridesmaids, minister, and Tom, all in place, and the double doors from the chapel opened for Tom's bride's entrance. She paused, absorbing the moment, and smiling happily, then slowly began the long walk down the aisle on her daddy's arm. Beautiful, yes, beautiful, but Bryant and I could not give her away as custom goes. Our choice was to present her to Tom instead.

Looking deep into each other's eyes, they repeated the vows softly — serious sweet promises of love and faith and hope, and a new life to be

Love is Magical

learned only by living it each day.

Chapter 93

Dreams a Reality

When the 1986-87 school year began in August, we were anxious to get started! During the summer break, Dan and I agreed this would be my last year to work outside the home. Susan would graduate from North Carolina State University in May of 1987, and I could become "a woman of leisure." When I told Jean of our decision, she said, "Wonderful! We'll have to do something to celebrate."

The past eight months had yielded a rare amount of sadness and joy. Jean and I felt it was time for the four of us to plan something fun and exciting to look forward to. When the school year ended in June of 1987, we did just that.

For years we had said, "When we get the children through college, we'll take a really fine trip." That time in our lives was now, and we were ready for a happy diversion. An adventure in some far away place! One evening as we enjoyed dinner together in the quietest place we could find, ideas for our excursion became the topic of conversation. Europe and Hawaii were our choices. We decided on Europe.

The next day, Jean and I went to a travel agent and began planning our trip. We decided on a fourteen day American Express "Tempo" tour of seven European countries. Dan and Bryant couldn't believe how fast we got the information together. Jean and I knew if we didn't get dates for them to put on their calendars they would find other things to fill their time. Jesse and Millie's deaths were a grim reminder of how all the tomorrows you may think you have can be gone in a moment. We were not going to wait any longer to do this. My mama would say on various occasions, "One of the best tricks the ole devil pulls on us is to make us think we have all the time in the world to do something, but we don't." She was right.

In a few weeks, our plans were finalized. The dates were set and deposits had been made. Happily, we had added two others to our "merry band" — Nancy and J.P., Bryant's sister and brother-in-law.

Dreams a Reality

It was hard for me to contain my excitement because, on the day that I would have been starting back to work in days' past, this year I would be in Europe with my "true love" and wonderful friends. It was still hard for me to believe.

On August 2nd, our journey began. The big Boeing 747, filled with folks from every walk of life, carried us across another time zone and landed us safely in London, England. The six hour flight had left J.P. stiff and barely able to walk. A few days before, he had fallen off the roof of his house while cleaning out gutters. He was being a good sport about it, but we all knew he was in pain. As Dan and I left the plane, we passed a room full of wheelchairs. "Dan, this was meant to be," I said. When we asked the kind, rosey-cheeked lady standing inside the door if we might use one for a friend who was injured, she answered cheerfully, "Yes, yes. Where is he?" As J. P. hobbled into view, we identified him. She took complete charge of the situation. Before J.P. could say a word, she had him seated. Her British accent was captivating. "Are you comfy, dearie?" she asked as she whisked him away. "We must get you through customs now," she announced. Over her shoulder, she said, "Come along now." The five of us obediently followed her and J.P. right up to the desk where our passports were checked. We were waved through customs in a matter of minutes. While our fellow passengers watched in amazement, we collected our luggage and were sent on our way by this angel of mercy.

Outside the air terminal, we boarded one of the big, red double-decked buses that were lined up waiting to transport travelers into the city. From the upper deck, our view of the picturesque landscape was unfurled before us. We were given a glimpse of what Londoners' early morning rush hour was like as we drew nearer the city. We passed neat, red brick houses that less than an hour before we had flown over. Huge limestone buildings lined the streets standing watch over the busy scene below. Bobbies in dark blue uniforms directed people and traffic like a precisioned drill team. We passed tree-filled squares and green parks warming in the morning sunshine. It was going to be a lovely day for the Queen Mother's 86th birthday.

Dan and I were not surprised to find London unchanged. The bright red coats of the guards at Buckingham Palace, Big Ben, Westminster Abbey, Hyde Park, and Trafalgar Square were familiar sights. Standing in all their splendor, these beautiful old buildings created the backdrop for millions of pictures snapped by tourists as they recorded their moment in time, while tour guides described their rich history.

A shopping spree at Harrods, London's largest department store, was a pleasant excursion. We could not believe how expensive everything was, but we enjoyed looking. We went to the theater one evening to see "Me and My Gal," a delightful and most entertaining play.

All of us wished our time in London could have been longer. As we ate a continental breakfast our last morning there, we became hysterical with laughter remembering Nancy that first day in London snapping pictures with her newly purchased camera everywhere we went, only to discover that evening she had not removed the lens cover.

Our trip from London to Dover took us southeast through small villages and a rolling landscape dotted with farms, grazing cattle and an occasional castle atop a high hill. Our journey through the county of Kent ended at the famous white cliffs with the remains of Dover Castle looking out over the little town below from one of the chalk hills towering above the shore line.

After lunch, we boarded a Hovercraft to take us across the English Channel to Calais, France, twenty-one miles away.

Paris was our destination now. The view from the wide windows on our large comfortable, air conditioned coach surrounded us with a continuation of the beauty we had enjoyed in England. The French farmland and countryside were covered with acres of blooming sunflowers. Patches of gold, stretching as far as the eye could see on either side of the four and six lane expressways, led us into the capital of France. Our first stop inside the city was at a cafeteria. France is famous for its elegant cuisine, but this place was not a good representation. We were all scared to death of eating something that would make us sick, so we tried to choose wisely from the selection we had. Jean's meal was a banana and an orange, a cup of yogurt, potato chips, and a Coke. Nancy and I followed suit, but the men were fearless. After our memorable cafeteria dinner, we spent the evening cruising on the river Seine. We understood why Paris is called the City of Light. Everything was illuminated — the Eiffel Tower and Notre Dame Cathedral, all bathed in bright lights. Our excitement was only heightened as we anticipated the walking tour scheduled for the next day. Notre Dame, the Louvre (we all finally saw the "Mona Lisa"), the Eiffel Tower, the Arc de Triomphe, and the Champs-Elysees, and lunch across from the Opera House at the Cafe de la Paix were wonderful! No trip to Paris would be complete without experiencing the can-can girls, which we did on our final evening, at the Nouvelle Eve Night Club. The excellent French wine and food, the comedians, and lively dancing gave us a small taste of Paris night life.

The beauty and majesty of the Swiss Alps encircled us as we drove

Dreams a Reality

toward Lausanne, Switzerland, located on the shore of picturesque Lake Geneva. One night was not enough time to spend in this impressive city built on five hills.

We began to understand why this tour was called "Tempo," for indeed the tempo was picking up. We spent less than twenty-four hours in Milan, Italy, but we toured the city including the seven hundred year old white marble Milan Cathedral and the Gallery of Victor Emmanuel, a one hundred year old shopping mall topped by a glass dome revealing to us further the creative ingenuity of minds so long ago.

The "Tempo" carried us to the leaning tower of Piza and farther south to Rome the next day. We began our first evening in Rome with a ride down the Appian Way to the Ristorante Tempio di Giove where we were treated to a lavish Italian dinner and entertained throughout by boisterous and lively musicians. They played violins, accordions, and tambourines while singing and dancing around the tables. After our evening meal, we strolled through narrow streets to the Trevi Fountain where we made a wish and tossed coins.

Rome was hot and crowded with tourists from all over the world, but Peter, our guide, a native Italian, moved us in and out of the Colosseum, St. Peter's Basillica, the Vatican Museum and the Sistine Chapel with the greatest of ease and efficiency.

"Thank the Lord, we've finally convinced Bryant and Dan to get on the bus first and hold us seats near the front, instead of standing aside in their southern gentlemanly way for everyone else to board," I told Jean one morning.

"Our politeness has put the six of us on the back seat for the last four days. This passenger rotation mess ain't working," she replied.

"We're not going to be the last ones in line at rest stops any more just because we're the last ones getting off that bus," I added.

"Let the others wait for a change," Jean concluded.

We were touring with people of many nationalities, all considerate in their own way, but each taking care of himself or herself before all others. It took us several days to realize that this was one of the very few disadvantages of traveling with a large tour group.

"Ruum, you're not going to believe this one," I told Jean, trying to keep a straight face as I came out of our last rest stop before entering the city of Florence. I couldn't wait to see the expression on her face. She emerged wide-eyed and grinning.

"Nancy is going to die! She won't believe it, Phoebe."

We went directly to Nancy who was still at the back of the line smoking her cigarettes.

"Nancy, this one is different!"

"What do you mean it's different?"

"I mean it's different from anything we've seen. It's just a hole in the ground!"

"Jean ain't lying, Nancy. You gotta stand on two raised footprints and pray you hit that hole!"

She dropped her cigarette into the dirt and put it out with the toe of her navy Keds saying, "I just can't do that, y'all! I just can't do that!"

"Well, you're goina have to if you go," Jean declared. "If we can do it, you can."

"Nancy, honey, you don't have a problem," I told her. "Look at those four nuns in flowing habits ahead of you. Now, they've got a problem!"

Our momentous European "pit stop" soon became history as we rode on toward Florence, Italy, and more ninety-five degree heat.

We stood in awe and gazed up at Michelangelo's David. He was only twenty-seven years old when he began to sculpt this work of art. In the afternoon, we browsed in elegant shops filled with fine hand-tooled leather and exquisite gold jewelry.

One night was spent in Florence, and then we went on to a day and night in Venice, a city that lies on a group of islands connected by four hundred bridges. Canals served as streets, and our means of transportation was a "waterbus," flat-bottomed boats, or gondolas. We found the Piazza of Saint Mark in the center of the city lined with interesting little shops full of Venetian lace and crystal. In the evening, we took a gondola ride along the Grand Canal, listening to voices and music blend in the night before returning to our four hundred year old hotel, the Al Sole, for a night of rest.

It was lunch in Innsbruck, Austria, the next day in the heart of the Bavarian Alps where we shopped for Hummel figurines and splurged on lederhose for Brandon and Taylor. Jean and I got excited trying to picture our little grandsons dressed in these short leather britches that we had seen worn by many Austrian children. Before leaving we treated ourselves to more Swiss chocolate.

Dinner that evening was in Munich, Germany. There was little evidence left of the destruction of World War II in this modern, clean city. It had been ninety-five percent destroyed during the war and was now almost completely reconstructed.

The next morning, we headed through immaculate farm lands of corn, red cabbage, tobacco, sunflowers, grain, and vineyards. Through

Dreams a Reality

Heidelburg and on to a cruise along the Rhein River we traveled before we arrived in Bonn, Germany, where we enjoyed the welcomed comforts of the western world.

Twenty-eight hundred miles and thirteen days later, the windmills and canals of Holland awaited us. Amsterdam, the Netherlands' capital and largest city, was busy and noisy. Our first stop was the Coster Diamond Factory where we were shown each step a diamond goes through before it ends up in one of the glittering show rooms. After a tour of the canals, we drove away from the city through the lush Dutch lowlands, stopping in a small village to watch wooden shoes being made, and to a farm where cheese was produced. By late afternoon, we were in Volemdam, a quaint little village on the Zuider Zee where we had a last minute shopping frenzy and then dinner.

Upon returning to the city, Peter, our guide, led us on a walking tour through the "red light" district of Amsterdam. He told us to walk quickly and stay close to him. We did as he told us because it was frightening to be in this shocking and unclean atmosphere. It was a relief to get back to the safe confines of our bus.

The next morning, we said farewell to our globe-trotting acquaintances and began our journey home.

Chapter 94

More Gifts from Heaven

After our revival from the draining and disorientating jet lag that accompanied our European trip, we remained on an emotional high for days, still a little dreamy from our marvelous and educational adventure. Our day-to-day schedules went quickly back into order, and September began again much the same as most Septembers do. One morning you wake up after a good night's sleep with a clear head, move slowly, and the splash of cold water on your still sleepy eyes refreshes you, giving you the needed surge of energy you need to move to the kitchen before starting the coffee. Suddenly, you become keenly aware of the hushed stillness in the air around you and recognize the fact that the sidewalks outside are empty, no bicycles or tricycles or strollers are wheeling by, and there are no sounds of children running and playing with neighborhood dogs barking at their heels. You stand and stare out the kitchen window after pouring two glasses of orange juice, and a big yellow school bus rolls by and on down the street carrying these summer sounds of lively children back to school leaving their pets in their pens; and it occurs to you that another school year has started.

This September and fall could be different for us. Phoebe and I were free for the first time to make great plans together, to enjoy thinking of just the four of us now. No more long working schedules for her, no more responsibility of caring for elderly parents, no more college tuition payments, and children settled happily, all of which moved us into a more relaxed and less demanding stage in our lives. We set out with regular aerobic classes and morning walks, determined to stay physically fit, planning early Christmas shopping jaunts and inspired to dream of traveling to even more exotic places with our sweet husbands. We appreciated this healthy stage in our lives and recognized the importance of slackening our pace with every emphasis on a more stress-free environment for us all.

More Gifts from Heaven

Imagining this is one thing but accomplishing it can be difficult. No one lives alone. Everyday something or someone contributes to the events of our lives. As the scope of life broadens for us, we know that we have control only of the choices we make and our attitudes, hopefully and positively teaching us to enjoy the peaceful and beautiful moments and gaining from this the leverage we need for balance.

In late September, Bryant and I were given another surprising level of balance in this newly begun stress-free program when our son called on a Monday night with the news that we were going to be grandparents again. Good stress you could call this. I quickly felt a surge of motherly anxieties, of added responsibilities for Bryant, Jr., of health and their well being, unconsciously praying that maybe this child would help with the seemingly incessant division in our family. Perhaps this blessed event would be the answer and not just another tainted sign of progress. Our hope was elevated once again with thoughts of another grandchild, a brother or sister to our wonderful little Taylor.

The next evening, Allison called and I quickly asked, "Did Bryant call you with their news?"

"Yes, Mama. Did he say the end of April? That's only seven months from now, isn't it? Is Diddy on the phone?"

"Here I am, Suzie. How's my little girl?" chimed in Bryant, grabbing his turn on the line.

"Hey, Diddy, I'm fine. Are you okay?"

"Yea, yea. Watcha know good?"

"Well, Tom and I have some news for you and Mama. I found out today that I'm going to have a baby; you're going to be grandparents a third time, and I think it's the exact same week that Bryant Jr. and his wife are expecting their baby."

Another flood of joy engulfed us. We could scarcely believe what she was saying but knew it was the truth. We were thrilled almost speechless as we listened to our angel spell out the details of her day. Allison a mother! And I thought, "Lord what a wonderful mother she will be." Not only would I have two babies to worry about in the next seven months but their mothers and fathers as well and specifically our daughter.

I stepped back immediately into the world of young motherhood with Allison, sharing my outdated knowledge and learning of the new and up-to-date from her. She carefully involved us in the entire procedure from maternity clothes to baby clothes, from doctors to diets, always genuinely boosting us as parents and role models for their lives. We suppressed any anxieties or fears with positive thoughts, and with each day we became more and more elated anticipating the arrival of two more grandbabies in the spring.

Not even the historical plunging of the stock market on October 19, 1987, dampened our high spirits. The entire world was shocked when the market crashed, pushing the Dow Jones average down 508 points and rivaling the crash of 1929 that sent our country into the Great Depression. Our generation had grown up listening to the sad and desperate stories from our parents of this era, and suddenly this drop in the market today injected a frightened uncertainty on the economy effecting everyone.

Bryant and I had always been too conservative to put much faith in the stock market, preferring other types of investments, but we both had a keen interest in it. My interest had come from Bryant's encouraging me to learn more about the investment world, and my involvement in a small investment club had opened up the intriguing world of business, of stocks and bonds, commodities and dividends, and highs and lows. I found it all very exciting and fascinating.

With the stunned disbelief and fears brought about from this astonishing crash, we trusted that the safeguards of our current economic systems and the Federal Deposit Insurance Corporation would prevent the banking system from collapsing, unlike the crippling Depression of 1929. Stocks began to rebound gradually, and the market leveled relieving fears and doubts of a global recession, and soon this crisis was behind us.

Our happiness during the months prior to the birth of our grandbabies gave us a new measure of an adventurous spirit. The demands on Bryant's time and energy seemed endless, and our only escape was to get out of town when possible. We had sorely missed our little haven at Gaston Lake, so the magnetic effect of the spectacular North Carolina coast drew us closer and closer, and the idea of our own place at the beach haunted us with each visit. We had an overwhelming desire to share a vacation home with our children, a place to build relaxing and happy memories, to hear the clamor of little feet echoing around us, to invest precious time in, and feel the calming effect of a brilliant orange and bronze sunset on Bogue sound.

We finally yielded to these desires in January of 1988 after finding a condominium overlooking the ever changing waters of Bogue Sound from the north and the mighty Atlantic Ocean from the south. We were shopping out of curiosity as we had done for years, but the beautiful panoramic view sold us immediately, and Bryant bought our home at the

More Gifts from Heaven

beach instinctively and on the spot.

Owning an empty home requires immediate and careful planning, much thought and a collection of furnishings we both agreed on, so with some persuasion I convinced Bryant that he needed to accompany me to Dallas on a shopping spree. My Christmas gift from Allison and Tom had been an airplane ticket with hotel reservations to join them in Dallas that January for the Dallas furniture market where Allison and I were to make it our special business to find the perfect crib for their forthcoming first baby. Now, it would be even more fun with the four of us together, a short winter holiday and the perfect opportunity to select furniture, also, for our newly purchased beach home.

I had never seen the de-icing of an airliner, and as we sat on the U.S. Air plane waiting for our flight to Dallas a few days later, we watched in amazement out the small windows the application of this pink, almost cotton candy-like, chemical being sprayed from a huge tanker truck onto the wings of this giant airliner as it was de-iced. We paid close attention to this different sight although there was never any question in our minds of the safety of flying in weather like this. Our main concern was doing whatever it took to be with our children. We left Rocky Mount on a commuter flight at 6:00 a.m. with a light snow falling peacefully like hominy, bound for Charlotte, then a quick change for Dallas, never expecting such an accumulation of snow and ice. Shortly after taking off from Charlotte, the pilot announced that the Charlotte airport had been closed because of ice, but he expected the Dallas airport to be opened before we arrived for our landing. It had been closed all night because of ice. At this particular point in our holiday, Bryant and I looked at each other and began to wonder about this memory we might be building. We tried to relax, knowing it was out of our hands completely and thought of Allison waiting for our safe arrival.

The ride from the Dallas/Forth Worth Airport into the city was slow and tedious. The freak ice storm and extremely low temperatures had turned the streets and highways into almost solid sheets of ice diminishing the traffic and bringing what little there was to a snail's pace in this southern city. All the while, Bryant's masterful handling maneuvered the Budget Rent-A-Car along the bleak streets toward a full view of the downtown skyline of Dallas and on to our hotel. We wondered what we were doing here. "Anybody has got to be crazy to be out like this," he kept saying over and over.

We knew she would be there waiting and she was. Pregnant women are supposed to be beautiful, but Allison standing with open arms and a wide smile of relief to greet us had to be the most gorgeous expectant little mother we had ever seen. If there were questions earlier in the day about why we had come, our answers were evident at the very first sight of her.

From the Lowe's Annatole Hotel, it was only a short walk to the huge complex housing the hundreds of varied furniture showrooms; so each day while Tom worked, Allison and I led Bryant in and out and back and forth studying prices and quality, beauty, and texture of the many different companies and unusual furniture available to us. Lunch with Tom, ice cream for Bryant, lovely dinners at Tom's favorite restaurants in the evening, entertaining us still; and after four days, our mission was accomplished and our decisions were made. We placed orders for condominium furnishings, and our new baby would sleep in a white enameled cast iron crib under a raised canopy that Allison and I would eventually sew and cover with yards of white eyelet.

It was now three months later, and during this time we had busily made ready for the arrival of another grandchild, and the time had passed quickly. Allison waited impatiently now three days past her due date, and with every ring of the telephone, I jumped anxiously hoping to hear news from her or Bryant, Jr. We had two babies coming within the same week, and each day was scheduled for a quick departure to be with our children.

On April 26, 1988, Bryant, Jr.'s call came exactly on time, announcing in his tender and soft voice, "Mama, you have another grandson, Robert David Aldridge. He's a big boy. Everything is fine. When are you and Daddy planning to come up here?"

Once again, my voice was almost gone as the lump in my throat swelled. I remembered our boy the day Taylor was born and the joy we all shared; now his second son, perfectly healthy, was here at last, and I thanked God for this precious little grandson and his safe arrival into the world.

The ride that afternoon through Wake Forest and Durham was familiar as we made our way to visit little Robert for the very first time. Lavender and pink candy tuft climbing the banks of drainage ditches along the way, dependable yellow jonquils greeting this fresh spring, and the dust flying behind a farmer's tractor in the fields scattering the smell of newly plowed land captured our attention. Only the seasons seemed to change along this route we so frequently traveled. In two and a half hours, we were in Greensboro and only minutes away from meeting Bryant, Jr. and

More Gifts from Heaven

his precious boys.

The halls of the hospital were crowded during visiting hours; and, as usual, when you're in a hurry, the elevators seem never to come. In just a short time, however, we found our son and his little family huddled lovingly over this tiny infant wrapped snugly in a blue receiving blanket sleeping quietly in a clear acrylic hospital bassinet. It was a happy moment and increased monumentally when Bryant, Jr. carefully lifted Robert from his little bed and offered him to me saying, "You hold him, Mama." With caution and grandmotherly pleasure, I cradled this precious little gift from heaven in my arms feeling his warmth. I held the tiny hands and fingers, smoothing his newborn skin and became hopelessly and instantly in love with our blessed little Robert.

After our brief visit, we left Taylor with his mommy in her hospital room watching television. Bryant draped his arm over Bryant, Jr.'s shoulder as he walked with us down the hall past the nurses' station toward the elevator. His face revealed the relief and pride of a new father, and we understood for our hearts were filled with pride, also. We knew that only in the years to come would he realize how this gift of devotion could increase.

We drove away through the rush of six o'clock traffic, catching every stop light it seemed, weaving our way to be with Allison and Tom for dinner and to spend the night. They wanted us to stay with them to wait out the remainder of time knowing that their baby could come at any moment. (Just as sure as we would go back home, they would call us to return.) She was ready — the white eyelet covered crib in place, everything just as we had planned, even the freezer loaded with easy to prepare food for our stay and her homecoming from the hospital. She was great with child, uncomfortable, anxious and glad to have us with her. For three days we waited, strolling the sidewalks in the warm sunlight, sending Tom and Bryant out on errands, arranging and rearranging baby needs and sitting on the sun porch sipping lemonade while Allison snacked on raisins from a large round paper Sun Maid canister. On Friday afternoon, Bryant and I decided to go shopping while Tom took Allison for her weekly doctor's appointment. I was sure the break would be good for her and help to pass the time for everyone. Bryant's idea of a shopping spree was finding a nice men's store and deciding on an entire spring and summer wardrobe in one fell swoop and be through. We weren't gone long which suited me just fine. Both of us were anxious to get back to Allison for a report from her doctor.

In only a few hours, our yearly spree was finished, and we went in search of our expectant mother. They hadn't returned home, so we settled down to wait, but the strange silence of the house sang out to me, and I went intuitively to their bedroom looking for the bag she had packed to carry to the hospital. It was gone.

"Bryant, Bryant, they've gone to the hospital. We need to go. They came back, and we weren't here. Suppose she has the baby before we get there?"

Bryant hardly had a chance to calm me before we leaped at the sound of the telephone ringing. It had to be Tom. I ran into the kitchen and jerked the phone from its cradle on the wall.

"Hey," I heard Tom's deep voice. "We're at the hospital. I brought Allison in around 5:30. She's fine; she's walking the halls. I've been busy checking her in, but the doctor says things seem to be moving along pretty quickly. You might want to come on."

"Tell Allison we're coming now."

Bryant took the phone from me, "Where do we meet you, Tom? We'll find it. We'll find you when we get there."

We were off in a matter of minutes, off again to another hospital, to another anxious wait for the relief that comes when prayers are answered, when tense souls can relax with the blessed news of a safe and normal delivery of a perfectly formed and healthy child. In only a few hours now, we would see our sweet daughter and greet our third grandchild, a gift from God that we already cherished.

The labor and delivery waiting room was overly crowded and unsettling. Young and old waited there for the same news that we all hoped for, sharing openly each birth and event one with the other. We immediately had a nurse notify Tom that we had arrived. He soon appeared with a brief on Allison's progress and suggested that we have a quick supper in the hospitality shop while we waited. There seemed to be plenty of time, so we found salads and hamburgers, coffee and ice cream, and a pay phone. I called Phoebe to give her the latest report, thinking that our baby might come on her Susan's birthday only hours away.

We roamed the halls of the Winston-Salem hospital, wandering freely-- Bryant never missing an opportunity to make a careful examination of different hospital surroundings--before finding our way back to the waiting area, looking for any idea to pass the time quickly. We waited nervously for a long time sitting side by side in a two seater niche opposite the busy waiting room, aimlessly flipping the dog-eared pages of outdated

Field and Stream and *Good Houskeeping* magazines.

Across the way, a tired toddler finally slept on a green naugahyde sofa stretched out with her head resting on her mother's lap. I looked away down the hall toward the double doors leading into the delivery suite, and at last we saw Tom coming toward us.

"You can go in to see Allison. Only husbands and mothers are allowed in there, so why don't you wait with her until I get back? I have to get something from the car. It won't take long. Come with me. I'll show you where she is."

Feeling excited and rather privileged, I followed Tom to Allison's room paying careful attention to his very precise instructions along the way.

"You'll have to watch the monitor beside the bed for any changes. Any change means that the baby is in distress, and you'll have to call the nurse immediately. I'll show you all of this when we get there. The doctor will be back soon to check to make sure Allison is all right. I don't think it'll be too much longer. Call the nurse if Allison needs anything."

I entered her room cautiously, and Tom explained the strange monitor to me. He was out the door, and I leaned over and kissed Allison and took her shivering hand. She smiled at me trying to make small talk, describing her feelings, asking about her daddy, answering my many questions, enduring the pain. Still shivering, she didn't feel the heat of the hospital room. Her doctor strolled into the room, and I introduced myself, firing concerned motherly questions at him. Tom had explained to us earlier that the doctor would be back to give Allison a second epidural. His initial anesthesia injection had not been completely successful, and this really concerned me. I lost little time in asking him just how long he had been doing these procedures.

"It'll be all right if you stay in here while I do this," he said. "You might want to move to the other side of the bed. Are you going to be okay?"

"I'm fine, just hot. I think I have on too many layers," I answered.

"Why don't you sit down?" he suggested.

"I'm fine. I'm just hot," I told him.

"Sit down and put your head between your knees. You'll feel better. Is that helping?" he asked.

"Mama, I'm sorry I can't help you," my smiling daughter said. "I'm so sorry I can't help you."

"I'm all right. I'm just hot," I explained confidently.

"Mrs. Miller, will you please come in here and help Mrs. Forrester's mother?" I heard the doctor calling, "Get her on the floor, put her feet up."

My head was swimming, and I knew the feeling. Only once before had I felt this way — the day I visited Bryant in Watts Hospital after his tonsillectomy in 1959. I knew what was coming.

"I'm going. I'm going," I muttered. I saw Allison's smile as I felt the fainting wave overcome me.

"She's gonna be okay. No, we won't need that. I think she'll be all right."

I could hear the doctor's words faintly off in the distance. I was so relaxed. I must be sleeping, resting. I opened my eyes and for a moment had to remember where I was. Certainly, I was on the floor flat of my back beside Allison's bed with all of them looking down at me. My daughter was having a baby, and I was out cold, struck senseless. She didn't need a doctor; I did.

"Well, I'm back," I uttered sheepishly.

"Mama, are you okay?" Allison asked.

"She's fine. Mrs. Miller, help Mrs. Aldridge up. I think she needs to go back to the waiting area. She'll be better off out there," the kind doctor said as he left the room, undoubtedly amuzed.

"Will you be all right?" the nurse asked me when we reached the empty chair beside Bryant.

"Thank you, I'm fine now."

"What's wrong? What happened?" Bryant asked in perplexity.

"Nothing. Allison's doing great. Oh, I just fainted."

"You what!" he blurted out. "I knew you shouldn't be back there. Family members just don't have any business in that area. I've told you that."

We sat quietly and had a Coke. It helped. We waited and listened to the many calls for different families to come to the delivery suite each time a baby was born, and the time passed. April 30, 1988, just before midnight, our call finally came.

"Will the Forrester family please come to the doors outside the delivery room?" the loud-speaker echoed through the halls.

We jumped up and walked excitedly to find them. My heart pounded as I saw Tom wheeling Allison toward us, caressing in her arms their bundle of joy.

"Mama, we have a little boy. He looks just like Tom."

Looking up at us from the warmth of his mother's arms was our newest gift, Thomas Allen Forrester, III, our wide-eyed, dimple cheeked, brown haired angel, safely in this big strange world ready for our caring and loving. The relief and happiness that comes at a moment like this is reserved for grandparents. Our hearts were so grateful, our eyes filled with tears as we praised our daughter; and for the second time in one week, we fell in love instantly — now with our newest angel.

Chapter 95

Dan

"You know, honey, I'm the luckiest man in the world!" Dan said as he headed for the door. "I get up every morning and go to a job I dearly love!"

I can still see him as he looked that morning in our sun-filled kitchen. I always teased that he "played hospital" because he enjoyed his work so much.

The move to Rocky Mount and Dan's affiliation with Nash General proved to be so right. Within three years, Dan moved from credit collection manager to personnel manager and was now one of Bryant's vice presidents in charge of administration.

The year 1988 had been a happy, busy year. Daniel was still an active Marine currently on a "float" in Okinawa. Susan was enjoying her first job since graduating from college; and in February, she and her "true love," Bob, had become engaged.

That spring, Jean and I spent happy hours at the beach in their beautiful new condo, decorating and "playing house" while waiting for Dan and Bryant to join us on the weekends. One morning Bryant called to check on us. I answered the phone because Jean was in the shower. During the course of our conversation, he said, "You need to make your husband go get a thorough physical."

"Why?" I asked.

"When he went down to give blood this morning, they wouldn't take his because he had low hemoglobin," he replied.

A twinge of fear rose in me, but I quickly dismissed it and said, "I'll make sure he gets a physical right away! Thanks for your concern and for letting me know."

The phone rang again within minutes of Bryant's call. "What are you girls up to this morning?" Dan's soft voice asked.

"Hi, honey. We're not up to much yet. What's going on with you? I understand they didn't want your blood this morning."

Dan

"Bryant called and told on me, didn't he?"

"Yes, and I'm glad he did. Please call today and make an appointment for a physical. I want you checked from head to toe."

"I'm fine, honey."

"Dan, call today and make that appointment! We need to find out why your hemoglobin is low. That explains why you are so tired lately. Now, promise me you'll call."

"All right. I'll call," he promised.

But he didn't. When I got home from the beach, he "had forgotten."

Two months passed and still no appointment was made, so I stopped nagging and tried tears. They worked! After my tearful outburst one morning, he called me later to say the doctor would see him the next day.

The results of his examination revealed very little. "Dan, I don't know what's wrong with you," his doctor mused. "Your hemoglobin's low, and your blood pressure's high. I want you to come back in for another blood test."

After the second test, the results were the same, and my concern for his health was rising.

The second weekend in August was so hot and so humid — typical eastern North Carolina weather. Dan came in from cutting the grass that Saturday and said, "I must have pulled something in my hip when I started that lawn mower. Every time I take a step, it hurts."

He looked very hot and tired. "Honey, go take your shower, then come get in your chair and rest. Maybe that will make it feel better."

There must be this little mechanism built deep within us that suddenly becomes active, opening our eyes, alerting our senses, raising red flags of alarm. For at that moment, watching Dan walk through our den, I saw and felt and remembered things I had tried to quell for months but could no longer. Like a giant wave crashing in on top of me, my mind was flooded with these thoughts: Dan's color has occasionally been poor. He looks older and has no energy. The moment he gets still, he falls asleep, and now this pain is in his hip. Was it a figment of my imagination? It had to be. I'll fix him a good lunch, make him take it easy, and he'll be as good as new by tomorrow, I thought.

The pain persisted, and Dan, once again, put off going to the doctor. By the next weekend, our son's homecoming occupied our thoughts. We drove to Jacksonville to meet him, and once again stood with other parents, sisters, sweethearts, and wives, all straining to catch that first glimpse of their marine. "There he is!" Susan cried out as she ran toward her brother. Tall, handsome, lean, and tanned, Daniel greeted us with his warm, familiar smile, and "Hey, family. What's happenin'?"

Thursday, Dan and I drove to Charleston to pick up Brandon. He and his daddy would be with us for the long Labor Day weekend. We had big plans, a State football game, church and a backyard cookout. The children and I were becoming increasingly concerned about Dan. By Monday, the pain in his hip was so bad that he could hardly walk. Finally, I said, "You must want me to break down and cry again."

"What makes you say that?"

"Well, that's what I had to do the last time to make you call the doctor, wasn't it?"

"Yes, but I won't make you do that this time."

Our orthopedic doctor saw Dan the next day and began treating him. When everything he tried failed to ease the pain, a bone scan was scheduled.

The technician in charge of giving the bone scan came to the waiting area to ask me if I had any immediate concerns about Dan. "He has lost eleven pounds in two weeks," was my answer.

I saw such kindness and compassion that day. There was a steady flow of Nash General employees who walked through the area where I waited. After a check on Dan, they spoke to me, expressing their care and concern. Still, I was spared the full realization of how serious the outcome could be. Bryant, however, carried the burden of knowing the awful truth while he came to encourage and support me whenever he could.

Late that afternoon, we met with the internist who put a name to our worst fears: renal cell carcinoma, kidney cancer. He felt that the removal of the kidney could halt the assault on Dan's body, which gave us a glimmer of hope.

After our talk with the doctor, I ran up to Dan's office to retrieve his sport coat, and then around to Bryant's office to let him know what the findings were. When I entered his office, Bryant was standing in front of his desk, hands in his pockets.

"It's bad, Bryant. Really bad."

"I know, and I'm so sorry."

Our small flicker of hope was grasped away the next day when we consulted the urologist who told us the cancer had spread throughout Dan's body and was rapidly taking his life.

The doctor began telling us about new drugs, still in the experimental stages being used at the National Institute of Health in Washington, DC, and Duke University. He made arrangements for Dan to be examined at Duke the following week.

Dan

Daniel and Susan would be home that evening. The grim task of telling them about their daddy lay ahead. In past weeks, they had shared our concern and were aware Dan was not well. Susan and I had dared to utter the word cancer a few days before, confessing to each other that the fear of it had crossed our minds. Now, it was a reality. When Dan explained his condition to our children, he was very positive.

"I want you to know that I am at peace about all this," he said. "I don't know what the future holds for us, but I do know who holds the future. The Lord we have depended on all our lives will be with us and see us through this. If I live, I win; if I die, I win. Either way, I'm a winner. I want you always to remember that."

Jean and Bryant drove us to Duke that next week, picking Susan up on the way, and lovingly saw to Dan's every comfort and need.

The doctor who examined Dan was compassionate but very frank. He could not be encouraging. When Dan asked, "How long do I have?" Without hesitation he replied, "Six months, Mr. Crouch." Susan's hand tightened on my arm.

Dan stood, shook the doctor's hand and said, "Thank you. I appreciate your time."

"I'm sorry, Mr. Crouch."

Dan smiled and said, "Either way...I win."

The trip home was subdued, but the five of us faced what was ahead. It hurt to leave Susan at her apartment, but she assured us that she would be fine.

For the remainder of the trip home, Jean, Bryant, and I listened to Dan. He discussed everything from finances to his feelings about being ill.

Settled in our family room later, the television droning in the background, Dan and I talked about the events that had unfolded in our lives one step at a time over the past few weeks. We had been spared the full brunt of it all hitting us at once.

While the wheels were set in motion for Dan to be accepted at NIH as a research patient, he set about to make sure his affairs were in order.

One evening, Dan told Jean and Bryant how grateful he was to have the time to get everything the way he wanted it. The four of us seized every opportunity to be together. We had gone through the loss of family members, but this time it was one of us. It was such a comfort to know that Jean and Bryant would be there with us no matter what.

Susan and Daniel came home every weekend. Our family drew closer as we tried to understand and support each other.

By late October, Dan's appointment at NIH was scheduled. As soon as

For All The World To See

Jean and Bryant heard the news, they came by to check on our plans for this first trip to Washington and to reiterate to us that the unknown ordeals we faced were not just our problems but theirs as well. From that moment on, there was never any doubt that they would be with us. Bryant had already made their reservations that afternoon, and added, "I'll drive. We'll pick you up in the morning."

A beautiful fall morning dawned the next day for our drive to Washington. Jean and Bryant arrived at eight o'clock on the dot. We were looking forward to being together. Jean was trying to finish up a roll of film in her camera, so we snapped a few pictures.

"Dan, you and Bryant stand over there," she directed. "Bryant, take one of Phoebe and me with Dan now."

Dan looked good. He still looked the same. I knew what Jean was doing.

We drove down familiar streets, leading away from our house, adjusting seat belts, settling ourselves comfortably for the ride ahead. On past Nash General, our community's sentinel of healing, with the morning sun reflecting in its tall narrow windows, to I-95 we moved along. This busy interstate highway that we had traveled many times before was somehow different today. We were on an uncharted quest this time.

Fall colors were aglow in all their splendor. The beauty and fellowship helped lift the heaviness in our hearts.

We pulled in to a Friendly Restaurant for lunch. A pleasant aroma of food greeted us as we entered and were seated. The atmosphere was warm and inviting. Dan and Bryant immediately noticed the picture of apple cobbler, advertising the restaurant's speciality desserts. It was agreed they would have to "sample" some after their usual hamburger.

"We need another bottle of mustard. I can't get any out of this one," Dan said.

Handing Dan the ketchup in exchange for the plastic mustard bottle, Bryant said, "Here, let me try it."

Jean and I were aware of the trade but weren't paying close attention. Suddenly, there was this SWOOSH-THUPP sound. In unison, the four of us jumped, trying to escape the yellow spray propelling toward us. The blitz ended in an instant. We froze in puzzled amazement. Every eye in the restaurant turned our way. Jean broke the silence with, "Bryant, what have you done? Made a mess it looks like."

Bryant was covered in mustard! Jean and I had random splotches in our hair, on our face and clothes. Dan was virtually untouched! The top on a full bottle of mustard had popped off when Bryant squeezed it!

Dan

The restaurant manager ran toward us with a handful of towels, apologizing profusely.

Seven towels and thirty minutes later with Bryant's appearance altered by a spattering of yellow, we began again. Seated in another booth with another order of food before Bryant, our waitress told him, "There will be no charge for you and your wife's meal, and the manager wants the four of you to have the dessert of your choice on the house."

As we were leaving, the manager handed Bryant a T-shirt with Friendly Restaurant across the front; he also asked that the cleaning bill be sent to him. We all agreed that they went beyond friendly to gracious and very generous. For a brief time, the purpose of our trip was forgotten because of this zany incident.

The afternoon appointments went well. Our request for Jean and Bryant to be with us for Dan's examination and interview was granted. We wanted them to hear, along with us, what was said. The four of us sat and listened while the doctors asked him questions in rapid succession with emotionless soft-toned voices, stopping only to listen, thump or probe the upper extremity of Dan's body.

"Mr. Crouch, we would like to see you again tomorrow. We need to run a few tests of our own and do an MRI, after which we can better evaluate your case."

The next day, we moved from one waiting room to another, each one filled with cancer patients and their anxious family members, people we had never met, yet we shared a common bond. Some were eager to tell their story, as though the telling would somehow ease the awful truth.

By late afternoon, they had compiled a sizeable file on Dan. A very neat, professional assistant informed us that they were through and dismissed us by saying, "You'll hear from us within a week, Mr. Crouch. Have a safe trip home."

The four of us were weary but decided it would be much nicer to sleep in our own beds that night. In five hours, we were home.

Dan received the call from NIH a week later, saying he had been accepted as a research patient.

On November 3, 1988, Dan entered the hospital at NIH. We drove two cars for this trip. Bryant's niece was getting married the next Saturday, necessitating their return to North Carolina before us. Dan had said to me the night before we left, "I tried to talk Bryant out of their going, but he wouldn't listen. I hate for them to make that trip and have to turn right around and come back."

The morning Dan was to enter the hospital, we arrived at our appointed time. Immediately, we learned there was some confusion about records and admitting Dan that morning. Within a matter of minutes, Bryant had it all worked out. Dan looked up at me from his wheelchair and said, "I'm so glad they're here with us."

Thus began a battery of tests to determine what treatment would help Dan most. The decision was made to operate on his hip and remove the tumor that was causing him so much pain. Surgery was scheduled for December 13th. This gave us three weeks at home before returning to Washington.

Our precious Brandon was with us for Thanksgiving. As always, the happiness and energy he brought flooded our hearts and lifted our spirits. It was a very special time for the five of us.

On December 7th, Dan and I drove to Washington for his preliminary examinations and another MRI. Susan flew up on Friday. In the midst of this really traumatic time, it was wonderful to have Susan there. It sustained us, and we were able to have some "happy time" together. A snow storm that blanketed the area Friday night, and my fear of his being on the highway in it, prevented Daniel from being with us that weekend, but his phone calls warmed our hearts and encouraged us so much.

Dan was to enter Washington Hospital Center Sunday afternoon. When the time came for us to leave, I said without looking at him, "Honey, are you ready? It takes forty-five minutes to get there. We better get started." He was sitting on the edge of the bed, he didn't answer, he didn't move. I walked over and stood in front of him; Susan joined me.

He looked up at us, his blue eyes brimming with tears, and said, "Guess I let fear of the unknown get to me for a minute. I'm fine. I really am. No matter what the outcome Tuesday, I'll be fine. I just hate putting everyone through this."

Jean and Bryant arrived Monday afternoon, our steadfast friends there once again to uplift and encourage us. We were so glad to see them.

The four and a half hour surgery went well. Dan's doctor told us, "I successfully removed the tumor; and if all goes well, he will be walking without pain as soon as he heals from the operation."

The next morning after a visit with Dan to say good-bye, Susan and Bryant left for North Carolina; Jean stayed with me.

Until Bryant's return on Thursday, we varied our routine very little that week. Each morning, we left our motel after the rush hour was over. This made our forty-five minute drive through a notoriously unsafe area of Washington easier. In the afternoon, our return trip was always made before dark. Outside that hospital room, the Christmas season was in full

Dan

swing. The mall across from our motel, where we had dinner each evening, was beautifully decorated. From the moment Jean and I walked through its doors, sights, sounds, and aromas befitting the holiday greeted us. There were thousands of tiny white lights, expertly twined in and out of red, green, and gold ornaments; wreaths; garlands and ribbons; carols playing; children waiting in line to tell Santa their wishes; and shoppers with their arms full of packages. We enjoyed an unhurried walk through some of the shops and stores before returning to our room. It helped ease the tension of the day. Once inside the safety of our room, we readied ourselves for bed. The weather outside was so cold it felt good to get in our beds and crawl between warm blankets to talk and watch TV.

Bryant returned Thursday; and when he and Jean left on Friday afternoon, I was on my own. Dan had improved each day; and if he continued to do well, they would release him to go home on the following Wednesday.

Tuesday night, I "broke camp"! There is a real art to packing a car, especially when you have everything but the kitchen sink with you! If I do say so myself, our car was a masterpiece when I finished loading it. Mama always said, "Self brag half scandal," but I didn't care. I had "done good"! Every inch of the trunk and back seat were full, and a feeling of relief settled over me knowing that what had seemed impossible a few hours before was now accomplished. I was ready to roll!

When I bounced into Dan's room the next morning, my high flying spirits nose-dived. The minute I looked at Dan, I knew something was wrong.

"I'm running a slight fever. They won't let me go home if I have one degree of fever."

"Has the doctor been in to see you?"

"No. Just pray this fever drops before he gets here. I'm having a problem with nausea, too, but I haven't mentioned it to the nurse. I just want to go home."

The look on his face broke my heart. I could tell he felt bad but did an excellent job of covering it when a nurse would appear.

At eleven thirty, the nurse took his temperature. It was normal! "Thank you, Lord! Please let that doctor come soon, and please let him release Dan," I prayed.

Five minutes later, his doctor entered the room, asked a few questions, looked at Dan's chart, and said, "Well, Mr. Crouch, it looks like you'll be spending Christmas at home. Have a merry one. We'll see you after the holidays."

They didn't see Dan after the holidays, or ever again. By the time we arrived home, he was very sick! Jean was waiting in our driveway when I pulled in.

"Bryant is on his way and can help you in the house in just a minute, Dan," she said as he started trying to get out of the car.

"Honey, let's wait for Bryant to get here. I'm so afraid you'll fall on these steps," I pleaded.

Jean and I realized he was not going to wait. We got on either side of him and miraculously got him inside and seated in his chair. He was so sick.

The next morning, I admitted Dan to Nash General. When he was settled in his room, he looked at me, smiled, and said, "I'm so glad we made it home, honey." The children and I celebrated Christmas at Dan's bedside, but one thing we meant not to change was our Christmas Eve get-together with the Aldridges. After we attended church, Jean, Bryant, Allison, Tom, and Thomas joined Susan, Daniel, and me at our house for dinner and to exchange gifts. We all felt Dan's absence, but at the same time knew he would be the first to agree that life goes on.

Brandon, our happy diversion, was with us on his granddaddy's fifty-seventh birthday, the day before a CT scan revealed a tumor on Dan's brain. This would end our trips to NIH. He would no longer be a candidate for their research program.

Our church family provided a continual network of prayers and support while the people at Nash General took every opportunity to show their love. The outpouring of cards, phone calls, and delicious food was such a blessing.

Dan was discharged from the hospital on New Year's Eve. Though he was having daily radiation treatments, he was able to go back to work a week later. Thankfully, the operation had eliminated the pain in his hip. For the next three weeks, our life was almost normal. Daniel brought his new girlfriend, Tadge, home for us to meet. We highly approved of this new relationship.

Jean, Bryant, Dan and I drove to their home at the beach for a quiet weekend. We slept late, watched basketball games on television, ate popcorn, talked, laughed, and each evening enjoyed a delicious seafood dinner at one of our favorite restaurants. It was a relaxed, easy time. The four of us hung on to each minute, hoping it would not pass too quickly; but it did. Once again, we logged another special time together in our book of memories.

Tadge's parents invited us to their home for lunch the end of January.

Dan

From the moment we met, it was like being with old friends. Dan knew this was a special day for Daniel and made every effort to cover the fact that he was having some discomfort in his left leg. However, on the way home, he could conceal it no longer. A week later, he was hospitalized with phlebitis. On February fourteenth, I brought my valentine home. The weather that week was unseasonably warm (around eighty degrees) and Dan observed, "This is my Spring!" Winter returned the next week with four inches of snow over ice. My heart was wintery, too, as I realized Dan was accepting the fact that he would not go back to work.

By the middle of March, Dan was very weak. Our sister-in-law, Betty Ann, and her husband, Bob Featherstone, flew in from their temporary home in Hawaii. Their visit was such a delight and lifted our spirits so much. Betty Ann and I shared a common bond now. We had always been close, but this went beyond anything we had ever experienced.

That same week, Henry and Jan brought Dad Crouch and Kitty for another visit. That weekend, Palm Sunday, Daniel and Susan were home as they had been every weekend.

As if he had said his last good-byes, Dan seemed to give up and stopped eating altogether. Sensing that I could no longer care for him at home, Bryant gently suggested that we re-admit Dan to the hospital on Maundy Thursday. Peacefully, with Susan, Daniel, Tadge, and me at his bedside, he died on Good Friday. I was numb as we drove home in the cold misty rain. Later that evening, alone in our bedroom sitting on the edge of our bed, I remembered Daniel at age ten asking, "Daddy, how does it feel to die? What is it like?"

"Son, I believe it's like going to sleep. You know when Mother and I take you and Susan over to stay with Grandmother while we go out for the evening? You go to sleep over there, don't you?"

"Yes."

"Well, while you are sleeping, I come in, pick you up, and bring you home. You went to sleep in one place but woke up in another. Right?"

"Right."

"I believe it's like that when our bodies die. We go to sleep here on earth. Our Heavenly Father picks us up in his loving arms, and when we wake up we are in heaven with Him."

"It doesn't hurt?"

"No, son, it doesn't hurt."

Miraculously, the cold rain that had been pouring down for days had stopped, and a crisp, sunny morning dawned the next day. As I stood on our front porch and felt the warmth of the sun, I was reminded of the lines of a poem Dad Crouch often used in sermons:

> *I saw God wash the world last night*
> *With his sweet showers on high,*
> *And then, when morning came, I saw*
> *Him hang it out to dry.*
> *He washed every tiny blade of grass, And every trembling tree;*
> *He flung his showers against the hill; And swept the billowing sea."*

> —William Leroy
> Stidger

Things looked clean, fresh, and alive. I thought of renewal and rejoiced that Dan would live eternally in heaven.

Wisely, Bryant had suggested we make some funeral arrangements and decisions in advance. I was so grateful we had. Our friend, Nina, knowing my wishes, took care of the music preparations for the service. Jean and Bryant moved quietly in the background overseeing things they saw to be done and helped in more ways than I'll ever know. The same friends who had been our support system in the past six months rallied around us. Our kitchen overflowed with food, and friends filled our house.

The day of the funeral, the moment I had dreaded, finally arrived. The funeral director came to pick us up. Bryant went ahead to join the other pallbearers, but Jean rode with me and the children. It seemed fitting that Jean be the one by my side now as she had been all along. We walked down the church aisle together followed by Daniel and Tadge, Susan and Bob, and the rest of our family. Entering the sanctuary, I was overwhelmed at the number of people attending. The funeral was truly a praise service. I had never heard the choir sing more beautifully, and our pastor's words were uplifting and comforting. The whole service was a testimony of Dan's Christian walk and a wonderful tribute to him.

After the service, we met downstairs in the fellowship hall. Loving hands had prepared a wonderful luncheon for family and out-of-town guests.

Immediately after lunch, we went home, changed clothes, and departed for Asheville to attend the burial service the following day.

Friends and family covered the burial site at the cemetery. It was a

Dan

gorgeous spring day, and the view of the mountains was breathtaking. Dogwood trees were in bloom filling the landscape with their mantle of white blossoms. Our nephew, Bill, lead the grave-side service, sharing personal and touching remarks about his Uncle Dan, as a light breeze softly sang in the pines surrounding us.

As we drove away from that hillside, I did not look back. Like a huge collage, pictures of our lives together flooded my mind. I was truly at peace for the first time in months, knowing that Dan was no longer suffering but at rest. It occurred to me that I was now beginning another phase of our life together. I would not be able to touch him, see him, or hear his sweet voice, but I would always feel his presence with me.

Chapter 96

Adding Chantilly Lace Memories

Eight months before Dan died, Susan walked into the kitchen and plopped herself up on the kitchen counter next to the sink where I was cutting up a salad for our supper. She reached over, retrieved a piece of carrot to nibble on, and asked, "Mama, where is your wedding dress?"

"In that old brown box under the bed in Daniel's room. Why?"

"Oh...I just thought I might try it on to see what it looks like on me."

"Thought you wanted your own dress."

"Well, I might. But I would like to see how yours looks on me before I decide. It just seems foolish to spend all that money on a dress you wear only once."

Since her engagement to Bob, plans for their wedding were discussed often. Even though a definite date had not been set, the dress and head piece were at the top of our list of things to be done. Having gone through Allison's wedding with Jean helped me know what to get done first. Looking back now it was hard to believe Allison and Tom had been married almost two years and were expecting their first child in April.

After supper that same night, we pulled the tattered box out from under the bed and carefully peeled away the layers of navy blue and black tissue paper my mother had always kept placed around the dress to protect it from light. Susan slowly, almost reverently, lifted the gown and held it up against her. Standing in front of the mirror, she said softly, "I remember playing dress-up in this gown at Grandmother Fair's house."

"See this little tear at the neckline?" I said. "That happened on one of those dress-up occasions. I remember saying to Mama, 'don't let her tear that dress up. She may want to wear it someday.' Your grandmother answered saying, 'You wouldn't want her to wear this ole dress; you would want her to have one of her own'."

"I can't believe she let me play in it!"

"Honey, your Grandmother Fair would let you and Daniel do anything

Adding Chantilly Lace Memories

you wanted to as long as it was safe."

The gown looked beautiful on Susan. It didn't take her long to decide.

"This is it, Mama! We won't find a dress any prettier or one that means as much to me. It's exactly what I want."

Because of the four inch difference in our height, there were some adjustments to be made. The next day, I asked Jean to come see the dress on Susan and assess the situation. She walked around Susan once and said, "All you have to do is open these side seams and put in a gusset." Before I could blink, she took my seam ripper, opened the seams, and showed me what she meant.

After shopping for satin and lace that blended with the old, I began mending places on the thirty-five year old gown that had deteriorated over the years. When it was time to insert the gussets, I asked my friend Nina to help. She was not intimidated one bit by this task. I was. Her talented nimble fingers had the material in place, sewn, and finished in no time. With that done, I sewed lace over the new satin, and the dress was finished. It was such a relief to have the gown completed and ready to wear.

Within a few weeks, I felt more than relief. I was exceedingly grateful, because we were suddenly confronted with Dan's illness, and the circumstances in our lives changed considerably. For the next six months, all of our attention centered on him and his needs. During quiet moments when we were alone, Susan and I still discussed wedding plans. She was so hopeful that her daddy would be able to walk her down the aisle.

On New Year's Day 1989, only three short months before he died, as we watched parades and football games on television and waited for Daniel to return from taking Brandon back to his mother, Dan looked at Susan and asked, "Why haven't I heard you girls talking about your wedding?"

Caught off guard, Susan replied, "I don't know, Daddy. Guess we've had other things on our mind."

With a warm expression of understanding, he smiled and said, "Sweetie, whether I'm here or not, I want you and Bob to go ahead with your wedding. So you girls get busy doing whatever you need to do. Okay?"

"Okay, Daddy," Susan answered tearfully as she got up to hug him. "If that's what you want, that's what we'll do."

Later that afternoon, Susan and I revamped our list of things to be done.

In January we still hoped that he would be with us, so Jean and I got busy. We checked out bridesmaids' dresses, bridesmaids' gifts, invitations, flowers, anything that would save time on the weekends when Susan was home. One day, Allison met us in Thomasville to shop for material to make a headpiece. There, sitting high on a shelf just waiting for us to buy it was one already made. Exactly what we wanted. When I held it next to the wedding gown, the three of us said in unison, "Was meant to be!" Jean added, "Tell Susan she has to like it because it's perfect."

When Susan got home that weekend, she did love it. "I have the best personal shoppers in the world!" she exclaimed.

Everything we did "clicked." It was amazing what was accomplished in just two weeks. We had fun, and for all of us, including Dan, it was a happy diversion.

By the end of February when the proofs of Susan's wedding portrait came, it was her daddy who chose the one we would hang in our home.

At this point in time, uncertain days followed. Dan's illness escalated. Nothing but his comfort and well-being filled our thoughts. After his death that spring, we all tried to get back to normal.

Nothing was normal to me. I was numb, immersed in a sea of loss and loneliness. Each day, I gave myself little pep talks. "Smile, count your blessings, life goes on, remember nobody wants to hear how you really feel, you're not the only widow in the world, don't let them know you're hurting, twinkle-toe it through, and Lord, please help me get through this day!"

April was a blur. Susan moved into the apartment she and Bob would occupy after their marriage, and Daniel became a civilian. Bryant patiently guided me through business affairs I had to learn. Jean, ever present and supportive, helped me think through things to be done right away. I began to ride this wave of stay busy, tuck your grief away until later, stay busy, stay strong for the children, stay busy. This seemed to work. By the time May rolled around, the wedding and all the joy connected with it consumed my days.

June 3rd was a beautiful sunspangled day. The temperature was just right. Allison, Susan's matron of honor, came by to take her to the church. What a picture they made going out the door. Both clad in shorts, Allison had the shoes she would wear in the wedding stuffed in her side pockets, and Susan's hooped skirt was hanging on one arm. Susan was laden with cosmetic bag, curling iron, and hair spray.

At two o'clock, all the hours of planning, all the anticipation was over. As I watched Allison take her place with the other attendants, I thought, "The circle is complete." The four of us, Susan, Allison, Jean and I have participated in each others' weddings, bonding us, once again, in a sweet memory. At the rehearsal party, the night before, Allison said it so well in a poem she had written for the occasion:

> *But although the blood*
> *is not really the same,*
> *the heartstrings could*
> *never be tighter.*
> *For the loving memories*
> *I've shared with Susan*
> *No real sister could*
> *ever make brighter.*

The church fell silent; Nina chimed the hour. At the altar, Bob stood tall and handsome, his two brothers by his side. The moment we were all waiting for was at hand. At the back of the church, Daniel and Susan stood poised, ready to enter the sanctuary. As they began their walk down the aisle, I felt an overwhelming sense of pride. They were a beautiful testimony of Dan's and my love. For a fleeting moment, I wished for Dan, I would always be wishing for Dan. No sadness allowed today, I thought, not on this blessed day. Their Uncle Henry, who was conducting the ceremony, gave them a reassuring smile as they took their positions in front of him. When he began to speak, each word was warm and personal, chosen especially for Susan and Bob. He spoke to them of the love, nurturing, heritage, life style, and roots that had brought them to this sacred moment.

We listened as Henry said, "Both of you have lost your fathers in death, but they have played a very important roll in your developments." (How perfectly Robert and Dan had been included. They too would have pledged their love and support.) "For in this hour, the courts of earth will recognize a union already made in heaven, so let us rejoice, for the spirit of Christ has taught us how to love."

Chapter 97

New Beginnings

The previous year held a number of incredible surprises for us, the most numbing being, of course, Dan's grave illness. His enormous courage and convictions had been an inspiration to those around him; and as we lived life with him to its inevitable end, this extraordinary influence raised us to a higher level of appreciation for God's great valuable gift of life and love and the world around us.

I was reminded of an adage I had learned in years past saying, "God gives us love, something to love He lends us"; therefore, I find a peace in believing that we and the things about us are all on loan, and with love and faith we are grateful for this divine gift for however long it may be. God gives and God takes away; and like the circular band of an endless wheel turning on its axle, the cycle of life revolves and continues.

Soon after Christmas, Bryant, Jr. gave us the surprising and unexpected news that another grandchild was on the way. Anticipation of this event brought concern and joy to our lives in the midst of sadness. We celebrated in April birthdays for little Robert and Thomas who were hardly able to comprehend their being a year old already. In June, Susan and Bob's wedding was a happy and emotional time for everyone. With mixed emotions, we continued to live and helped Phoebe carry out these plans just as Dan wanted, suppressing waves of despondency knowing he was not with us. He would have been proud of his family. I'd like to think he was watching over us with that satisfying little smile on his face as he nibbled on even bigger and better chocolate chip cookies.

Two days after Susan's wedding, Allison and I left Rocky Mount in the background. Quite often, plans don't work out as you hope, but today they had. Hurried schedules, dressy clothes, rich food, chit chat, stress, and tears were uninvited quests on the vacation that awaited us. With Thomas belted safely in his blue padded car seat, we happily let the winding two lane road lead us away through Kinston and out past King's Barbecue, on to Trenton and beyond the mill pond looking so restful with its Spanish

New Beginnings

moss covered cypress trees shading the slick waters. We took the short cut on curvy back country roads cutting their way through freshly plowed fields of new green corn, soy beans, tobacco, and tall pine tree woods leading us as quickly as possible to our escape. Just the three of us, mother and daughter and grandson, cares behind us, were on our way just to enjoy being together, to do as we pleased at our own pace.

Minutes later, we delighted in seeing the wide concrete and steel bridge at Emerald Isle rise high in front of us drawing us to its view of splendor. The glistening different shades of water, lightened with shallow sand bars and patches of tall sea grasses, confident fishermen casting and reeling in the mid-day sun and standing tall in their fishing boats with steadfast hope of the big catch, all of the warm summery sights we so loved carried us away from any difficulties or pressures, much like the graceful grey and white sea gulls flying freely overhead.

Our baby had slept all of the way, giving Allison and me a quiet time to reflect, to visit, and to think on the coming week together. He was awake now just as we arrived to park at our condominium and second home, rested, and ready for his time. Allison gently lifted him out of the restraining car seat and cheerfully said to him, "Thomas, we're at the beach. Look, we're at the beach. Isn't this wonderful?" And it was wonderful. Our welcomed summer vacation began encompassed with young life and beauty and happiness galore.

The laid plans for the summer thankfully continued for us. Our holiday ended, Allison and Thomas went home with Tom, and it was Phoebe's turn for a visit. We had ten whole days free and felt very blessed, even though we knew it would be difficult. Her first trip back to the beach without Dan would not be easy. There were reminders everywhere of his last visit, the restaurants where the four of us enjoyed dinner together, a slow walk around the marina, the many steps he was determined to climb, and, the most outstanding, Dan meditating quietly, resting on the sofa telling us of how we had everything as he gazed out over the expanse of waters still before him.

It wasn't easy, though, as our hearts filled with nostalgia and our eyes filled with tears. Phoebe and I drew deep from our basic values and appreciated the fact that he no longer suffered, allowing the warm and fond memories he left with us to dominate. It was the beginning of a long and difficult adjustment period but maybe a good place to start. Quiet walks along the strand watching little sand fiddlers running, or just feeling the warmth of summer sand under your feet can often relieve the desperate pain of loneliness somewhat when you're confident of a friend

For All The World To See

walking beside you. It helps to have someone you can trust to share the fears and anxieties of mounting and perplexing decisions thrust upon you suddenly.

Phoebe and I knew the importance of these quiet precious interludes in our lives. This time for the rekindling of values and sentiments served as an avenue for us always to gain a deeper and clearer understanding of our state of existence and the control that we have over its quality.

The first weeks of summer passed quickly, and it was July almost before we knew it. We celebrated the independence of our great country that July with eastern North Carolina barbecue and fried chicken, cole slaw, and slices of watermelon at our annual picnic at Beacon's Reach, crowding in the gazebo overlooking the boat slip-filled marina in an attempt to escape the threatening grey skies overhead. Allison and Tom and Thomas were there for the long weekend, celebrating and waiting with us in excited anticipation of news of the birth of our fourth grandchild. No news came on July 4, but the afternoon brought strong winds and rushing black clouds. The lightning crackled and soon the heavy summer rain fell, breaking the thick humid heat just as our children departed for home and another trip to the Dallas furniture market. Bryant and I were alone again, snug and safe, with a few days left to rest and wait before our vacation would end.

Two days later on July 6, 1989, our telephone rang, and the voice on the end of the line was our son saying, "Mama, you have another grandson. He's fine. Everything is fine! We missed July 4 and your birthday on the eleventh, but he's great."

I breathed a huge sigh of relief. More prayers had been answered, and we made plans for a trip to see our boys.

The rainy skies had cleared, and the early morning was bright as we drove away from the beach toward Greensboro on Friday. Leaving early always gave us a clear-conscience excuse to stop for hot sausage biscuits, orange juice, and coffee along the way, and it did help to pass the time. We stopped briefly for gas and cold soft drinks and soon the four and a half hour drive was but another chapter in history.

Bryant, Jr. was waiting for us once again at the hospital and so was our beautiful, perfectly formed and healthy little Jesse Joseph Aldridge, named proudly for his father's late uncles and great grandfathers. We held our baby, touching him tenderly, feeling the softness of God's gift to us all. The miracle of this new birth and the joy and warmth of our spirits were broken only by the icy atmosphere in the hospital room.

Our visit was brief but our mission had been accomplished, and the

New Beginnings

long ride from the coast was safe and well worth our time. We had seen our proud son and Jesse, our newest little boy.

Chapter 98

Hawaii

As I walked through the airport in San Francisco I thought, "So far, so good." My confidence level was on the rise. Not being a seasoned traveler, I had been anxious about taking this long trip alone, but here I was, with my new Samsonite overnight bag slung over my shoulder, striding along in my new Easy Spirits appearing to know exactly where I was going. "Thank goodness I have a longer layover here than I did in Charlotte," was my next thought, as I continued the silent conversation with myself.

After locating my departure gate, I was able to have a relaxed lunch. Perched on a tall stool at a table overlooking the runways, I watched planes take off and land while I drank a Coke and ate a turkey sandwich and chips. By the time my flight was called, I was ready to begin the last half of my journey.

As the big plane soared out over the Pacific Ocean, I stared down at the vast body of water below and still could not believe that in a few hours I would be landing in Honolulu, Hawaii.

It felt good to lay my head back and rest my eyes. My thoughts drifted back to an evening only a year ago when Jean and Bryant and Dan and I agreed that Hawaii would be the next trip the four of us would take. We had tentatively planned it for this summer, but now it would only be the three of us.

The pilot's voice on the intercom interrupted my reflection by drawing our attention to the scene below. There was Pearl Harbor, sparkling and serene, the Arizona Memorial only a white dot, and I said softly, "December 7, 1941, A day that will go down in infamy."

I breathed a prayer of thanks and gratitude as the wheels of the plane touched the runway. I felt a rush of excitement.

As I emerged from the tunnel leading into the airport, there was Bob snapping my picture while Betty Ann placed a beautiful lei around my neck. Amid the hugs and alohas, I was so glad I had accepted their

Hawaii

invitation and taken Betty's advice not to cancel our plans to come to Hawaii. Jean and Bryant would join me here next week when we would begin a three island tour together.

For the next seven days, Bob proved to be the perfect tour guide as he and Betty showed me all the places of interest in Honolulu and around the Island of Oahu. Saturday evening, they took me to dinner at the elegant Monarch Room at the Royal Hawaiian Hotel where, after our meal, we were entertained by Hawaii's famous recording artists, The Brothers Cazimero.

Sunday morning, we worshipped at The Westminster Abbey of Hawaii, Kawaiahao Church. After the service, that was in both Hawaiian and English, we enjoyed lunch at the Hanohano Room in the Sheraton Hotel overlooking Waikiki Beach and Diamond Head.

Each day, I wished Jean and Bryant could see all the sights I was being treated to. On Friday, September 1st, they arrived. That evening the five of us enjoyed dinner together, and the next day Bob and Betty graciously played tour guide and host and hostess to me and the Aldridges for the last time before we said our good-byes.

For the next nine days, we turned ourselves over to Tauck Tours.

The first thing on our sightseeing agenda the next day was Pearl Harbor. What we saw and heard that morning stirred our hearts and refreshed our memories of what took place on that fatal day when we were only children. After an informative movie about December 7, 1941, and the events leading up to it, we boarded a Navy launch that took us out to the memorial, gleaming white in the morning sun with dark blue water gently lapping at its sides. Jean turned to me and whispered, "Have you noticed how many Japanese are here?"

"Yes, I have! We're surrounded by them. We seem to be the only American group here this morning."

We also noticed that their mood seemed to be that of the conqueror, while ours was quiet and somber. It was a moving experience to stand there looking down at the twisted, rusty hull of the Arizona, with oil slowly seeping from it, knowing that the remains of eleven hundred men were still entombed there.

Our next stop was Punch Bowl, an extinct volcano crater that became the National Memorial Cemetery of the Pacific.

Our excursion continued through downtown Honolulu, Waikiki, and Diamond Head before we returned to the Hilton Hawaiian Village.

Our flight the next day took us to Kauai, The Garden Isle. We visited the missionary town of Old Hanalei, Hanalei valley where "Puff the Magic

For All The World To See

Dragon" played by the sea, and where, it is said, rainbows are born. Together we took an unforgettable helicopter ride through Waimea Canyon, over beaches, cliffs, and valleys along the secluded Na Pali Coast.

In the evenings, we enjoyed the hotel's excellent cuisine, ocean views, and watched sunsets that left us at a loss for words to describe their beauty.

After a night of rest and a sunrise breakfast, we were taken to the airport for our flight to the Valley Island, Maui. We were, once again, met with a display of earth, sky, and sea blending perfectly to form an offering of unparalleled beauty. Our first stop was Lahaina, once a port of call for whaling fleets. Today, its old streets are lined with quaint shops and restaurants, filled with tourists enjoying Polynesian hospitality.

The next morning, we climbed the winding, narrow, scenic road to the top of Haleakala Crater, now a national park. The Island of Maui was formed by this sleeping volcano eons ago.

We were told by our native Hawaiian guide that the plant we were all so fascinated with was called the Silversword.

"It blooms only once, then dies. Then, it grows five to twenty years before blooming again. You are most fortunate," he continued, "because these are the first to bloom in forty years because of our threatened environment." The red and yellow, black and grey lava of the crater made a colorful setting for the pictures we took of this delicate plant with its dagger-like silvery leaves and yellow and reddish-purple flower.

The day before our departure from this island paradise, we rented a car and leisurely explored areas not included on our tour.

The ninth day of our tour came all too soon. We said our final aloha and mahalo nue, farewell and many thanks to this land of gentle sea breezes and soft rain showers, to giant, misty waterfalls casting rainbows while their waters flow to the blue green sea, and to tall mountains covered with cloaks of green tropical vegetation. I left wishing that everybody I knew would someday be able to experience "This loveliest fleet of islands that lies anchored in any ocean," as described by Mark Twain — and is so true.

My walk through the San Francisco Airport was better this time with Jean and Bryant at my side. We were spending a couple of days here to break the trip home and to give me a chance to see a little of this famous city. The Monticello Inn was located in the heart of San Francisco's Union Square. As we entered the lobby, its old world charm warmed us as did the fire burning in the library fireplace close by. It was quite a contrast to warm, sunny Hawaii.

After a short rest, we took a cable car to the Mark Hopkins Hotel. At the Top of the Mark, we drank a glass of wine and watched a grey misty fog cover the city. We walked through the lobby and gift shops of the Fairmont Hotel — better known to TV viewers as the St. Gregory Hotel in the ABC TV series "Hotel." After dinner, we retired to our rooms to catch up on our sleep and adjust to a different time zone.

We did not let the gloomy grey day that greeted us the next morning dampen our spirits. After our continental breakfast served in the library of the hotel by a glowing fire, we took a brief Gray Line tour around the City by the Bay. Golden Gate Park, Japanese Tea Gardens, Seal Rock, a drive across the Golden Gate Bridge, and Fisherman's Wharf, to name a few, were places we touched to give me a glimpse of San Francisco.

The flight back home was smooth and uneventful. We had all missed Dan terribly. The trip had not been without moments of sadness. It would have been nice if Dan had been with us, but we knew in our hearts he would have been glad we had gone on.

Chapter 99

Tadge and Daniel

It had to be the coldest December 15th on record! Jean, Susan, and I thought we would freeze as we ran back and forth to the car in the biting wind unloading boxes of greenery, candles, and red velvet ribbon and bows. We had only a few hours to turn this cold, stark banquet hall into a warm and inviting room for Tadge and Daniel's rehearsal dinner. I stood watching Jean place greenery and a red ribbon at the base of a hurricane globe and said, "Ruum, can you believe all that has happened to us this year?" Her hands stopped working, and her brown eyes stared into space.

"When I think back, it is hard to remember everything. It all happened so fast," Jean said.

"And nearly all of it without Dan," I stated. "I'm so glad he got to know Tadge and her family. He was finally at peace with the direction Daniel's life was taking."

Susan handed Jean and me greenery and bows, candles, and hurricane globes as we moved from table to table around the room. When at last we finished and surveyed our work, Jean said, "It ain't half bad, Ruum. It looks pretty!"

"It looks great to me," Susan said.

Pleased with our handiwork, we rushed to find a cup of hot coffee, braced ourselves against the cold, and returned to my motel room to put our feet up before having to get dressed for the evening.

As the wedding party and other guests began to arrive, festive sounds filled the room. I greeted friends and family as they entered, accepting their congratulations, compliments, and Christmas greetings when suddenly the thought of Dan popped through a door in my mind, a door I was sure I had shut and locked up tight for this evening and the wedding tomorrow: "You should be here, honey. You should be here with me and our children." A wave of loneliness engulfed me. I wondered how in the world I would get through another wedding without him, but things are

Tadge and Daniel

always brighter in the morning. With the dawn, bright sunlight did come but along with another bitter cold day and happy voices and laughter filling the air, lifting my spirits to carry me through the hours ahead.

Tadge was a lovely bride, fair and petite, a real contrast as she stood beside our tall son with his coal black hair. Bryant, as Daniel's best man, was where Dan would have been, and Uncle Henry helped Keithen, his son-in-law, perform the ceremony.

The service was a reflection of family and Christian values Tadge possessed, and all we had always hoped Daniel would find in a wife. It thrilled me to see such a sense of family in the wedding party — Susan and Bob, Tadge's brother, Todd, Sarah, Keithen, and their little girls, and Perry, Daniel's cousins. Each one was a wonderful reminder of the importance of family support.

God continued his goodness to me. I had lost Dan, but he had given me two new children in Tadge and Bob, and they came at exactly the right time.

One week after the wedding, I celebrated Christmas with Susan and Bob in Raleigh. Tadge and Daniel had returned safely from their honeymoon Christmas Eve. They, like Susan and Bob, were excited about their first Christmas as husband and wife, and the beginning of their lives together.

As a New Year began, I resolved to visit Kitty and Dad Crouch as soon as possible. Just before Dan's death was the last time we had seen them, and I would not allow another week to pass without a visit. Dad's illness had prevented them from attending Susan and Daniel's weddings, and they had been greatly missed.

Kitty was so glad to see me. Lonely and tired, she knew she was facing the loss of her husband, and more years alone. Each day, we stayed with Dad who was now in a nursing home. On the third day of my visit, the 12th of January, 1990, Dad died. He was eighty-two. It was good that I was there. Jan and Henry, Kitty, and I were a source of strength for each other. It was sad, but our family would be together again.

I came back to Rocky Mount shortly after the service for Dad, and this was the first time in almost a year that I was glad to be home alone and to have a quiet, calm day. I had been on a roller coaster, staying busy, fleeing my grief, but today I planned to sit in front of the television, undisturbed to watch the inauguration of George Bush, the forty-first President of our country.

As I watched the parade of limousines carrying his entourage to the Capitol, I had an unexpected thought of curiosity. Wonder how many

Presidents have been sworn in since Jean and I attended Peace College? I counted back and concluded Bush was the ninth one.

Today, a new era began for all of us.

Chapter 100

Inspiration

"For All the World to See"

"For all the world to see" — the words kept coming back like the ebbing of a tide — "for all the world to see." I stood in the quietness of our home, motionless, staring out the kitchen window, my right hand resting on the still warm faucet as I watched Bryant back out of the driveway, turn the car in a straight direction and leave for work.

"For all the world to see" — it was back.

The trees outside were wrapped in a dense mist that late January morning, creating another foggy and gloomy day. Everything seemed quiet and peaceful. I don't know how long I stood there just gazing into the bleakness. The heat flowing from the vent under the kitchen counter felt warm to my feet and ankles, so I just stood there being lazy.

"For all the world to see, the simple joy of you and me" — there was more, and I began to think and listen.

Why not? I thought. We have shared so much, and nearly everything that has happened in our lives has effected us all, good and bad; we walked through it together and for such a long time. We've laughed until we've cried, we've cried until we've laughed, we endured and learned from criticizing and analyzing each other. We have faced reality together, and through it all our lives were always strengthened because of our friendship.

"For all the world to see, the simple joy of you and me."

Yes, I thought, we long for this for everyone, yet we know it cannot be. There it was again.

I moved and opened the drawer in my kitchen desk and found a dull pencil and a small legal pad. "Phoebe and I have to do it," I told myself out loud. "We've been teased about it, and we've joked about it long enough. We have a lot to write about, and we can do it. We can record it together for our children."

It was nearly noon before I realized the time. I had been at our kitchen table leaning over a legal pad writing all morning without hesitation and enjoying it. The words flowed, and my thoughts raced. When I finally rose from the table, I had written the first two chapters of this book and could hardly wait to tell Phoebe. Still clad in my gown and warm winter robe, teeth unbrushed and bed unmade, I went to the telephone and called Phoebe only to realize she was at school that day. I had to talk to someone and was satisfied momentarily with her telephone answering machine.

"Phoebe, I need you to come over today as soon as you get free. We need to talk. I've had a crazy brainstorm. I'll be at home all afternoon."

She was there by four o'clock, curious, wondering what I was thinking.

"Phoebe, we've got to write a book! I know it sounds crazy, but I really think we can do it. It won't be easy, but we have a lot we can write about."

"Ruum," she exclaimed, and looked at me in amazement!

"Here," I said. "I have something I want you to read."

I handed her the few pages I had been led to write and waited for her reaction. After a brief time, she looked up from the pages and laid them in her lap. She was sitting on the floral sofa in our den across the room from me. I smiled and waited, and with eyes brimming, her voice broke as she said, "Ruum, I honestly think these words are inspired. When did you do this?"

"Today." And I described my day to her. "What do you think? I honestly think we can write a book for ourselves and our children. We've got to do it, Phoebe!"

"Well, writing a book is the last thing I had on my mind today, but I really do believe you've been inspired. You know Dan and Bryant have teased us a million times about writing a book, so we might as well try."

"I know we can do it. It'll be our secret. We'll get Bryant to read and proof it for us. We'll just get to work. We have almost forty years to recapture — not many friends can claim that."

For the next two hours, we discussed and planned this crazy venture. The more we talked, the more excited we became. Bryant came in from work, and we ran our ideas by him. He good naturedly wanted some credit for our actions, reminding us of how he and Dan had tried to get us to write our thoughts down in book form; so with his immediate approval and encouragement, we made this commitment. Thus began the story you now

Inspiration

hold in your hands.

> *Go now, write it on a tablet for them, inscribe it on a scroll, that for the days to come it may be an everlasting witness.*
>
> Isaiah 30:8 NIV

Chapter 101

Seeking Direction

During the weeks that followed, Phoebe and I charted our course searching for the right direction. We began with pocket tape recorders, organizing, and recording our working conversations, taking us back to our Peace College days, exercising our recall abilities to the utmost. We lost ourselves reflecting on dates and events, sentiment and nostalgia; and with our meditating, we became increasingly more and more amazed at the drama of life we had experienced together.

We were filled with an unbelievable measure of enthusiasm for our secret project but found ourselves plagued with interruptions preventing any progress toward writing. Up until then a lot of talk without much to show for it, so in March of 1990, we broke away from routine and schedules, from telephones and television, and with feeble excuses of needing to get away for a rest, we drove to the beach seeking an uninterrupted and hasty retreat. Here, we buried ourselves for ten days, and from the third floor window of our condominium, we were once again surrounded only by quietness, the slight swaying of weathered youpon tree tops, the gentle motion of the butterflies and sea gulls, and the ever constant beauty of the sea all around us. Here, we finally began to write, to think, to laugh, to cry, to encourage as we shared our meager creative writing abilities.

Equipped with new pencils and erasers, legal pads, an electric pencil sharpener, and a dictionary and thesaurus, we worked from morning until sometimes very late at night filling our hearts and minds with nostalgia — that which looks over the rough spots and pot holes of the past we've been told, but we had our start and there was no turning back. We had no modern word processor, only many, many handwritten pages, the desire to complete our project, and with perseverance we set our goals and assignments for the months ahead. We took our breaks in the evening with seafood dinners and chilled wine and often with other friends who seemed

Seeking Direction

perfectly satisfied thinking we had been reading, relaxing, or shopping all day. At the end of our stay, we were mentally drained and ready to go home, ready to resume our usual schedules, free of the frustrations we had questioned, and confident we could accomplish the goal we had set for ourselves.

Before we left the beach on that last day, I watched Phoebe from across the room and could tell she was daydreaming. It was easy to do in this surrounding. I looked out the big window at the view that mesmerized her, a clear crisp early spring day stretching her vision past the marina over rippling waters to the tree lined banks on the other side of the sound.

She eventually spoke. "You know what I wish I could do?" she said. I waited for her answer. "Take Susan to New York. She's always wanted to go."

"Why don't we do it?" I said. "Wouldn't that be a great birthday present? It'll be Allison's thirtieth birthday, Susan's twenty-sixth! The four of us, you and Susan, and Allison and me. A girl trip! Let's do it! We have plenty of time to plan it for the summer, and it will be a gift they'll always remember."

She liked the idea and knew I was serious. Without hesitation, our thoughts excitedly turned from reminiscing and writing to planning a holiday with our girls.

Two days later, they received silly birthday cards, weeks before their birthdays, inviting them to join us for their birthday celebration in New York City. They thought we were crazy, but they knew we were serious.

Phoebe and I returned to the beach in June for another week of concentrated work on our book, vividly aware of the freedoms we take for granted and grateful for this land we are fortunate to live in. We are still constantly amazed as we see face to face, through the median we know as television, the best of the world and the worst of the world as we watch our world changing rapidly right before our eyes. On the night following the first anniversary of Susan and Bob's wedding, the nightly news brought to us a grim reminder of the massacre in Tianamen Square in Beijing, China. This too had taken place on June 3 the previous year, and the replays of this tragedy sickened us still.

The Chinese student movement had occupied Tianamen Square for weeks prior to the riot in a quest for freedom and democracy, questioning the deeply held conviction of the Communist People's Republic, wondering if it was fundamentally wrong. As the signs of democracy simmered and the support for this movement grew stronger, armored Chinese troops moved in shooting and killing not only their own intellectuals and students, but workers and businessmen as well, in a ruthless slaughter that captured the attention of the world. This military might shattered dreams of idealism and a better way of life. Now the youth of China still wait for relief from communism and hope for a democratic future.

The scenes of horror in China were a direct contrast to the jubilation we watched on television just seven short months earlier. In October, the nightly news once again had carried us straight to Germany and the collapse of the Berlin Wall. The reunification of East and West Germany was at last a reality after four decades. In absolute awe, we watched the German people, armed with chisels and hammers and a new freedom, knock and hammer, beat, stomp, and kick until portions of the gigantic wall fell in joyous celebration. "Checkpoint Charlie" no longer existed, and the citizens moved freely across the forty year old barrier that had separated their worlds for so long, bringing to an end still another unbelievable and extraordinary chapter in world history. Amid the joy, trouble still existed as fellow citizens confronted their extreme differences and doubts building a new life in a united nation.

We reminded each other that we were at the beach to work, so with the remote control we drew the curtain on world events temporarily, feeling fortunate that we could do just that. We were safe and blessed, free to express ourselves, free to come and go and make our own choices, free to live our lives without any threat of intimidation.

The next week, Phoebe and I traveled to Raleigh and back to the roots of our friendship. The students were away for the summer, so we were free to roam. We climbed round and round the familiar old stairs in the Main central hall of our beloved Peace College, exploring the corridors, looking, seeking out our old room, and her halls echoed with fond priceless memories of 1952 and our past. We were saddened to find that Miss Lucy's memorial room no longer existed, and the only evidence of her was the portrait hanging in one of the parlors.

The same narrow hidden back stairs took us down where we had another glimpse of the modern fast track cafeteria now occupying much of the area we knew in the fifties as an orderly and refined dining room. Styrofoam cups and paper napkins had replaced the white and green trimmed china and linens. The changes were all there, thirty-eight years of change and progress, and we felt that the warm, rich traditions had slipped away. Everyone accepted the changes.

Two blocks away, we ordered toasted pimento cheese sandwiches and cherry Cokes at the lunch counter at Person Street Drug. Sitting now at altogether new tables, we remembered the days before graduation, eating

Seeking Direction

this same lunch clad in Bermuda shorts, bobbie socks and saddle oxfords, dreaming of Bryant and Dan, and hopes for the future. Now, the future was the past.

By late afternoon, the traffic began to build, and we planned to be on our way home before the rush. There was still one thing left to do before we ended our step back in time. We walked from our parked car away from Peace College up Wilmington Street until we came to the home we were sure was Dr. Pressly's. Cautiously, we approached the front door of the stately and still grand old home. We entered freely as we realized that the once elegantly furnished rooms now housed offices with desks, clicking typewriters, and humming computers. There were no oriental rugs but bare hardwood floors in need of refinishing. Signs of progress!

We returned to the car and went home to write.

Chapter 102

New York, New York

With help and good suggestions from Bryant and Tom and a host of friends, Phoebe and I carefully planned our birthday trip to New York with our girls. On August 2, 1990, we met Allison and Susan at the Raleigh/Durham Airport where their celebration began. Giggly, silly, filled with a teenage excitement, organized, and well stocked with an extra carry-on stuffed with instant Tang, granola bars, raisin bran muffins, "four corner" nabs, and a six-pack of diet Pepsi, we boarded the plane for our brief flight to the Big Apple.

"Mama, can you believe this? I can't believe this. Look at all these people, Mama. This is just wild! Allison, can you believe we're here? I'm not believing this!" Susan could hardly contain herself as we obediently followed behind Allison, our appointed tour guide, through the crowded maze of different people at La Guardia.

"Now, Alece (our pet name for Allison), you do know where to meet him, don't you?" Phoebe had to ask only once.

"Yes, Phoebe, don't worry. He'll be there! You and Mama just hold hands and follow me. He'll be holding a sign up with my name on it."

Tom had arranged earlier to have a chauffeur driven limousine at our disposal for transportation during our four-day stay in New York, and in a matter of minutes, we were greeted by James, a greying middle-aged gentleman straight out of South Carolina but who was familiar with this big city after having worked as a chauffeur here for twenty years. We followed his instructions and made our way to the parked limousine eager to get started.

"Mrs. Forrester, I have your champagne whenever you are ready," we heard James say to Allison after we were comfortably seated (giggling still) in the sleek black limousine.

"Now will be fine, James," we listened as Allison answered him politely.

Susan, Phoebe, and I were all shocked!

New York, New York

"Alece, I can't believe this. Champagne! Does that come with the limo?" I asked naively.

"No, Mama, I ordered it! This is my surprise," she explained to us as James served the chilled Korbel for our enjoyment before the drive into the city. We toasted each other and everything else we could think of, Susan and Phoebe's first trip to New York, and each was thrilled to be building and sharing another special memory. At our hotel, we watched while James and the doorman unloaded our luggage and soon realized that Allison was tipping the doorman or whomever when needed and always a step ahead of us. Phoebe and I decided to give her our tipping money, and she became our official designated tipper. She knew how and when to do it.

Our suite of rooms at the Salisbury Hotel on 57th Street was beautiful. A huge bedroom with queen size beds, bath, dining room and efficiency kitchen, and living room (where we eventually sent Phoebe to sleep by herself because her snoring kept us awake) were a delightful surprise. After settling in, Allison led us a few blocks away to the Hard Rock Cafe for lunch, and that evening we were off to the "Phantom of the Opera" and a late supper after the theater at Un, Deux, Trois, a trendy little restaurant.

The next morning, we walked taking in as many of the sights as possible from Central Park and Park Avenue, Fifth Avenue, and Bergdorf Goodman's to Rockefeller Center where we dropped at last for lunch on the Plaza. On the sidewalk in front of Saks Fifth Avenue, Allison made us stop again for hot pretzels and soft drinks exclaiming, "Everyone who comes to New York has to eat a hot pretzel with mustard! Here, Susan, try one!" From there, we cruised Tiffany's, FAO Swartz, and did more shopping and looking till the afternoon with only enough energy left to get to the theater for "Cats" that evening.

James arrived promptly at 10:00 on Saturday morning for our four-hour limousine ride and tour. He knew exactly where to take us. We ate Italian pastries in Little Italy. Then we went to China Town (with Susan standing and leaning out the sun roof to get better pictures of the colorful oriental community), the World Trade Center, the Statue of Liberty, Central Park, Wall Street, and all points of interest in between before he deposited us in the theater district for an afternoon matinee of "Grand Hotel."

We saved our birthday dinner for the last evening in the elegant atmosphere at The Top of the Sixes at 666 Fifth Avenue, Tom's recommendation for our big dinner out. With reservations in Mrs. Forrester's name, we again followed Allison and the maitre d' to our prearranged table by the window overlooking the brilliantly lit skyline of New York. We had played tourist long enough. We were ready to slow our pace, relax, and savor every moment left together. Phoebe and I especially knew that this could be a once in a lifetime experience.

Ever faithful James was again prompt on Sunday morning in ample time to get us to the airport for our flight home. By now, he had become our friend, our guide and guardian away from home. He took us on a different route on our return trip to La Guardia, still guiding and showing us the sights; and from the rear window of the limousine, we said farewell to our whirlwind birthday celebration and New York City.

On Monday morning, our giddy New York memories of joy and harmony were hushed. From this point, all of our thoughts leaped in near panic to gather the details and reasons for another unreasonable outburst.

Eager to entertain Thomas after being away from him for four days and wanting to fulfill a promise made to Taylor weeks before to take him for a bike ride on his new bicycle, Allison had decided that this warm and beautiful August Monday morning was the perfect day for such an excursion. Thomas loved to ride in his rumble seat on his mommy's bicycle; so with heads covered in safety helmets, off they peddled to issue an invitation to Taylor. He was thrilled, dressed quickly, and with permission from his mother and firm instructions to have him home in exactly twenty minutes, they rode away happily.

Allison insisted that Taylor wear his watch to keep the time. He was seven and a half years old now, a very bright little boy, telling time, and delighted to be the keeper of the clock. They sought out the quiet neighborhood streets as they peddled close to the curb, giving Taylor the opportunity to show proudly to his aunt and cousin how well he had learned to ride his shiny new bicycle; and in precisely twenty minutes, they rode back into Taylor's driveway where their fun had started. Their fun ended abruptly, however, for waiting for them was a very angry mother who expressed her displeasure vehemently about Allison's presence and at any happiness that she and Thomas had given to Taylor. Stunned and shocked, Allison calmly hugged Taylor, kissed him good-bye, and hurriedly peddled Thomas away carrying with her a painful and heart-wrenching memory. Needless-to-say, this incident continued the strain on many family relationships.

Chapter 103

Changing Positions

Trying desperately to understand the "driveway" incident, we again made adjustments and turned our thoughts and sights toward the upcoming pleasant events our family could look forward to. Our lives had always been so intimately interwoven — a canvas of sad and happy days, with coping and resolving, caring and communicating. Life is at best a constant game of coping. Whenever we had been confronted with a problem, we had always been able to settle it, but now we found a jagged rip in the dream of stability we had spent our lifetime building. We felt there was no thread strong enough to repair the damage far, far beneath the surface. Henceforth, there would always be something in a day to remind us of the wrenching pain deep within our hearts.

Only one week had passed when Allison gave us the wonderful news of her second pregnancy. She suspected it in New York but said nothing. "Pretzels"? Now, I know why she kept wanting to eat hot pretzels! Another child, another new little life, and again God's timing was perfect. There was always something good to think about.

We now had before us not only the glorious expectation of another grandchild but a family wedding to help plan in the coming months. Our niece Millicent had finally been able to set the date for her wedding after waiting for the U.S. Navy to settle on a leave time for Steve, her fiance. Sweet Millicent and her sister Sally Ann had adjusted well to the tragic loss of their parents, a loss we cannot begin to comprehend. Bryant and I were gratified and complimented that she turned now to us for advice and guidance, and we wanted to do everything we could to help make her wedding day a happy one.

In September, Bryant, Jr. came to his sister's surprise thirtieth birthday party alone and for only a few minutes. He was so handsome, but the strain on his face now brought a choking lump in my throat every time I saw him. It was not easy to celebrate a birthday or any occasion when this burden of the unknown was so evident. It broke our hearts to think that here we were celebrating another beautiful occasion with our daughter and that we had never been allowed to do the same with our son or his children during nine long years. Difficult as it was for him, I knew that it was this unbreakable thread of love and loyalty instilled in him long ago that always drew him back to us if only for a few minutes.

We were deeply concerned as we watched his family, a part of us, continue to drift away. It had been nearly two years since we had had an extended visit with Taylor, our first grandson; so with Bryant Jr.'s permission, we were able to take him on a fun-filled five day trip to Disney World in January. I will never forget the uninhibited delight in his big brown eyes on that Wednesday afternoon when we met him and his daddy at the airport to leave. His little duffle bag was loaded with special things. He wore a stuffed fanny pack, all prepared, and his face beamed with childlike excitement. This was the greatest gift he could give to us. How wonderful it was to see this look on his innocent face, free from the uncomfortable expression of anxiety he had learned to greet us with these last few years. (We would eventually see in the faces of his little brothers as they grew older not only anxiety but fear each time they saw us. We hoped the future held a remedy.)

The flight to Orlando was exhilarating for Taylor. He sat with his granddaddy on the way down and promised to sit with me on the return trip. He was oblivious to our feelings of apprehension caused by the chaos and the threat of impending war for our country in the Persian Gulf. This possibility had been building for months, but we hoped to be back at home before it actually happened.

We were taxiing in from the airport to our hotel in Disney World when the news broke. Shocked by what we thought we had heard on the car radio, the driver turned the volume higher, and we listened as the announcer said over and over, "They're bombing Baghdad! They're bombing Baghdad! It's war. It's true. The news is coming in from everywhere!"

The thudding in my heart increased. Nobody knew what to expect, and we were miles away from the security of our home. Allison and Thomas were due to join us the next day for the rest of the week, and she would be traveling pregnant and alone with two year old Thomas. We had already been warned, and rumors were circulating about possible terrorist attacks in our local airports. We were frightened, and my mind literally raced as I waited for Bryant to check us into the hotel. Taylor, full of excitement, went from window to window in the lobby peering out trying

Changing Positions

to see all around him. We could hardly wait to get to our room, turn on the news, and call home.

* * *

As I walked through the back door, coming in from choir practice, the phone was ringing. It was Jean.

"Hey, we're here."

"Ruum, I'm so glad to hear your voice and know that you all are there. Have you heard the news? We're at war," I said to Jean.

"Yes, we're in our room and have the television on right now," she told me.

"I just walked in the house from church, so I haven't seen any of it until right this minute. Isn't it something when we can sit in our family room and watch a war?"

We had been aware since August of our country and its allies launching a massive build-up of troops and high-tech equipment in the Saudi Arabian desert. Day after day, we watched as young men and women said brave, tearful good-byes to their families, and left for a foreign land where they battled not man but relentless heat and sand. For weeks, the news media spanned the miles to bring Desert Shield into our homes in vivid detail.

Patriotism was at an all time high. The American people had not been this united since World War II, and our service men and women never failed to mention their gratitude for the support back home when interviewed.

None of us really believed there would be a war. We were convinced Saddam Hussein would back down, but mad men seldom do, and he was no exception. The looting and murdering of the people of Kuwait had continued. The United Nations' deadline for Hussein to stop this madness was January 15, 1991. Hussein refused, and Desert Shield became Desert Storm. While Americans ate dinner the evening of January sixteenth, they watched the allied air strike over Baghdad. We saw fireworks, unequaled by any we had ever seen, as tracers darted across the dark sky, and Patriot missiles rose to meet incoming Iraqi scud missiles. People's lives and the oil fields of Kuwait were in harms way.

We were told that the relentless air attacks being ordered would pave the way for a possible ground war. We waited eagerly for press conferences by General Colin Powell and General Norman Schwarzkopf to be announced to gain further information. It was a tense and strangely

For All The World To See

exciting time.

Jean ended our conversation that night by saying, "I'll call you again before we leave to come home."

As we hung up the phone, I thought how glad I would be when they would get back home and how wonderful it would be to have everybody back safely in the fold.

* * *

The joy of a child and the magic of Disney World took over the following day. From the new MGM Studios and the unveiling of Hollywood film making secrets to the monorail whisking us away to the beauty of the Magic Kingdom, we allowed ourselves to slip away again into this incredible fantasyland.

Allison and Thomas arrived safely in the afternoon, and for three days the five of us enjoyed the security of one another and explored every avenue of joy rides and exhibits in this kingdom of theme parks. Breakfast with Mickey Mouse and the other Disney characters was a highlight for young and old as we began our second day. Swimming in the hotel pools, kicking sand, and running on the man-made beach, fried chicken, french fries, ice cream, sailor hats, and spectacular firework displays at Epcot made for long days and tired, sleepy little cousins, not to mention a pregnant mother and weary grandparents. Feeling the warmth of a child's tiny hand in yours and the spontaneous teddy bear hugs of love and gratitude during a day of enchantment easily made up for aching backs and tired sore feet at day's end. Taylor's Kodak fun-saver camera clicked feverishly until there was no film left. It's interesting what an eight year old sees at eye level — the tops of garbage cans, a lunch table covered with dirty plates and cups, the back side of a man's waist, and the many different feet of people standing in a line.

It was a moment of wonder although clouded by the news of the raging war, and by week's end we could no longer escape from the real world. On Sunday, we were greeted by dramatically increased security when we arrived at the Orlando Airport for departure. Two to three hour waits in lines for security checks on all incoming and outgoing passengers and luggage irritated very few as all seemed thankful for the added scrutiny. An uneasy quietness prevailed in the terminal while busy travelers anxiously tried to get to their destinations. Eastern Air Lines chose only the day before to go out of business, grounding all their planes and leaving Allison and Thomas, along with many others, stranded with

Changing Positions

Eastern tickets. She was eventually able to change to another airline with yet another delayed schedule.

Taylor sat with me on our return trip just as he had promised. Bryant and I rested that night only after taking Taylor to his daddy and hearing from Allison and Thomas. Our children were safe, and we possessed a memorable and endearing gift.

Chapter 104

Easter Angel

The raging of Desert Storm came to a surprisingly quick end just as we had all hoped and prayed for. For nearly six weeks, we were taken daily to the shores of the Persian Gulf and the sand covered land of Saudi Arabia, Iran, and Iraq by continuous twenty-four hour coverage from the television networks to witness face to face the magnitude of this disaster. The citizens of the world had access to live pictures of the battling and suffering when during the final days of February the Kuwaiti people were at last liberated. February 26, 1991, brought the ceasing of guns firing, but the beginning of a monumental clean-up in a land ravaged by war and a calamity of suffering, of human health, and of animal and plant life increased by Iraq's senseless burning of the Kuwaiti oil wells. For decades, the environment will be marred from the scars and contamination of this battle.

The war ending brought a colossal relief to the entire world, and our consciences were now able to enjoy totally the euphoria during the weeks of March as we waited for our fifth grandson's birth while we watched the Duke Blue Devils march on the road to the final four in a basketball frenzy. Our plans were to gather at Allison and Tom's home for the Easter weekend in March to wait for baby and watch basketball.

Our wait this time was different. Allison and Tom were calm and free of questions. They knew what to expect as she sat uncomfortable and great with child, and Thomas was our main distraction. Bryant and I had come to enjoy our grandson and to take care of him while Allison was in the hospital. (There would be no labor room visits for me this time around!)

On Saturday night, we settled down after a pizza dinner to watch the Duke vs UNLV basketball game; and as the final buzzer sounded with the Blue Devils the winner, Allison clearly jumped to the ceiling in the den of their home with joy and excitement! Duke had made it to the final game, and Allison promised to have her baby soon, so no one would have to miss the championship game on the following Monday night.

At two o'clock in the morning, the jubilant scenes of celebration had been quiet for only about two hours when we were gently awakened by our expectant mother saying they were on their way to the hospital.

"I'm sorry I have to disturb you, Mama, but we're leaving. Yes, we're leaving. I'm on my way! Pretty good timing, huh? Thomas is asleep and just fine. Tom will call you. I love you. Go back to sleep."

Her instructions telling me to go back to sleep were fruitless. My heart began to pound. I could not lie there. I prayed and paced from Thomas' bed back to ours until the light of dawn began to appear. Bryant slept, and Thomas was still sleeping when Tom called at 7:00 a.m.

"He's here and fine. He's really different — doesn't look anything like Thomas did — he's fair and blond. Allison is doing well, just tired. She's anxious to see you. I'm going to stay here with them until you come."

We breathed a sigh of relief and thanked God for our new baby, another grandson, another miracle, and brought to us on this glorious Easter morning. Soon, we heard the waking sounds of Thomas and went to give him the good news of his little baby brother and attempt to keep his world as natural and normal as possible. I called Phoebe and Bryant, Jr.; and later in the morning, we took Thomas to spend the day with Allison and Tom's good friends where he would play with their twins. Bryant and I went straight to the hospital to share this Easter elation with our children.

The halls of the hospital were familiar to us now. We passed the hospitality shop, teeming with visitors, its windows filled with spring flower bouquets, balloons and Easter bunnies, reminding me of the surprise Easter baskets Allison had set out for Thomas and us before leaving for the hospital. I could hardly wait to get to her as we waited for an elevator.

Allison, smiling but with chin trembling, turned and looked at us when we entered the room but was unable to speak. She began to cry softly.

"Honey, what's wrong?" I asked as we went to her bedside.

"Oh, Mama, something is wrong with our baby." She could say no more. Her heart was breaking, and I was engulfed instantly with fear. We turned to Tom as he quickly began to speak.

"He's been taken to the Intensive Care Nursery. They say he should be okay, but his lungs apparently did not clear of fluid during the birth because he came so fast. In recovery, he stopped breathing, but he's breathing now and is on oxygen and being monitored constantly. The doctor says that this is not unusual when a baby is large and born quickly. He'll have to stay in the nursery until his lungs clear. We'll just have to wait, but he's going to be okay."

Tom's words were reassuring, and Allison gained composure, still beautiful in all her anguish.

"You'll be able to see him when they call. Daddy, don't you want to know what we named him?" Her blue eyes glistened, and she looked up at Tom who did most of the talking.

"Bryant Aldridge Forrester. We thought we would call him Aldridge. We hope you like that."

With that, the flood of emotion could be restrained no longer. Bryant took his daughter in his strong arms for a big daddy hug as I had seen him do so many times, and with misty eyes and his voice overcome with gratitude, he thanked them for yet another gift of love.

I tried hard not to allow myself to think of the realm of possibilities but only of the reassurances Tom kept giving to us. I was holding her warm hand. Her long slender fingers kept squeezing mine as we tried to comfort each other. The sun flooded the cold hospital room, and I remembered again what day it was and how quickly our mood had changed. I leaned down and gave my baby a hug.

"We're going to see Aldridge. I can't wait any longer. I know he's beautiful. Try to stop worrying, Allison. He's going to be fine. You'll see. We'll be back soon. I love you. You rest."

Before we entered the nursery, a nurse gave us faded olive green sterile hospital gowns and masks to wear and led us through the unit filled with sick and premature babies until our eyes fell on our Aldridge. It was March 31, 1991, as I stood over the bassinet and talked silently with God, watching this beautiful fair haired child, his tiny chest rising and collapsing as he struggled for each breath. Our first sight of this baby boy, nine pounds and thirteen ounces, and I couldn't understand how such a big baby could have this trouble.

The doctor explained everything, why the oxygen tent was necessary, the tiny IV connected to his scalp, the heart monitoring, giving us answers to every question for the reassurance we needed so desperately.

For two days, we watched and waited. Seeing Duke beat Kansas on Monday night to become the 1991 National Champions thrilled us, but our real thrill that day had come with the news of Aldridge's improvement and the possibility that he would be released soon.

After what seemed like forever, on Tuesday, this angel's tiny lungs were clear, he stabilized and was brought finally to his longing mother and father. How grateful we were to have the medical care readily available to us, saving our precious little boy when we know that there are thousands of children around the world who are not as fortunate.

Easter Angel

Our beautiful Easter baby came home, and the glory of that day will never be forgotten.

Chapter 105

1991 Progressing

Millicent and Sally Ann were waiting for us in Roanoke Rapids in late April when Phoebe and I arrived at the hotel. It was a wonderful warm and sunny spring day, and with each new day Aldridge grew stronger, and my heart and thoughts could focus more on helping Millicent finalize plans for her upcoming wedding in June. We could at last relax with relief and feel some of Millicent's excitement.

We had spent much of the winter having her mother's wedding dress altered to fit her. This was done, and now it was time for the last details of parties, guest lists, hotel arrangements, music and flowers, and a conference with her church minister concerning the direction of the ceremony. Over lunch that day, we listened as Millicent went over all the orderly and precisely organized specifics before we began moving from place to place with her checklist. With mature efficiency, she had taken care of every possible detail, and all she really needed from us was our approval.

She wanted Phoebe to be her wedding director and Bryant to give her away and wanted me to sit where her mother would have been. We were, therefore, a significant part of her plans, and she and Steve were eager to share every aspect of this special day in their lives. Millie and Jesse would have been very pleased and proud of her. We were, and it was a satisfying and good feeling seeing her so in love, so happy, and so secure.

The sun was setting as we drove back home that evening, and Phoebe and I, full of memories, wondered how we could get through another emotion-filled wedding ceremony.

On June 8, the carefully planned events began to unfold in perfect order. Family, friends, the beauty and reverence of their lovely church, the love and support for a young couple beginning a life together created exactly the atmosphere Millicent had hoped for. I choked back the usual lump in my throat as I watched Bryant bring her down the aisle and give

1991 Progressing

her away, the privilege long reserved for her own father. I watched the single candle, lit in memory of her parents, flicker peacefully as she and Steve said their vows, making the same serious promises and giving their lives to each other.

After the festive and elaborate reception that Millicent had planned carefully, we waved them off amid a shower of bird seed and blessings to begin their new life in San Diego, California, where Steve would be stationed for the next four years with the U.S. Navy.

* * *

There are some things you think you will never see in your lifetime. On August 19, 1991, such a happening occurred. We, the world, listened as the Soviet Union began to crumble after seventy years of communist rule.

Top Soviet leaders attempted to remove President Gorbachev, but the coup failed as quickly as it began two days later. Led by Boris Yeltsin, the Russian Republic president, thousands of Russian people dared to defy the coup leaders. The yoke of communism had been around their necks for too long. They were being fed bits of freedom and democracy, and they liked it. Yeltsin urged them to begin a general strike against the Communist Committee to show their opposition. Under Yeltsin's leadership and approval from the majority of Russian citizens, their efforts to establish democracy were realized, overcoming communism but leaving the Soviet Union riddled with turmoil.

In September, Jean and I plucked a few days from our calendars and went to the beach to work on our book. Our book. Just saying those two words made us tingle with excitement! We had surprised ourselves and shocked Bryant with our ability to recall so many varied events in our lives. When we first began, we prayed we would be able to write at least two hundred pages, but now we prayed we could find an end. After our usual bowl of oat bran and a few cups of coffee, we began a day of remembering and weaving words and memories.

"It's not going to mean anything to anybody but us. I don't know why we keep torturing ourselves like this," Jean would say.

"Our children will appreciate it, and just think how much fun it will be to sit around in our old age and read it to each other. It's probably the only way we'll remember anything, so don't knock it," I told Jean.

As we wrote, we relived and traveled back through each event. Places and people floated in and out of our minds. We worked hard to hold them there long enough to record our experiences with them. Sometimes, it was like knowing you still had this wonderful treasure, but you couldn't remember where you put it. We kept working and pushing, and the stories somehow surfaced.

"Just think, Ruum," I said, "Our friends think we're down here playing."

"Yeah, what a hoot! They won't believe it."

I was doing a lot of substitute teaching now, so Jean and I set aside Thursdays that fall to work on our project. Finding the time to break away from our daily routines to work uninterrupted wasn't easy. At times, it was difficult to find believable excuses to give to our other friends for the concentrated time we were spending together.

"You're going to the beach again!" they would exclaim. "Yes, I'm helping Jean with a project she's working on down there," was my usual answer, and Jean used, "Phoebe's been having some low days lately, and the beach will cheer her up." They probably thought the Aldridges had the most decorated condo on the Crystal Coast and that I was the biggest whinebox of the century. But if it sufficed, so be it. They would understand later.

* * *

An autumn chill was still in the air, and I hoped that the cold blast of winter would hold off now until after Thanksgiving. In North Carolina, we are often that fortunate, and as I busied myself in the kitchen on that Tuesday before Thanksgiving, I pictured Thomas running and playing on the sand at the beach. The aroma of roasted turkey filled the house, my almond pound cake and pumpkin pie were ready, and I was waiting for the sweet potato casserole that Tom loved to finish baking. I began to relax as most of my cooking came to an end, and all that was left to do was organize our packing for what had become our annual trip to the beach for the Thanksgiving holiday. I found that cooking before going was easier and gave us more time to enjoy each other.

Allison and Tom were to meet us on Wednesday, and we loved this last long weekend together away from our usual busy schedules before the bitter cold weather set in. The telephone began to ring just as the timer on my oven started buzzing. I couldn't decide which to get first; then I reached for the telephone and stretched the long spiral cord to the oven with me and took the casserole out as I heard Allison's voice on the line.

"Hey, Mama. I bet you're cooking."

"You're right. I just finished. Where are you? When are you coming?

1991 Progressing

The weather's gorgeous. I hope it stays this way for the remainder of the week."

"Mama, would you mind if we didn't go to the beach, and we came to Rocky Mount?"

"No, certainly not, if that's what you all want to do."

"I hope you won't be too disappointed, Mama, but I have some news. I'm okay, but I'm at the doctor's office now in Winston, and I wanted to call you now."

I turned off the oven and pulled out a kitchen chair to sit in.

"What is wrong? Are the boys okay?"

"Yes, they're fine. It's me. I've known since Friday but waited until today to get the results before calling you and Daddy. I have a giant cell tumor on my knee and the doctors say it has to be removed as soon as possible. All of the tests thus far indicate that it is not malignant. They are ninety-five percent sure, but we can't be positive until after surgery."

I was petrified with fear and tried to keep my composure as she continued. This just couldn't be happening, but, oh, God, please God, don't let this happen to my baby. I was thankful she did the talking and was unable to see my distress. She didn't need that.

"Mama, remember how I complained of my knee bothering me all summer? Well, after a game of tennis on Friday, it was hurting so bad that I went straight to the doctor's office. He sent me to an orthopedic oncologist here at Baptist Hospital. He's very nice and supposed to be one of the best. Daddy can check that out for us. I want it done immediately. I've already told him that I didn't want to wait any longer than necessary. It could be as early as Friday."

"Allison, it's going to be all right, honey. We'll do everything that we have to do to take care of you. I'll come and take care of the boys. Maybe, Phoebe will go and help us. I know she will."

"Mama, I'll have to be in the hospital for seven days, then in bed propped up most of the time for another week. That's too much to ask of you and Phoebe, but, Mama, I don't know what to do. I really do need you to keep my boys."

"Don't you worry for another minute. You know I'm coming. You just come on to Rocky Mount tomorrow, and we'll work it all out. I love you, sweetie pie."

On Friday, the call came giving her the surgery schedule, and we spent the remainder of that day in Rocky Mount finishing their Christmas shopping, knowing that this would be the last chance she had. When I talked to Phoebe, her first reaction was just as I expected.

"Ruum, I'm going with you. You'll need my help. There's no way I'll stay here and let you go alone to keep those babies. I wouldn't be worth two cents sitting here worrying my head off. That's all there is to it. Anything I have to do can wait."

Monday morning, December 2 at five o'clock, came early, but we couldn't sleep anyway. Bryant went with Tom to take Allison to the hospital for the dreaded major surgery scheduled for seven, and Phoebe and I drank coffee on the sun porch talking quietly, trying not to wake the boys as we began the final wait. Soon, the little voices of children drew us to their bedsides and became that precious distraction that playful children can be at a time of sadness or sorrow. We had finished giving Thomas and Aldridge breakfast and had them dressed when the long awaited ring of the telephone made us jump.

Tom's voice was filled with relief. I began to cry and Phoebe did too as I listened to him, motioning at the same time to Phoebe that Allison was okay.

"It wasn't malignant, and she's going to be all right. She'll be on crutches for two or three months and will have to be checked periodically to be sure that another cell has not recurred somewhere else, but she's okay."

I repeated the message from Tom to Phoebe, and we both said, "Oh, thank you, God, thank you, thank you, thank you!"

With this wonderful relief, it was easier for us to assume the duties and responsibilities of Allison and Tom's household. Babysitting was a pleasure always, and the cooking was made easier by their many friends who kept bringing in food. Phoebe's being there allowed me the freedom to sit with Allison at the hospital during that first week of recovery, but by nightfall each day we were weary. We soon found ourselves on our knees a lot, as our backs wouldn't bend, due to the strain of tending to an energetic eight month old baby and an active two year old.

We had established in the beginning with Tom that it would be more convenient and comfortable for all if Bryant and Phoebe and I moved into his company's condominium where we could spend the nights leaving Tom the privacy he needed. Bryant returned to Rocky Mount when he was sure that Allison was all right, and Phoebe and I arrived at Tom and Allison's house each morning at six, slow, but ready to begin the day.

For two weeks, our schedule varied little. Allison finally came home, and her company was welcomed by everyone. Thomas wouldn't leave her side, and with each new day she became more mobile. Tom was able to find pleasant and efficient help for her, help she could depend on during the months of recuperation; and our second week of nursing and caretaking, gratification and delight soon began to wind down.

We were true believers in signs, meant to be, as we say so often, and on the morning of our last day with Allison, the real sign of our departure appeared. Phoebe and I went early to help Allison and her new maid get organized for the day, returned to the condominium around nine a.m. to gather our belongings for the trip back home, and the sign appeared as plain as day! We were joined on the elevator for our ride up to the twelfth floor by a short black lady, apparently domestic help, clad in a heavy winter coat with a toboggan pulled down over her ears, and carrying a tattered shopping bag in each hand. As the door of the elevator closed and we began ascending, she spoke.

"Mornin'."

"Good morning," we replied.

"What flo' y'all work on?"

"Twelve," I unhesitatingly answered, keeping a straight face not daring to look at Phoebe.

The ding of the bell signalling the twelfth floor broke the silence. The door opened and closed behind us as we fell against the wall in uncontrollable laughter.

"We must really look bad, Ruum. Do you really think she thought we work here?"

"Well, look at us, no make-up, warm-up suits, hair not coiffed, bleary-eyed, even with tote bags. We look exactly like what she thought we were."

"Man, it's really time for us to go home and regroup."

Chapter 106

Capturing the Surprise

Aedh Wishes for the Cloths of Heaven

Had I the heavens' embroidered cloths, Enwrought with golden and silver light,
The blue and the dim and the dark cloths of night and light and the half light,
I would spread the cloths under your feet: But I, being poor, have only my dreams;
I have spread my dreams under your feet;
Tread softly because you tread on my dreams.

—W. B. Yeates

Twelve new months, 1992, our brand new year. At the beginning of each new year, as a child, I remember my mother saying, "Wonder what's in store for us this year? Guess it's good we don't know." Now I heard myself saying these same words to my little grandson, Brandon, as we spent this New Year's Day together.

January and February moved along quickly, and when the cool, windy days of March arrived, Jean and I decided we would spend a few days in Williamsburg. We had not been since long before Dan's death. The weather was cold and rainy, but it didn't bother us. We made the rounds of all our favorite places as well as some of the new. In the evenings after dinner, we sat on our beds facing each other, like we did at Peace when we studied and like we did at the beach when we worked on the book. We had panic attacks about finishing our story more often now but kept them

Capturing the Surprise

subdued with our tried and true philosophy of "one day at a time."

At the end of March, we celebrated Aldridge's first birthday; and on April sixth we watched the ACC's shining star, Duke, win its second National Basketball Championship. Jean and Bryant were in Minneapolis to see this back-to-back victory. When they returned from this exciting experience, Jean and I slipped away for a few more days of work at the beach. On the 30th, we were back at Allison and Tom's to be with Thomas on his fourth birthday. Millicent and Steve were visiting from California, and we were glad to be together on this occasion. There were pony rides and popcorn, cowboy cookies and lemonade, ten gallon hats, little toy guns and holsters, cowboys and cowgirls bobbing for apples and pinning the tail on the donkey, and Thomas walking tall in his daddy's cowboy boots. The yard was a patchwork of colorful quilts spread for the children, friends, and family where they could sit relaxed and watch the action — sticky little hands, bright-eyed faces, a springtime picture of cherished moments on another happy day.

In May, Tadge's graduation from nursing school was a joyous event, and all of us were looking forward to the coming months of summer. We welcomed this warm, relaxed time of the year.

* * *

In September of 1992, Phoebe and I realized that for the last two and a half years we had relived together much of our past, not without frustrations, disappointments, or disagreements. We know that the strength of our relationship comes from our ability to tolerate our differences, thus allowing for continued growth and better understanding.

Our thoughts turned now to the future. It is good not to know what the days ahead hold for us, knowing would only rob us of the countless number of miracles and surprises that wait for us, and in not knowing we have the gift to dream and hope for a myriad of grand things. How grand it would be to live to see a safe and peaceful world, a drug free and disease free world, a more compassionate and less materialistic world for our grandchildren to grow in. How grand it would be to live a long and healthy life free of disability or pain, free to hold on to each day for as long as possible, stretching out the beauty of it like a kite on a string until all length and joy were realized.

We dream and hope for all of this and more, time with our families, and safety always for our loved ones, more years of birthday luncheons with our dear friends, of relaxing walks along the beach, even two mile hikes in Tarrytown Mall, and maybe the loss of a pound or two. Our dreams are endless, perhaps waiting for us is another trip to New York with our girls or even another trip abroad, more grandchildren, maybe even twins. Surprises, all out there waiting for us.

Who knows, some day, one of you might look out from your kitchen or living room window and watch a second-hand Winnebego coming into your driveway, and you'll say, "Oh, my gosh, there comes Jean and Phoebe, surely building another memory!"

Forty years have passed, and time has caught up with us. We've shared with you a flavor of our past, some of the events of our lives and the fundamental principles that bring us peace. We hope we've sewn the seeds of good values, that they will grow profusely, and although trampled at times their roots will remain deep and strong allowing them to flourish and continue to multiply. We have seen material things come and go, power rise and fall, human suffering, death, and happiness. Life is an intriguing and continuous game of coping, and we have learned that the real foundation for much needed inner strength comes from sound principles that endure and an unending faith.

This is our story. It's different, or it may not be, but it's our expression written with pride and happiness. We have captured on paper this treasure of vivid and human memories that can never be taken away from us. Our wish for you is one friend in your lifetime, one above all the friendly people surrounding you, one who is honest and loyal, one you will respect, enjoy, and love.

Acknowledgements

We are indebted to David Maryland Webb, our editor, our mentor, and friend, for his sincerity, direction, and constant encouragement; to Anita Williams for her sweet spirit, patience, and superb typing talents; to Sue Hayworth for her genuine warmth, wisdom, and support; to Alma Murchison for her enthusiasm and encouragement; to Carol Pattilo for the original writing on the cover; to Bill Goode for the photographs used on the cover; and to Walker-Ross Printers of Rocky Mount, North Carolina. Their contributions and enthusiasm to our effort made our work an even greater joy, and we are extremely grateful.

Additional Acknowledgements

Holy Bible, New International Version; *National Geographic; National Register of Historic Places Inventory; News-Times,* Carteret County, North Carolina; *Roget's College Thesaurus; Time; Webster's Dictionary and Thesaurus; World Book Encyclopedia; World News Digest.*

"How dear to this heart are the scenes of my childhood," "Like warp and woof all destinies are woven fast," "I miss thee, my mother," *Forty Thousand Quotations,* compiled by Charles Noel Douglas, 1940, Blue Ribbon Books, Garden City, New York, and Little, Brown and Company, Publishers, Boston, Massachusetts; "Aedh Wishes for the Cloths of Heaven," *Norton Anthology of Modern Poetry,* edited by Richard Ellmann, 1973, W.W. Norton and Company, New York, New York, and Macmillan Publishing Company, New York; "I Saw God Wash the World," William Leroy Stidger, *The Best Loved Poems of the American People,* 1936, Doubleday and Company, Inc., New York, and Fleming H. Revell Company, Tarrytown, New York; *The Treasury of Religious Verse,* Donald T. Kauffman, Sherman, Connecticut; "Oh my son's my son till he gets him a wife," *The Quotable Woman,* Corwin Books, Los Angeles, California.

Further Acknowledgements

The authors and publishers have made every effort to trace the ownership of all copyrighted material as well as non-copyrighted information and to indicate proper credit. Should there prove to be any question, however, regarding the use of any material or information, the authors and publishers herewith express regret for such unconscious error. Upon notification of any error, the publishers will be pleased to make proper acknowledgement in future editions of this book.